Praise for THE FOUR IN

Every so often, it does Christians good to stand back from the four Gospels and get a sense of how the whole story might work as a continuous narrative. Nikola Dimitrov has done a remarkable service in producing this compilation of all four Gospels so that the reader can feel the full impact of the unique and explosive story they tell.

— N. T. WRIGHT, *former Bishop of Durham (England),*
Professor of New Testament and Early Christianity,
University of St Andrews

Sometimes the serious reader of Matthew, Mark, Luke, and John can get confused by tiny apparent discrepancies in the order of events as presented in the four Gospels. Yet these minor discrepancies actually bolster the case for the reliability of the Gospel-writers. They were not colluding with each other. Instead, they provide four separate and distinct pictures of Jesus, the Christ. It's helpful to see this new work by Bulgarian pastor and scholar Nikola Dimitrov, who has attempted to provide a chronological picture of the life of Christ in this new book, *The Four in One Gospel of Jesus.* I welcome this book and efforts like it to shed light on the history-changing events of God in human flesh coming into our world.

— DR. JERRY NEWCOMBE, *Christian author,*
columnist, TV producer, and talk host

The Four in One Gospel of Jesus is a unique chronological presentation of the Gospels useful to scholars as well as Christians seeking greater understanding. Author and scholar Nikola Dimitrov has combined Matthew, Mark, Luke and John into subject chapters following a timeline that presents comparisons and insights not previously available. Dimitrov's work is excellent and well worth the investment.

— WILLIAM J. MURRAY, *Chairman, Religious Freedom Coalition*
www.ReligiousFreedomCoalition.org

THE FOUR IN ONE
GOSPEL *of*

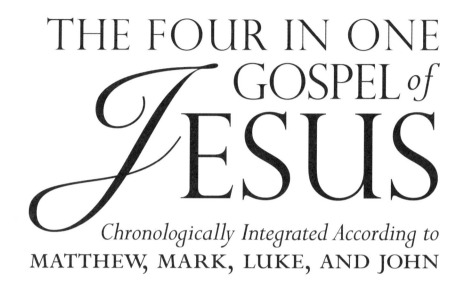

JESUS

Chronologically Integrated According to
MATTHEW, MARK, LUKE, AND JOHN

NIKOLA DIMITROV

Nordskog
Publishing inc.

VENTURA, CALIFORNIA

THE FOUR IN ONE GOSPEL OF JESUS
*Chronologically Integrated According to
Matthew, Mark, Luke, and John*

Enhanced Second Edition

Compiled by Nikola Donchev Dimitrov

Copyright © 2017 by Nikola Dimitrov

First printing 2017 in USA by Versa Press
Second printing 2018 in USA by Versa Press

ISBN: 978-0-9903774-7-4
Library of Congress Control Number: 2017903288

Scripture from the Authorized King James Version of the Holy Bible.
(Some words have been modified to contemporary English for easier reading.)

Cover art: Elena Perfanova, www.elenaarts.com
Cover design and interior layout: Diakonia Bookworks

Editing and Production
Desta Garrett, Managing Editor
Michelle Shelfer, Copy Editor
Ronald Kirk, Theology Editor

Published by

2716 Sailor Avenue, Ventura, California
www.NordskogPublishing.com

MEMBER

CHRISTIAN SMALL PUBLISHERS
ASSOCIATION

DEDICATION

I dedicate *The Four in One Gospel of Jesus* entirely and completely to my Lord Jesus Christ. He is everything to me—my life, my love, my passion, and the reason for my existence.

I have long desired to make this chronological piece of work on the life of Jesus, and have actually worked on it for a decade. Now I am blessed to present it ready before the Lord and before you—His people.

Thank You, Lord, for the grace that You have given me to be able to do this work for Your Glory! Amen!

N. D. D.

ACKNOWLEDGMENTS

All my thanks go to the Lord Jesus Christ, as this whole material is about Him, because of Him, and for His Glory. May more and more people get to know You intimately, receiving You as their personal Lord and Saviour. May You open our spirits, hearts, minds, souls, emotions, and strength, so we can fulfill Your will and purpose for the generation we are living in. May Your Glory fill this Earth, as the waters cover the Seas. May You rule and reign over our world, as You do in Heaven! Amen!

I would like to express my heart-felt gratitude to Mr. Jerry Nordskog, the *best* Publisher in the world, *ever*. His generosity, humility and desire to review my manuscript based on its own merit and not based on my being famous, in this mammon-driven business world, is unheard of. Thank you, Sir. Throughout the whole process you *never ever* made a mistake in your speaking, writing, or actions. I admire you and am so grateful to God for crossing our paths.

My deepest gratitude goes also to Mr. Ron Kirk, Theology Editor, for your wealth of wisdom; I've learned from you and appreciate the character you display. You are an encouragement that the Lord has *more than enough* great people on earth today through whom to transform everything around us.

Mrs. Desta Garrett, Biblicist at Nordskog, thank you so much for the encouragement and super-fast work in turning my manuscript into a full blown book.

Mrs. Michelle Shelfer, I can't even qualify the greatness of your work. I was *most honored* to work with you, because you are the fastest and most detail-oriented editor I have ever seen.

Mr. Kyle Shepherd, thank you so much for turning all our corrections and additions into a finished product, along with the cover art. You and your wife have been *such* a blessing, through all the cover-to-cover revisions. I am humbled.

To the whole team at Nordskog Publishing—a *big* Thank You, from my whole heart!!!

Nikola Dimitrov
March, 2017

TABLE OF CONTENTS

INTRODUCTION

The book that you hold in your hands right now is the story of the life of our Lord Jesus Christ, exactly as it is narrated in the Holy Bible, in the Gospels of Matthew, Mark, Luke, and John. The uniqueness of this material is the chronological mixing and blending of the four Gospels. Nothing has been added and nothing has been deleted; it has instead been blended and set in chronological order.

This book is in no way meant to be a substitute for the four Gospels, since each Gospel has its own style and context, and is serving for the fulfillment of a definite purpose of God. And most of all, we wholly believe that every jot and tittle in each Gospel has been Divinely placed where it stands, by God Himself (Matthew 5:18). So this material may likely serve as a help book and a reference, revealing the whole story in chronological order for each and every event in the Gospels, giving the reader a more complete perspective of how the stories unfolded. The following example provides clarity:

The Gospel of Matthew says that Jesus touched the hand of Simon Peter's mother-in-law, and the fever left her (8:15). In Mark's Gospel, it is written that Jesus took Simon Peter's mother-in-law by the hand, and lifted her up; and immediately the fever left her (1:31). Luke says that Jesus stood over her, and rebuked the fever; and it left her (4:39). See how the fact that the fever left Peter's mother-in-law is the same, while each Gospel writer adds a new element to the "process" of her healing and thus, to the whole picture?

In this four-in-one Gospel of Jesus, this passage would look like this: "Jesus came, stood over her, rebuked the fever, took her by the hand, and lifted her up; and immediately the fever left her" *[paraphrased]*. So, we get the complete picture by adding and mixing all the words and details that are unique in each of the four Gospels. When the chronology is applied to the whole story of the life of Jesus, *The Four in One Gospel of Jesus* emerges. We believe it will bless and enrich your life and your walk with God.

EXPLANATIONS

1. There are thirty-one chapters, as well as many subtitles for quicker and easier reference.

2. *Italicized words* (without parentheses) are a part of the original Authorized King James Version text of the Gospels, where they are also italicized to indicate that they are not part of the original language but were added by the translators for greater clarity.

3. *Italicized words [in brackets]* have been added by the compiler of this volume for clarification and information. They are, for the most part, words such as "a," "and," "the," which help connect the words and sentences from the different Gospels.

4. There are several Old Testament prophecies that have been fulfilled in the New Testament. Their references are footnoted, and a table of Old Testament prophecies and their respective Scripture references in the New Testament can be found in Appendices IV and V.

5. The actual blending of the Gospels is twofold:

> First, the Gospel of Mark is used as a base Gospel, since it recounts events virtually in chronological order. Different Biblical elements, details, stories, and words of Jesus from John, Matthew, and Luke that do not appear in the Gospel of Mark have been blended into the text and have been inserted in their chronological place. This is especially true for the Gospel of John, since it has many elements that are not found in the other three Gospels.

> Second, when there is a story in two or more Gospels, but not in Mark, another Gospel is used as the base, and the blending method is applied. When another Gospel is selected as the base, the resulting mixture is blended into the chronological road map of Mark, resulting in *The Four in One Gospel of Jesus*. In this way, a more complete story is told with details from all the Gospel writers, without repetition.

6. Blending where two Gospels imply the same meaning:

Where two Gospels describe the same thing with different words, a parenthetical reference is included to point out the difference. This does not include cases where the same words are used in a different order. For example, if one Gospel says "Then he went," and the other says "Then went he," only one version has been used, because both have the same meaning. Nothing could be added or better explained by the different order of the words, or by the different way of saying the same thing.

7. Since many words, phrases, sentences, or even whole verses or sections can be the same in two, three, or four Gospels, only one Gospel has been chosen. This may leave the impression that there are Bible verses (or parts of verses or words) that are missing from the references which are in parenthesis after each paragraph or group of paragraphs. That's because:

- They say ABSOLUTELY the same thing—word for word. For example, Matthew 11:6 says absolutely the same thing as Luke 7:23, so we have used only one of the Gospel Scriptures, in this case Luke, and we define the verse from Matthew as identical.
- One whole verse from one Gospel may be identical with parts of a longer verse from another Gospel, e.g., the longer verse includes the shorter one. In this case we have used the longer verse, and have defined the shorter one as identical. One such example is Luke 6:28, which is shorter as a verse and is included in Matthew 5:44.
- Bible verses from different Gospels may say the same thing but for some similar words, e.g., one Gospel uses the word "for" and the other uses the word "because." Other such similar words and phrases are "clothes" and "garments," "forsook" and "left," "arise" and "rise," "for him alone" and "for him only." Also, tense variations fall into this category, e.g., "come" and "came." John 5:14, for example, uses two tenses in the same verse—"finds" and "said."

In all these cases, we have used one of the Gospels, and identi-fied as identical the other verses that are the same, but for the par-ticular similar word. On the other hand, all the different words, sentences, phrases, or sections that add to the meaning of the Gos-pel text used, even if it is in a small way, are placed in parenthesis with their Scripture references, as explained in point 6 above. All the "missing in the references" identical Scriptures you can find in Appendix III.

8. In some cases, only a part of the referenced Scripture has been used, because the remainder is identical to a different Scrip-ture that has been used in the Gospel mixture, although it may be used in another paragraph. One example is Mark 1:13, which says, "And he was there in the wilderness forty days, tempted of Satan; and was with the wild beasts; and the angels ministered unto him." We know though, that between "And he was there in the wilderness forty days, tempted of Satan; and was with the wild beasts;" and "and the angels ministered unto him," there are temptations described by Matthew and Luke.

So, we have used the first part of Mark 1:13 in one paragraph, and, since the other part of the same verse is identical with Mat-thew 4:11, we have not included a second reference to Mark 1:13 after the next paragraph which references Matthew 4:11.

9. In the King James Version of the Bible, each verse begins with a capital letter, regardless of whether it begins a new sen-tence. We have not followed the convention of capitalizing words which are not the beginning of sentences unless the words are specified as the beginning of a dialogue or monologue. As in the Authorized King James Version there are long sentences which are connected with commas, semi-colons, and colons. We have followed this convention as much as possible. In the process of blending, we have added punctuation such as commas, exclama-tion points, semi-colons, and dashes.

10. The actual blending begins in chapter 3.

11. References within the text are as follows:

- The verse number is referenced at the beginning of each paragraph, sentence, phrase, or word.
- The corresponding Gospel and chapter number are referenced in parenthesis after the word, sentence or paragraph(s).
- The name of the Gospel/Gospels used for each subtitle mixture is parenthetically referenced at the end of each paragraph or group of paragraphs.

Some archaic word forms have been modified to contemporary English for easier readability, including verbs with "est" and "eth" endings, and "thee" and "thou" pronouns, for example. Some of the King James spellings of Old Testament names and places that we retained may not be familiar to readers of more modern versions. For this reason we offer the following chart. Although not exhaustive (as can be seen by looking at Appendix I, The Lineage of Jesus Christ), we hope it is a help:

KING JAMES SPELLING	MODERN SPELLING
Aser	Asher
Elias	Elijah
Elisabeth	Elizabeth
Eliseus	Elisha
Esaias	Isaiah
Jeremy, Jeremias	Jeremiah
Jona, Jonas	Jonah
Juda	Judah
Judaea	Judea
Messias	Messiah
Nephtalim	Naphtali
Noe	Noah
Sion	Zion
Zabulon	Zebulun

Further explanation and detail can be found in Appendix II.

THE FOUR IN ONE

GOSPEL *of*

*J*ESUS

Chronologically Integrated According to
MATTHEW, MARK, LUKE, AND JOHN

CHAPTER ONE

Things Which We Believe

¹ FORASMUCH as many have taken in hand to set forth in order a declaration of those things which are most surely believed among us, ² even as they delivered them unto us, which from the beginning were eyewitnesses, and ministers of the word; ³ it seemed good to me also, having had perfect understanding of all things from the very first, to write unto you in order, most excellent Theophilus, ⁴ that you might know the certainty of those things, wherein you have been instructed. (Luke 1)

(LUKE 1:1–4)

In the Beginning Was the Word

¹ IN the beginning was the Word, and the Word was with God, and the Word was God. ² The same was in the beginning with God. ³ All things were made by him; and without him was not any thing made that was made. ⁴ In him was life; and the life was the light of men. ⁵ And the light shone in darkness; and the darkness comprehended it not. (John 1)

⁶ There was a man sent from God, whose name *was* John. ⁷ The same came for a witness, to bear witness of the Light, that all *men* through him might believe. ⁸ He was not that Light, but *was sent* to bear witness of that Light. ⁹ *That* was the true Light, which lights every man that comes into the world. ¹⁰ He was in the world, and the world was made by him, and the world knew him not. ¹¹ He came unto his own, and his own received him not. ¹² But as many as received him, to them gave he power to become the sons of God, *even* to them that believe on his name: ¹³ which were born,

not of blood, nor of the will of the flesh, nor of the will of man, but of God. (John 1)

¹⁴ And the Word was made flesh, and dwelt among us, (and we beheld his glory, the glory as of the only begotten of the Father,) full of grace and truth. ¹⁵ John bore witness of him, and cried, saying, This was he of whom I spoke, He that comes after me is preferred before me: for he was before me. ¹⁶ And of his fulness have all we received, and grace for grace. ¹⁷ For the law was given by Moses, *but* grace and truth came by Jesus Christ. ¹⁸ No man has seen God at any time; the only begotten Son, which is in the bosom of the Father, he has declared *him*. (John 1)

(JOHN 1:1–18)

MOSES
JESUS

A Priest Named Zacharias

⁵ THERE was in the days of Herod, the king of Judaea, a certain priest named Zacharias, of the course of Abia: and his wife *was* of the daughters of Aaron, and her name *was* Elisabeth. ⁶ And they were both righteous before God, walking in all the commandments and ordinances of the Lord blameless. ⁷ And they had no child, because that Elisabeth was barren, and they both were *now* well stricken in years. (Luke 1)

⁸ And it came to pass, that while he executed the priest's office before God in the order of his course, ⁹ according to the custom of the priest's office, his lot was to burn incense when he went into the temple of the Lord. ¹⁰ And the whole multitude of the people were praying without at the time of incense. (Luke 1)

¹¹ And there appeared unto him an angel of the Lord standing on the right side of the altar of incense. ¹² And when Zacharias saw *him*, he was troubled, and fear fell upon him. ¹³ But the angel said unto him, Fear not, Zacharias: for your prayer is heard; and your wife Elisabeth shall bear you a son, and you shall call his name John. ¹⁴ And you shall have joy and gladness; and many shall rejoice at his birth. ¹⁵ For he shall be great in the sight of the Lord, and

shall drink neither wine nor strong drink; and he shall be filled with the Holy Ghost, even from his mother's womb. [16] And many of the children of Israel shall he turn to the Lord their God. [17] And he shall go before him in the spirit and power of Elias, to turn the hearts of the fathers to the children, and the disobedient to the wisdom of the just; to make ready a people prepared for the Lord. (Luke 1)

[18] And Zacharias said unto the angel, Whereby shall I know this? For I am an old man, and my wife well stricken in years. [19] And the angel answering said unto him, I am Gabriel, that stand in the presence of God; and am sent to speak unto you, and to show you these glad tidings. [20] And, behold, you shall be dumb, and not able to speak, until the day that these things shall be performed, because you believed not my words, which shall be fulfilled in their season. (Luke 1)

[21] And the people waited for Zacharias, and marvelled that he tarried so long in the temple. [22] And when he came out, he could not speak unto them: and they perceived that he had seen a vision in the temple: for he beckoned unto them, and remained speechless. [23] And it came to pass, that, as soon as the days of his ministration were accomplished, he departed to his own house. [24] And after those days his wife Elisabeth conceived, and hid herself five months, saying, [25] Thus has the Lord dealt with me in the days wherein he looked on *me*, to take away my reproach among men. (Luke 1)

(LUKE 1:5–25)

The Angel Gabriel

[26] AND in the sixth month the angel Gabriel was sent from God unto a city of Galilee, named Nazareth, [27] to a virgin espoused to a man whose name was Joseph, of the house of David; and the virgin's name *was* Mary. [28] And the angel came in unto her, and said, Hail, *you that are* highly favoured, the Lord *is* with you: blessed *are* you among women. (Luke 1)

[29] And when she saw *him*, she was troubled at his saying, and

cast in her mind what manner of salutation this should be. ³⁰ And the angel said unto her, Fear not, Mary: for you have found favour with God. ³¹ And, behold, you shall conceive in your womb, and bring forth a son, and shall call his name Jesus. ³² He shall be great, and shall be called the Son of the Highest: and the Lord God shall give unto him the throne of his father David: ³³ and he shall reign over the house of Jacob for ever; and of his kingdom there shall be no end. ³⁴ Then said Mary unto the angel, How shall this be, seeing I know not a man? (Luke 1)

³⁵ And the angel answered and said unto her, The Holy Ghost shall come upon you, and the power of the Highest shall overshadow you: therefore also that holy thing which shall be born of you shall be called the Son of God. ³⁶ And, behold, your cousin Elisabeth, she has also conceived a son in her old age: and this is the sixth month with her, who was called barren. ³⁷ For with God nothing shall be impossible. ³⁸ And Mary said, Behold the handmaid of the Lord; be it unto me according to your word. And the angel departed from her. (Luke 1)

(LUKE 1:26–38)

Mary Goes to Elisabeth

³⁹ AND Mary arose in those days, and went into the hill country with haste, into a city of Juda; ⁴⁰ and entered into the house of Zacharias, and saluted Elisabeth. ⁴¹ And it came to pass, that, when Elisabeth heard the salutation of Mary, the babe leaped in her womb; and Elisabeth was filled with the Holy Ghost: ⁴² and she spoke out with a loud voice, and said, Blessed are you among women, and blessed is the fruit of your womb. ⁴³ And whence is this to me, that the mother of my Lord should come to me? ⁴⁴ For, lo, as soon as the voice of your salutation sounded in my ears, the babe leaped in my womb for joy. ⁴⁵ And blessed is she that believed: for there shall be a performance of those things which were told her from the Lord. (Luke 1)

⁴⁶ And Mary said, My soul does magnify the Lord, ⁴⁷ and my spirit has rejoiced in God my Saviour. ⁴⁸ For he has regarded the low estate of his handmaiden: for, behold, from henceforth all generations shall call me blessed. ⁴⁹ For he that *is* mighty has done to me great things; and holy *is* his name. ⁵⁰ And his mercy *is* on them that fear him from generation to generation. ⁵¹ He has showed strength with his arm; he has scattered the proud in the imagination of their hearts. ⁵² He has put down the mighty from *their* seats, and exalted them of low degree. ⁵³ He has filled the hungry with good things; and the rich he has sent empty away. *Ps107* ⁵⁴ He has helped his servant Israel, in remembrance of *his* mercy; ⁵⁵ as he spoke to our fathers, to Abraham, and to his seed for ever. ⁵⁶ And Mary abode with her about three months, and returned to her own house. (Luke 1)

(LUKE 1:39–56)

Elisabeth Delivers a Son

⁵⁷ Now Elisabeth's full time came that she should be delivered; and she brought forth a son. ⁵⁸ And her neighbours and her cousins heard how the Lord had showed great mercy upon her; and they rejoiced with her. ⁵⁹ And it came to pass, that on the eighth day they came to circumcise the child; and they called him Zacharias, after the name of his father. ⁶⁰ And his mother answered and said, Not *so*; but he shall be called John. (Luke 1)

⁶¹ And they said unto her, There is none of your kindred that is called by this name. ⁶² And they made signs to his father, how he would have him called. ⁶³ And he asked for a writing table, and wrote, saying, His name is John. And they marvelled all. ⁶⁴ And his mouth was opened immediately, and his tongue *loosed, and he* spoke, and praised God. ⁶⁵ And fear came on all that dwelt round about them: and all these sayings were noised abroad throughout all the hill country of Judaea. ⁶⁶ And all they that heard *them* laid *them* up in their hearts, saying, What manner of child shall this

be! And the hand of the Lord was with him. (Luke 1)

67 And his father Zacharias was filled with the Holy Ghost, and prophesied, saying, 68 Blessed *be* the Lord God of Israel; for he has visited and redeemed his people, 69 and has raised up an horn of salvation for us in the house of his servant David; 70 as he spoke by the mouth of his holy prophets, which have been since the world began: 71 that we should be saved from our enemies, and from the hand of all that hate us; 72 to perform the mercy *promised* to our fathers, and to remember his holy covenant; 73 the oath which he swore to our father Abraham, 74 that he would grant unto us, that we being delivered out of the hand of our enemies might serve him without fear, 75 in holiness and righteousness before him, all the days of our life. (Luke 1)

76 And you, child, shall be called the prophet of the Highest: *Highest* for you shall go before the face of the Lord to prepare his ways; 77 to give knowledge of salvation unto his people by the remission of their sins, 78 through the tender mercy of our God; whereby the dayspring from on high has visited us, 79 to give light to them that sit in darkness and *in* the shadow of death, to guide our feet into the way of peace. 80 And the child grew, and waxed strong in spirit, and was in the deserts till the day of his showing unto Israel. (Luke 1)

(LUKE 1:57–80)

The Highest - referring to God

CHAPTER TWO

The Conception of Jesus

¹⁸ Now the birth of Jesus Christ was on this wise: When as his mother Mary was espoused to Joseph, before they came together, she was found with child of the Holy Ghost. ¹⁹ Then Joseph her husband, being a just *man*, and not willing to make her a public example, was minded to put her away privately. ^(Matthew 1)

²⁰ But while he thought on these things, behold, the angel of the Lord appeared unto him in a dream, saying, Joseph, you son of David, fear not to take unto you Mary your wife: for that which is conceived in her is of the Holy Ghost. ²¹ And she shall bring forth a son, and you shall call his name JESUS: for he shall save his people from their sins. ^(Matthew 1)

²² Now all this was done, that it might be fulfilled which was spoken of the Lord by the prophet, saying, ²³ Behold, a virgin shall be with child, and shall bring forth a son, and they shall call his name Emmanuel, which being interpreted is, God with us.^a ²⁴ Then Joseph being raised from sleep did as the angel of the Lord had bidden him, and took unto him his wife: ²⁵ and knew her not till she had brought forth her firstborn son: and he called his name JESUS. ^(Matthew 1)

(MATTHEW 1:18–25)

The Birth of Jesus

¹ AND it came to pass in those days, that there went out a decree from Caesar Augustus, that all the world should be taxed. ² (*And* this taxing was first made when Cyrenius was governor of Syria.)

---

a. O.T. prophecy in Isaiah 7:14.

³ And all went to be taxed, every one into his own city. ⁴ And Joseph also went up from Galilee, out of the city of Nazareth, into Judaea, unto the city of David, which is called Bethlehem; (because he was of the house and lineage of David:) ⁵ to be taxed with Mary his espoused wife, being great with child. ⁶ And so it was, that, while they were there, the days were accomplished that she should be delivered. ⁷ And she brought forth her firstborn son, and wrapped him in swaddling clothes, and laid him in a manger; because there was no room for them in the inn. (Luke 2)

⁸ And there were in the same country shepherds abiding in the field, keeping watch over their flock by night. ⁹ And, lo, the angel of the Lord came upon them, and the glory of the Lord shone round about them: and they were sore afraid. ¹⁰ And the angel said unto them, Fear not: for, behold, I bring you good tidings of great joy, which shall be to all people. ¹¹ For unto you is born this day in the city of David a Saviour, which is Christ the Lord. ¹² And this *shall be* a sign unto you; You shall find the babe wrapped in swaddling clothes, lying in a manger. (Luke 2)

¹³ And suddenly there was with the angel a multitude of the heavenly host praising God, and saying, ¹⁴ Glory to God in the highest, and on earth peace, good will toward men. ¹⁵ And it came to pass, as the angels were gone away from them into heaven, the shepherds said one to another, Let us now go even unto Bethlehem, and see this thing which is come to pass, which the Lord has made known unto us. (Luke 2)

¹⁶ And they came with haste, and found Mary, and Joseph, and the babe lying in a manger. ¹⁷ And when they had seen *it*, they made known abroad the saying which was told them concerning this child. ¹⁸ And all they that heard *it* wondered at those things which were told them by the shepherds. ¹⁹ But Mary kept all these things, and pondered *them* in her heart. ²⁰ And the shepherds returned, glorifying and praising God for all the things that they had heard and seen, as it was told unto them. (Luke 2)

(LUKE 2:1–20)

The Child Jesus to Jerusalem

²¹ AND when eight days were accomplished for the circumcising of the child, his name was called JESUS, which was so named of the angel before he was conceived in the womb. ²² And when the days of her purification according to the law of Moses were accomplished, they brought him to Jerusalem, to present *him* to the Lord; ²³ (As it is written in the law of the Lord, Every male that opens the womb shall be called holy to the Lord;) ²⁴ and to offer a sacrifice according to that which is said in the law of the Lord, A pair of turtledoves, or two young pigeons. (Luke 2)

²⁵ And, behold, there was a man in Jerusalem, whose name *was* Simeon; and the same man *was* just and devout, waiting for the consolation of Israel: and the Holy Ghost was upon him. ²⁶ And it was revealed unto him by the Holy Ghost, that he should not see death, before he had seen the Lord's Christ. ²⁷ And he came by the Spirit into the temple: and when the parents brought in the child Jesus, to do for him after the custom of the law, ²⁸ then took he him up in his arms, and blessed God, and said, ²⁹ Lord, now let your servant depart in peace, according to your word: ³⁰ for my eyes have seen your salvation, ³¹ which you have prepared before the face of all people; ³² a light to lighten the Gentiles, and the glory of your people Israel. (Luke 2) *Gentiles and Israel*

³³ And Joseph and his mother marvelled at those things which were spoken of him. ³⁴ And Simeon blessed them, and said unto Mary his mother, Behold, this *child* is set for the fall and rising again of many in Israel; and for a sign which shall be spoken against; ³⁵ (Yea, a sword shall pierce through your own soul also,) that the thoughts of many hearts may be revealed. (Luke 2)

³⁶ And there was one Anna, a prophetess, the daughter of Phanuel, of the tribe of Aser: she was of a great age, and had lived with an husband seven years from her virginity; ³⁷ and she *was* a widow of about fourscore and four *[eighty-four]* years, which departed not from the temple, but served *God* with fastings and prayers night and day. ³⁸ And she coming in that instant gave

thanks likewise unto the Lord, and spoke of him to all them that
looked for redemption in Jerusalem. ³⁹ And when they had performed all things according to the law of the Lord, they returned
into Galilee, to their own city Nazareth. ^(Luke 2)

(LUKE 2:21–39)

Wise Men from the East

¹ Now when Jesus was born in Bethlehem of Judaea in the days
of Herod the king, behold, there came wise men from the east to
Jerusalem, ² saying, Where is he that is born King of the Jews? For
we have seen his star in the east, and have come to worship him.
^(Matthew 2)

³ When Herod the king had heard *these things,* he was troubled,
and all Jerusalem with him. ⁴ And when he had gathered all the
chief priests and scribes of the people together, he demanded of
them where Christ should be born. ^(Matthew 2)

⁵ And they said unto him, In Bethlehem of Judaea: for thus it is
written by the prophet, ⁶ And you Bethlehem, *in* the land of Juda,
are not the least among the princes of Juda: for out of you shall
come a Governor, that shall rule my people Israel.ᵃ ^(Matthew 2)

⁷ Then Herod, when he had privately called the wise men, enquired of them diligently what time the star appeared. ⁸ And he
sent them to Bethlehem, and said, Go and search diligently for the
young child; and when you have found *him,* bring me word again,
that I may come and worship him also. ^(Matthew 2)

⁹ When they had heard the king, they departed; and, lo, the
star, which they saw in the east, went before them, till it came
and stood over where the young child was. ¹⁰ When they saw the
star, they rejoiced with exceeding great joy. ¹¹ And when they were
come into the house, they saw the young child with Mary his
mother, and fell down, and worshipped him: and when they had
opened their treasures, they presented unto him gifts; gold, and

---

a. O.T. prophecy in Micah 5:2.

frankincense, and myrrh. [12] And being <u>warned of God</u> in a dream that they should not return to Herod, they departed into their own country another way. (Matthew 2)

(MATTHEW 2:1–12)

Flee into Egypt

[13] AND when they were departed, behold, the angel of the Lord appeared to Joseph in a dream, saying, Arise, and take the young child and his mother, and flee into Egypt, and be there until I bring you word: for Herod will seek the young child to destroy him. (Matthew 2)

[14] When he arose, he took the young child and his mother by night, and departed into <u>Egypt</u>: [15] and was there until the death of Herod: that it might be <u>fulfilled</u> which was spoken of the Lord by the prophet, saying, <u>Out of Egypt have I called my son.</u>[a] (Matthew 2)

Moses
Egypt
Jesus

[16] Then Herod, when he saw that he was mocked of the wise men, was exceeding wroth, and sent forth, and slew all the children that were in Bethlehem, and in all the coasts thereof, from two years old and under, according to the time which he had diligently enquired of the wise men. (Matthew 2)

[17] Then was fulfilled that which was spoken by Jeremy the prophet, saying, [18] In Rama was there a voice heard, lamentation, and weeping, and great mourning, Rachel weeping *for* her children, and would not be comforted, because they are not.[b] (Matthew 2)

[19] But when Herod was dead, behold, an angel of the Lord appeared in a dream to Joseph in Egypt, [20] saying, Arise, and take the young child and his mother, and go into the land of Israel: for they are dead which sought the young child's life. (Matthew 2)

[21] And he arose, and took the young child and his mother, and came into the land of Israel. [22] But when he heard that Archelaus did reign in Judaea in the room of his father Herod, he was afraid

---

a. O.T. prophecy in Hosea 11:1.
b. O.T. prophecy in Jeremiah 31:15.

to go thither: notwithstanding, being warned of God in a dream, he turned aside into the parts of Galilee: ²³ and he came and dwelt in a city called Nazareth: that it might be fulfilled which was spoken by the prophets, He shall be called a Nazarene. ^(Matthew 2) ⁴⁰ And the child grew, and waxed strong in spirit, filled with wisdom: and the grace of God was upon him. ^(Luke 2)

(MATTHEW 2:13–23; LUKE 2:40)

The Feast of the Passover

⁴¹ Now his parents went to Jerusalem every year at the feast of the passover. ⁴² And when he was twelve years old, they went up to Jerusalem after the custom of the feast. ⁴³ And when they had fulfilled the days, as they returned, the child Jesus tarried behind in Jerusalem; and Joseph and his mother knew not *of it*. ⁴⁴ But they, supposing him to have been in the company, went a day's journey; and they sought him among *their* kinsfolk and acquaintance. ⁴⁵ And when they found him not, they turned back again to Jerusalem, seeking him. ⁴⁶ And it came to pass, that after three days they found him in the temple, sitting in the midst of the doctors, both hearing them, and asking them questions. ⁴⁷ And all that heard him were astonished at his understanding and answers. ^(Luke 2)

⁴⁸ And when they saw him, they were amazed: and his mother said unto him, Son, why have you thus dealt with us? Behold, your father and I have sought you sorrowing. ⁴⁹ And he said unto them, How is it that you sought me? Knew you not that I must be about my Father's business? ⁵⁰ And they understood not the saying which he spoke unto them. ⁵¹ And he went down with them, and came to Nazareth, and was subject unto them: but his mother kept all these sayings in her heart. ⁵² And Jesus increased in wisdom and stature, and in favour with God and man. ^(Luke 2)

(LUKE 2:41–52)

CHAPTER THREE

John the Baptist

¹ THE beginning of the gospel of Jesus Christ, the Son of God. (Mark 1) ¹ Now in the fifteenth year of the reign of Tiberius Caesar, Pontius Pilate being governor of Judaea, and Herod being tetrarch of Galilee, and his brother Philip tetrarch of Ituraea and of the region of Trachonitis, and Lysanias the tetrarch of Abilene, ² Annas and Caiaphas being the high priests, the word of God came unto John the son of Zacharias in the wilderness. (Luke 3) ¹ In those days came John the Baptist. (Matthew 3) ³ And he came into all the country about Jordan, (Luke 3) ¹ in the wilderness of Judaea, (Matthew 3) ³ preaching the baptism of repentance for the remission of sins, (Luke 3) ² and saying, Repent: for the kingdom of heaven is at hand. (Matthew 3)

³ For this is he that was spoken of by (Matthew 3) *[and]* ⁴ as it is written in the book of the words of Esaias the prophet, saying, (Luke 3) ² Behold, I send my messenger before your face, which shall prepare your way before you. ³ The voice of one crying in the wilderness, Prepare the way of the Lord, make his paths straight. (Mark 1) ⁵ Every valley shall be filled, and every mountain and hill shall be brought low; and the crooked shall be made straight, and the rough ways *shall be* made smooth; ⁶ and all flesh shall see the salvation of God.ª (Luke 3)

⁴ And the same John had his raiment of camel's hair, and a leather girdle (Matthew 3) ⁶ of a skin (Mark 1) ⁴ about his loins; and his meat was locusts and wild honey. (Matthew 3) ⁴ John did baptize in the wilderness, and preach the baptism of repentance for the remission of sins. ⁵ And there went out unto him all the land of Judaea, and they of Jerusalem, (Mark 1) ⁵ and all the region round about Jordan, (Matthew 3) ⁵ and were all baptized of him in the river of Jordan, confessing their sins. (Mark 1)

(MARK 1:1–6; MATTHEW 3:1–5; LUKE 3:1–6)

---

a. O.T. prophecy in Isaiah 40:3–5 and Malachi 3:1.

John's Exhortation

⁷ BUT when he saw many of the Pharisees and Sadducees come to his baptism, he said unto them (Matthew 3) *[and]* ⁷ to the multitude that came forth to be baptized of him, O generation of vipers, who has warned you to flee from the wrath to come? ⁸ Bring forth therefore fruits worthy of repentance, (Luke 3) ⁹ and think not to say within yourselves, We have Abraham to *our* father: for I say unto you, that God is able of these stones to raise up children unto Abraham. ¹⁰ And now also the axe is laid unto the root of the trees: therefore every tree which brings not forth good fruit is hewn down, and cast into the fire. (Matthew 3)

¹⁰ And the people asked him, saying, What shall we do then? ¹¹ He answered and said unto them, He that has two coats, let him impart to him that has none; and he that has meat, let him do likewise. ¹² Then came also publicans to be baptized, and said unto him, Master, what shall we do? ¹³ And he said unto them, Exact no more than that which is appointed you. ¹⁴ And the soldiers likewise demanded of him, saying, And what shall we do? And he said unto them, Do violence to no man, neither accuse *any* falsely; and be content with your wages. ¹⁵ And as the people were in expectation, and all men mused in their hearts of John, whether he were the Christ, or not; (Luke 3)

¹⁶ John answered, saying unto *them* all, (Luke 3) ¹¹ I indeed baptize you with water unto repentance: but he that comes after me is mightier than I, (Matthew 3) ⁷ the latchet of whose shoes I am not worthy to stoop down and unloose, (Mark 1) *[and]* ¹¹ whose shoes I am not worthy to bear: he shall baptize you with the Holy Ghost and *with* fire: ¹² whose fan *is* in his hand, and he will throughly purge his floor, and gather his wheat into the garner; but he will burn up the chaff with unquenchable fire. (Matthew 3) ¹⁸ And many other things in his exhortation preached he unto the people. (Luke 3)

(MATTHEW 3:7–12; LUKE 3:7–8, 10–16, 18; MARK 1:7)

John Baptizes Jesus

⁹ AND it came to pass in those days, that Jesus came from Nazareth of Galilee, (Mark 1) 13 to Jordan unto John, to be baptized of him. ¹⁴ But John forbad him, saying, I have need to be baptized of you, and come you to me? ¹⁵ And Jesus answering said unto him, Suffer *it to be so* now: for thus it becomes us to fulfil all righteousness. Then he suffered him. (Matthew 3)

²¹ Now when all the people were baptized, it came to pass, that Jesus also being baptized (Luke 3) 9 of John in Jordan (Mark 1) 21 and praying, (Luke 3) 16 went up straightway out of the water: and, lo, the heavens were opened unto him, and he saw the Spirit of God descending (Matthew 3) 22 in a bodily shape like a dove, (Luke 3) 16 and lighting upon him. (Matthew 3) 11 And there came a voice from heaven, *saying*, You are my beloved Son, (Mark 1) 22 in you I am well pleased. (Luke 3)

Beloved
we are called beloved

(MARK 1:9, 11; MATTHEW 3:13–16; LUKE 3:21–22)

Jesus Is Tempted of the Devil

¹ AND Jesus being full of the Holy Ghost returned from Jordan, (Luke 4) 12 and immediately the spirit drove him into the wilderness. MOSES
(Mark 1) 1 Then was Jesus led up of the Spirit into the wilderness to JESUS be tempted of the devil. (Matthew 4) 13 And he was there in the wilderness forty days, tempted of Satan; and was with the wild beasts. 40
(Mark 1) 2 And in those days he did eat nothing. (Luke 4) 2 And when he had fasted forty days and forty nights, (Matthew 4) 2 and when they were ended, he afterward hungered. (Luke 4) 3 And when the tempter (the devil, Luke 4:3) came to him, he said, If you be the Son of God, command that these stones be made bread. (Matthew 4) 4 And Jesus answered him, saying, It is written, That man shall not live by bread alone, but by every word (Luke 4) 4 that proceeds out of the mouth of God. (Matthew 4)

⁵ Then the devil took him up into the holy city (Matthew 4)

[9] Jerusalem, (Luke 4) [5] and set him on a pinnacle of the temple, [6] and said unto him, If you be the Son of God, (Matthew 4) [9] cast yourself down from hence: (Luke 4) [6] for it is written, He shall give his angels charge (Matthew 4) [10] over you, to keep you: [11] and in *their* hands they shall bear you up, lest at any time you dash your foot against a stone. [12] And Jesus answering said unto him, (Luke 4) [7] It is written again, You shall not tempt the Lord your God. (Matthew 4)

[8] Again the devil took him up into an exceeding high mountain, and showed him all the kingdoms of the world, and the glory of them (Matthew 4) [5] in a moment of time. [6] And the devil said unto him, All this power (Luke 4) *[and]* [9] all these things will I give you, (Matthew 4) [6] and the glory of them: for that is delivered unto me; and to whomsoever I will I give it. [7] If you therefore will (Luke 4) [9] fall down and (Matthew 4) [7] worship me, all shall be yours. [8] And Jesus answered and said unto him, Get behind me, Satan: for it is written, You shall worship the Lord your God, and him only shall you serve. (Luke 4) [13] And when the devil had ended all the temptation, he departed from him for a season, (Luke 4) [11] and, behold, angels came and ministered unto him. (Matthew 4)

(LUKE 4:1–13; MARK 1:12–13; MATTHEW 4:1–9, 11)

John Testifies of Jesus

[19] AND this is the record of John, when the Jews sent priests and Levites from Jerusalem to ask him, Who are you? [20] And he confessed, and denied not; but confessed, I am not the Christ. [21] And they asked him, What then? Are you Elias? And he said, I am not. Are you that prophet? And he answered, No. [22] Then said they unto him, Who are you? That we may give an answer to them that sent us. What say you of yourself? [23] He said, I *am* the voice of one crying in the wilderness, Make straight the way of the Lord, as said the prophet Esaias.[a] [24] And they which were sent were of the Pharisees. [25] And they asked him, and said unto him, Why

a. O.T. prophecy in Isaiah 40:3.

baptize you then, if you be not that Christ, nor Elias, neither that prophet? ²⁶ John answered them, saying, I baptize with water: but there stands one among you, whom you know not; ²⁷ he it is, who coming after me is preferred before me, whose shoe's latchet I am not worthy to unloose. ²⁸ These things were done in Bethabara beyond Jordan, where John was baptizing. (John 1)

²⁹ The next day John saw Jesus coming unto him, and said, Behold the Lamb of God, which takes away the sin of the world. ³⁰ This is he of whom I said, After me comes a man which is preferred before me: for he was before me. ³¹ And I knew him not: but that he should be made manifest to Israel, therefore am I come baptizing with water. ³² And John bore record, saying, I saw the Spirit descending from heaven like a dove, and it abode upon him. ³³ And I knew him not: but he that sent me to baptize with water, the same said unto me, Upon whom you shall see the Spirit descending, and remaining on him, the same is he which baptizes with the Holy Ghost. ³⁴ And I saw, and bore record that this is the Son of God. (John 1)

(JOHN 1:19–34)

John's Two Disciples Follow Jesus

³⁵ AGAIN the next day after John stood, and two of his disciples; ³⁶ and looking upon Jesus as he walked, he said, Behold the Lamb of God! ³⁷ And the two disciples heard him speak, and they followed Jesus. ³⁸ Then Jesus turned, and saw them following, and said unto them, What seek you? They said unto him, Rabbi, (which is to say, being interpreted, Master,) where dwell you? ³⁹ He said unto them, Come and see. They came and saw where he dwelt, and abode with him that day: for it was about the tenth hour. (John 1)

⁴⁰ One of the two which heard John *speak*, and followed him, was Andrew, Simon Peter's brother. ⁴¹ He first found his own brother Simon, and said unto him, We have found the Messias, which is, being interpreted, the Christ. ⁴² And he brought him to

Jesus. And when Jesus beheld him, he said, You are Simon the son of Jona: you shall be called Cephas, which is by interpretation, A stone. (John 1)

⁴³ The day following Jesus would go forth into Galilee, and found Philip, and said unto him, Follow me. ⁴⁴ Now Philip was of Bethsaida, the city of Andrew and Peter. ⁴⁵ Philip found Nathanael, and said unto him, We have found him, of whom Moses in the law, and the prophets, did write, Jesus of Nazareth, the son of Joseph. ⁴⁶ And Nathanael said unto him, Can there any good thing come out of Nazareth? Philip said unto him, Come and see. (John 1)

⁴⁷ Jesus saw Nathanael coming to him, and said of him, Behold an Israelite indeed, in whom is no guile! ⁴⁸ Nathanael said unto him, Whence know you me? Jesus answered and said unto him, Before that Philip called you, when you were under the fig tree, I saw you. ⁴⁹ Nathanael answered and said unto him, Rabbi, you are the Son of God; you are the King of Israel. ⁵⁰ Jesus answered and said unto him, Because I said unto you, I saw you under the fig tree, believe you? You shall see greater things than these. ⁵¹ And he said unto him, Verily, verily, I say unto you, hereafter you shall see heaven open, and the angels of God ascending and descending upon the Son of man. (John 1)

(JOHN 1:35–51)

The Wedding Feast in Cana

¹ AND the third day there was a marriage in Cana of Galilee; and the mother of Jesus was there: ² and both Jesus was called, and his disciples, to the marriage. ³ And when they wanted wine, the mother of Jesus said unto him, They have no wine. ⁴ Jesus said unto her, Woman, what have I to do with you? My hour is not yet come. ⁵ His mother said unto the servants, Whatsoever he says unto you, do *it*. ⁶ And there were set there six waterpots of stone, after the manner of the purifying of the Jews, containing two or three firkins apiece. ⁷ Jesus said unto them, Fill the waterpots with

water. And they filled them up to the brim. [8] And he said unto them, Draw out now, and bear unto the governor of the feast. And they bore *it*. (John 2)

[9] When the ruler of the feast had tasted the water that was made wine, and knew not whence it was: (but the servants which drew the water knew;) the governor of the feast called the bridegroom, [10] and said unto him, Every man at the beginning does set forth good wine; and when men have well drunk, then that which is worse: *but* you have kept the good wine until now. [11] This beginning of miracles did Jesus in Cana of Galilee, and manifested forth his glory; and his disciples believed on him. [12] After this he went down to Capernaum, he, and his mother, and his brethren, and his disciples: and they continued there not many days. (John 2)

(JOHN 2:1–12)

CHAPTER FOUR

Jesus Drives Out the Money Changers

¹³ AND the Jews' passover was at hand, and Jesus went up to Jerusalem, ¹⁴ and found in the temple those that sold oxen and sheep and doves, and the changers of money sitting: ¹⁵ and when he had made a scourge of small cords, he drove them all out of the temple, and the sheep, and the oxen; and poured out the changers' money, and overthrew the tables; ¹⁶ and said unto them that sold doves, Take these things hence; make not my Father's house an house of merchandise. ¹⁷ And his disciples remembered that it was written, The zeal of your house has eaten me up.ᵃ ⁽ᴶᵒʰⁿ ²⁾

¹⁸ Then answered the Jews and said unto him, What sign show you unto us, seeing that you do these things? ¹⁹ Jesus answered and said unto them, Destroy this temple, and in three days I will raise it up. ²⁰ Then said the Jews, Forty and six years was this temple in building, and will you rear it up in three days? ⁽ᴶᵒʰⁿ ²⁾

²¹ But he spoke of the temple of his body. ²² When therefore he was risen from the dead, his disciples remembered that he had said this unto them; and they believed the scripture, and the word which Jesus had said. ⁽ᴶᵒʰⁿ ²⁾

(JOHN 2:13–22)

Jesus with Nicodemus

²³ Now when he was in Jerusalem at the passover, in the feast *day,* many believed in his name, when they saw the miracles which he did. ²⁴ But Jesus did not commit himself unto them, because he knew all *men,* ²⁵ and needed not that any should testify of man:

---

a. O.T. prophecy in Psalm 69:9.

for he knew what was in man. (John 2)

¹ There was a man of the Pharisees, named Nicodemus, a ruler of the Jews: ² the same came to Jesus by night, and said unto him, Rabbi, we know that you are a teacher come from God: for no man can do these miracles that you do, except God be with him. ³ Jesus answered and said unto him, Verily, verily, I say unto you, except a man be born again, he cannot see the kingdom of God. ⁴ Nicodemus said unto him, How can a man be born when he is old? Can he enter the second time into his mother's womb, and be born? (John 3)

⁵ Jesus answered, Verily, verily, I say unto you, except a man be born of water and of the Spirit, he cannot enter into the kingdom of God. ⁶ That which is born of the flesh is flesh; and that which is born of the Spirit is spirit. ⁷ Marvel not that I said unto you, You must be born again. ⁸ The wind blows where it lists, and you hear the sound thereof, but can not tell whence it comes and whither it goes: so is every one that is born of the Spirit. ⁹ Nicodemus answered and said unto him, How can these things be? (John 3)

¹⁰ Jesus answered and said unto him, Are you a master of Israel, and know not these things? ¹¹ Verily, verily, I say unto you, we speak that we do know, and testify that we have seen; and you receive not our witness. ¹² If I have told you earthly things, and you believe not, how shall you believe, if I tell you of heavenly things? ¹³ And no man has ascended up to heaven, but he that came down from heaven, even the Son of man which is in heaven. ¹⁴ And as Moses lifted up the serpent in the wilderness, even so must the Son of man be lifted up: ¹⁵ that whosoever believes in him should not perish, but have eternal life. (John 3)

¹⁶ For God so loved the world, that he gave his only begotten Son, that whosoever believes in him should not perish, but have everlasting life. ¹⁷ For God sent not his Son into the world to condemn the world; but that the world through him might be saved. ¹⁸ He that believes on him is not condemned: but he that believes not is condemned already, because he has not believed in the name of the only begotten Son of God. ¹⁹ And this is the condemnation,

that light is come into the world, and men loved darkness rather than light, because their deeds were evil. [20] For every one that does evil hates the light, neither comes to the light, lest his deeds should be reproved. [21] But he that does truth comes to the light, that his deeds may be made manifest, that they are wrought in God. (John 3)

(JOHN 2:23–25; 3:1–21)

John Bears Witness of Jesus

[22] AFTER these things came Jesus and his disciples into the land of Judaea; and there he tarried with them, and baptized. [23] And John also was baptizing in Aenon near to Salim, because there was much water there: and they came, and were baptized. [24] For John was not yet cast into prison. (John 3)

[25] Then there arose a question between *some* of John's disciples and the Jews about purifying. [26] And they came unto John, and said unto him, Rabbi, he that was with you beyond Jordan, to whom you bore witness, behold, the same baptizes, and all *men* come to him. (John 3)

[27] John answered and said, A man can receive nothing, except it be given him from heaven. [28] You yourselves bear me witness, that I said, I am not the Christ, but that I am sent before him. [29] He that has the bride is the bridegroom: but the friend of the bridegroom, which stands and hears him, rejoices greatly because of the bridegroom's voice: this my joy therefore is fulfilled. [30] He must increase, but I *must* decrease. [31] He that comes from above is above all: he that is of the earth is earthly, and speaks of the earth: he that comes from heaven is above all. (John 3)

[32] And what he has seen and heard, that he testifies; and no man receives his testimony. [33] He that has received his testimony has set to his seal that God is true. [34] For he whom God has sent speaks the words of God: for God gives not the Spirit by measure *unto him.* [35] The Father loves the Son, and has given all things into his hand. [36] He that believes on the Son has everlasting life: and he

that believes not the Son shall not see life; but the wrath of God abides on him. (John 3)

[19] But Herod the tetrarch, being reproved by him [John the Baptist] for Herodias his brother Philip's wife, and for all the evils which Herod had done, [20] added yet this above all, that he shut up John in prison. (Luke 3) [12] Now when Jesus had heard that John was cast into prison, he departed into Galilee; (Matthew 4) [14] preaching the gospel of the kingdom of God. (Mark 1)

[17] From that time Jesus began to preach, and to say, (Matthew 4) [15] The time is fulfilled, and the kingdom of God is at hand: repent, and believe the gospel. (Mark 1)

Repent
Believe

[14] And Jesus returned in the power of the Spirit into Galilee: and there went out a fame of him through all the region round about. [15] And he taught in their synagogues, being glorified of all. (Luke 4)

(JOHN 3:22–36; LUKE 3:19–20; 4:14–15;
MATTHEW 4:12, 17; MARK 1:14–15)

Samaritan Woman at the Well

[1] WHEN therefore the Lord knew how the Pharisees had heard that Jesus made and baptized more disciples than John, [2] (Though Jesus himself baptized not, but his disciples,) [3] he left Judaea, and departed again into Galilee. [4] And he must needs go through Samaria. [5] Then came he to a city of Samaria, which is called Sychar, near to the parcel of ground that Jacob gave to his son Joseph. [6] Now Jacob's well was there. Jesus therefore, being wearied with *his* journey, sat thus on the well: *and* it was about the sixth hour. (John 4)

[7] There came a woman of Samaria to draw water: Jesus said unto her, Give me to drink. [8] (For his disciples were gone away unto the city to buy meat.) [9] Then said the woman of Samaria unto him, How is it that you, being a Jew, asks drink of me, which am a woman of Samaria? For the Jews have no dealings with the Samaritans. [10] Jesus answered and said unto her, If you knew the gift

of God, and who it is that says to you, Give me to drink; you would have asked of him, and he would have given you living water. (John 4)

¹¹ The woman said unto him, Sir, you have nothing to draw with, and the well is deep: from whence then have you that living water? ¹² Are you greater than our father Jacob, which gave us the well, and drank thereof himself, and his children, and his cattle? ¹³ Jesus answered and said unto her, Whosoever drinks of this water shall thirst again: ¹⁴ but whosoever drinks of the water that I shall give him shall never thirst; but the water that I shall give him shall be in him a well of water springing up into everlasting life. (John 4)

¹⁵ The woman said unto him, Sir, give me this water, that I thirst not, neither come hither to draw. ¹⁶ Jesus said unto her, Go, call your husband, and come hither. ¹⁷ The woman answered and said, I have no husband. Jesus said unto her, You have well said, I have no husband: ¹⁸ for you have had five husbands; and he whom you now have is not your husband: in that said you truly. ¹⁹ The woman said unto him, Sir, I perceive that you are a prophet. ²⁰ Our fathers worshipped in this mountain; and you say, that in Jerusalem is the place where men ought to worship. (John 4)

²¹ Jesus said unto her, Woman, believe me, the hour comes, when you shall neither in this mountain, nor yet at Jerusalem, worship the Father. ²² You worship you know not what: we know what we worship: for salvation is of the Jews. ²³ But the hour comes, and now is, when the true worshippers shall worship the Father in spirit and in truth: for the Father seeks such to worship him. ²⁴ God is a Spirit: and they that worship him must worship *him* in spirit and in truth. (John 4)

²⁵ The woman said unto him, I know that Messias comes, which is called Christ: when he is come, he will tell us all things. ²⁶ Jesus said unto her, I that speak unto you am *he*. ²⁷ And upon this came his disciples, and marvelled that he talked with the woman: yet no man said, What seek you? Or, Why talk you with her? ²⁸ The woman then left her waterpot, and went her way into the city, and said to the men, ²⁹ Come, see a man, which told me all things that ever I did: is not this the Christ? (John 4)

³⁰ Then they went out of the city, and came unto him. ³¹ In the mean while his disciples prayed him, saying, Master, eat. ³² But he said unto them, I have meat to eat that you know not of. ³³ Therefore said the disciples one to another, Has any man brought him ought to eat? (John 4)

³⁴ Jesus said unto them, My meat is to do the will of him that sent me, and to finish his work. ³⁵ Say not you, There are yet four months, and *then* comes harvest? Behold, I say unto you, lift up your eyes, and look on the fields; for they are white already to harvest. ³⁶ And he that reaps receives wages, and gathers fruit unto life eternal: that both he that sows and he that reaps may rejoice together. ³⁷ And herein is that saying true, One sows, and another reaps. ³⁸ I sent you to reap that whereon you bestowed no labour: other men laboured, and you are entered into their labours. (John 4)

³⁹ And many of the Samaritans of that city believed on him for the saying of the woman, which testified, He told me all that ever I did. ⁴⁰ So when the Samaritans were come unto him, they besought him that he would tarry with them: and he abode there two days. ⁴¹ And many more believed because of his own word; ⁴² and said unto the woman, Now we believe, not because of your saying: for we have heard *him* ourselves, and know that this is indeed the Christ, the Saviour of the world. (John 4)

(JOHN 4:1–42)

CHAPTER FIVE

Galilaeans Receive Jesus

⁴³ Now after two days he departed thence, and went into Galilee. ⁴⁴ For Jesus himself testified, that a prophet has no honour in his own country. ⁴⁵ Then when he was come into Galilee, the Galilaeans received him, having seen all the things that he did at Jerusalem at the feast: for they also went unto the feast. ⁴⁶ So Jesus came again into Cana of Galilee, where he made the water wine. And there was a certain nobleman, whose son was sick at Capernaum. ⁴⁷ When he heard that Jesus was come out of Judaea into Galilee, he went unto him, and besought him that he would come down, and heal his son: for he was at the point of death. (John 4)

⁴⁸ Then said Jesus unto him, Except you see signs and wonders, you will not believe. ⁴⁹ The nobleman said unto him, Sir, come down ere my child die. ⁵⁰ Jesus said unto him, Go your way; your son lives. And the man believed the word that Jesus had spoken unto him, and he went his way. ⁵¹ And as he was now going down, his servants met him, and told *him*, saying, Your son lives. ⁵² Then enquired he of them the hour when he began to amend. And they said unto him, Yesterday at the seventh hour the fever left him. ⁵³ So the father knew that *it was* at the same hour, in the which Jesus said unto him, Your son lives: and himself believed, and his whole house. ⁵⁴ This *is* again the second miracle *that* Jesus did, when he was come out of Judaea into Galilee. (John 4)

(JOHN 4:43–54)

Jesus at the Synagogue in Nazareth

¹⁶ AND he came to Nazareth, where he had been brought up: and,

as his custom was, he went into the synagogue on the sabbath day, and stood up for to read. ¹⁷ And there was delivered unto him the book of the prophet Esaias. And when he had opened the book, he found the place where it was written, ¹⁸ The Spirit of the Lord *is* upon me, because he has anointed me to preach the gospel to the poor; he has sent me to heal the brokenhearted, to preach deliverance to the captives, and recovering of sight to the blind, to set at liberty them that are bruised, ¹⁹ to preach the acceptable year of the Lord.ᵃ (Luke 4)

²⁰ And he closed the book, and he gave *it* again to the minister, and sat down. And the eyes of all them that were in the synagogue were fastened on him. (Luke 4)

²¹ And he began to say unto them, This day is this scripture fulfilled in your ears. ²² And all bore him witness, and wondered at the gracious words which proceeded out of his mouth. And they said, Is not this Joseph's son? (Luke 4)

²³ And he said unto them, You will surely say unto me this proverb, Physician, heal yourself: whatsoever we have heard done in Capernaum, do also here in your country. ²⁴ And he said, Verily I say unto you, no prophet is accepted in his own country. ²⁵ But I tell you of a truth, many widows were in Israel in the days of Elias, when the heaven was shut up three years and six months, when great famine was throughout all the land; ²⁶ but unto none of them was Elias sent, save unto Sarepta, *a city* of Sidon, unto a woman *that was* a widow. ²⁷ And many lepers were in Israel in the time of Eliseus the prophet; and none of them was cleansed, saving Naaman the Syrian. (Luke 4)

²⁸ And all they in the synagogue, when they heard these things, were filled with wrath, ²⁹ and rose up, and thrust him out of the city, and led him unto the brow of the hill whereon their city was built, that they might cast him down headlong. ³⁰ But he passing through the midst of them went his way. (Luke 4)

¹³ And leaving Nazareth, he came and dwelt in Capernaum, (Matthew 4) ³¹ a city of Galilee, (Luke 4) ¹³ which is upon the sea coast,

---

a. O.T. prophecy in Isaiah 61:1–2.

in the borders of Zabulon and Nephthalim: [(Matthew 4)] 31 and taught them on the sabbath days, [(Luke 4)] 14 that it might be fulfilled which was spoken by Esaias the prophet, saying, 15 The land of Zabulon, and the land of Nephthalim, *by* the way of the sea, beyond Jordan, Galilee of the Gentiles; 16 the people which sat in darkness saw great light; and to them which sat in the region and shadow of death light is sprung up.[a] [(Matthew 4)]

(LUKE 4:16–31; MATTHEW 4:13–16)

Jesus at the Lake of Gennesaret

18 AND Jesus, walking by the sea of Galilee, saw two brethren, Simon called Peter, and Andrew his brother, casting a net into the sea: for they were fishers. [(Matthew 4)] 1 And it came to pass, that, as the people pressed upon him to hear the word of God, he stood by the lake of Gennesaret, 2 and saw two ships standing by the lake: but the fishermen were gone out of them, and were washing *their* nets. 3 And he entered into one of the ships, which was Simon's, and prayed him that he would thrust out a little from the land. And he sat down, and taught the people out of the ship. [(Luke 5)]

4 Now when he had left speaking, he said unto Simon, Launch out into the deep, and let down your nets for a draught. [(Luke 5)]

5 And Simon answering said unto him, Master, we have toiled all the night, and have taken nothing: nevertheless at your word I will let down the net. 6 And when they had this done, they inclosed a great multitude of fishes: and their net broke. 7 And they beckoned unto *their* partners, which were in the other ship, that they should come and help them. And they came, and filled both the ships, so that they began to sink. [(Luke 5)]

8 When Simon Peter saw *it*, he fell down at Jesus' knees, saying, Depart from me; for I am a sinful man, O Lord. 9 For he was astonished, and all that were with him, at the draught of the fishes which they had taken: 10 and so *was* also James, and John,

---

a. O.T. prophecy in Isaiah 9:1–2.

the sons of Zebedee, which were partners with Simon. And Jesus said unto Simon, Fear not; from henceforth you shall catch men. [11] And when they had brought their ships to land, (Luke 5) [17] Jesus said unto them *[Simon called Peter and Andrew]*, Come after me, (Mark 1) [19] follow me, (Matthew 4) [17] and I will make you to become fishers of men. [18] And straightway they forsook their nets, and followed him. (Mark 1)

[19] And when he had gone a little farther thence, (Mark 1) [21] he saw other two brethren, James *the son* of Zebedee, and John his brother, (Matthew 4) [19] who also were (Mark 1) [21] in a ship with Zebedee their father, mending their nets. (Matthew 4) [20] And straightway he called them: (Mark 1) [22] and they immediately (Matthew 4) [20] left their father Zebedee in the ship with the hired servants, and went after him. (Mark 1) [11] They forsook all, and followed him. (Luke 5)

(MATTHEW 4:18–22; LUKE 5:1–11; MARK 1:17–20)

They forsook all, and followed Him.

Jesus in Capernaum

[21] AND they went into Capernaum; and straightway on the sabbath day he entered into the synagogue, and taught. (Mark 1) [32] And they were astonished at his doctrine: for his word was with power, (Luke 4) [22] for he taught them as one that had authority, and not as the scribes. (Mark 1) [33] And in the synagogue there was a man, which had a spirit of an unclean devil, (Luke 4) [23] and he cried out (Mark 1) [33] with a loud voice, [34] saying, Let *us* alone; what have we to do with you, *you* Jesus of Nazareth? Are you come to destroy us? I know you who you are; the Holy One of God. (Luke 4)

[35] And Jesus rebuked him, saying, Hold your peace, and come out of him. And when the devil had thrown him in the midst, (Luke 4) [26] had torn him and cried with a loud voice, (Mark 1) [35] he came out of him, and hurt him not. (Luke 4) [27] And they were all amazed, insomuch that they questioned among themselves, saying, What thing is this? What new doctrine *is* this? (Mark 1) [36] What a word *is* this! For with authority and power (Luke 4) [27] commands he even the

unclean spirits, and they do obey him ^(Mark 1) ³⁶ and they come out. ^(Luke 4) ²⁸ And immediately his fame spread abroad throughout all the region round about Galilee. ^(Mark 1)

(MARK 1:21–23, 26–28; LUKE 4:32–36)

Jesus Heals Many

²⁹ AND forthwith, when they were come out of the synagogue, they entered into the house of Simon and Andrew, with James and John. ³⁰ But Simon's wife's mother lay sick, ^(Mark 1) ³⁸ taken with a great fever; ^(Luke 4) ³⁰ and anon *[soon]* they tell him of her. ³¹ And he came, ^(Mark 1) ³⁹ stood over her, and rebuked the fever; ^(Luke 4) ³¹ and took her by the hand (touched her hand, ^{Matthew 8:15}), and lifted her up; and immediately the fever left her, ^(Mark 1) ³⁹ and immediately she arose and ministered unto them. ^(Luke 4)

³² And at even, when the sun did set, ^(Mark 1) ⁴⁰ all they that had any sick with divers diseases ^(Luke 4) ³² and them that were possessed with devils, ^(Mark 1) ⁴⁰ brought them unto him; and he laid his hands on every one of them, ^(Luke 4) ¹⁶ and he cast out the spirits with *his* word, and healed all that were sick. ^(Matthew 8) ³³ And all the city was gathered together at the door. ^(Mark 1) ⁴¹ And devils also came out of many, crying out, and saying, You are Christ the Son of God. And he rebuking *them* suffered them not to speak: for they knew that he was Christ. ^(Luke 4)

[All this happened] ¹⁷ That it might be fulfilled which was spoken by Esaias the prophet, saying, Himself took our infirmities, and bore our sicknesses.^a ^(Matthew 8)

(MARK 1:29–33; LUKE 4:38–41; MATTHEW 8:15–17)

---

a. O.T. prophecy in Isaiah 53:4.

Jesus Teaches and Preaches the Gospel

³⁵ AND in the morning, rising up a great while before day, he went out, and departed into a solitary place, and there prayed. ³⁶ And Simon and they that were with him followed after him. ³⁷ And when they had found him, they said unto him, All *men* seek for you. ³⁸ And he said unto them, Let us go into the next towns, that I may preach there also: for therefore came I forth. (Mark 1)

⁴² And the people sought him, and came unto him, and stayed him, that he should not depart from them. ⁴³ And he said unto them, I must preach the kingdom of God to other cities also: for therefore am I sent. (Luke 4)

²³ And Jesus went about all Galilee, teaching in their synagogues, and preaching the gospel of the kingdom, and healing all manner of sickness and all manner of disease among the people, (Matthew 4) ³⁹ and cast*[ing]* out devils. (Mark 1) ²⁴ And his fame went throughout all Syria: and they brought unto him all sick people that were taken with divers diseases and torments, and those which were possessed with devils, and those which were lunatic, and those that had the palsy; and he healed them. ²⁵ And there followed him great multitudes of people from Galilee, and *from* Decapolis, and *from* Jerusalem, and *from* Judaea, and *from* beyond Jordan. (Matthew 4)

(MARK 1:35–39; LUKE 4:42–43; MATTHEW 4:23–25)

Jesus Heals a Man with Palsy

¹² AND it came to pass, when he was in a certain city, behold a man full of leprosy: who seeing Jesus, (Luke 5) ² came (Matthew 8) ⁴⁰ and kneeling down to him, (Mark 1) ¹² fell on *his* face, (Luke 5) ² worshipped him, (Matthew 8) ¹² and besought him, saying, Lord, (Luke 5) ⁴⁰ if you will, you can make me clean. ⁴¹ And Jesus, moved with compassion, put forth *his* hand, and touched him, and said unto him, I will; be clean. ⁴² And as soon as he had spoken, immediately the leprosy departed from him, and he was cleansed. (Mark 1)

⁴³ And he straitly charged him, and forthwith sent him away, ⁴⁴ and said unto him, See you say nothing to any man: but go your way, show yourself to the priest, and offer for your cleansing those things (the gift, ⁽Matthew 8:4⁾) which Moses commanded, for a testimony unto them. ⁽Mark 1⁾

⁴⁵ But he went out, and began to publish *it* much, and to blaze abroad the matter. ⁽Mark 1⁾ ¹⁵ But so much the more went there a fame abroad of him: and great multitudes came together to hear, and to be healed by him of their infirmities, ⁽Luke 5⁾ ⁴⁵ insomuch that Jesus could no more openly enter into the city, but was without in desert places. ⁽Mark 1⁾ ¹⁶ He withdrew himself into the wilderness, and prayed. ⁽Luke 5⁾ ⁴⁵ And they came to him from every quarter. ⁽Mark 1⁾

¹⁷ And it came to pass on a certain day, ⁽Luke 5⁾ ¹ he entered into a ship ⁽Matthew 9⁾ ¹ after *some* days; ⁽Mark 2⁾ ¹ and passed over, and came into his own city ⁽Matthew 9⁾ ¹ Capernaum, and it was noised that he was in the house. ² And straightway many were gathered together, insomuch that there was no room to receive *them*, no, not so much as about the door: and he preached the word unto them. ⁽Mark 2⁾ ¹⁷ As he was teaching, there were Pharisees and doctors of the law sitting by, which were come out of every town of Galilee, and Judaea, and Jerusalem: and the power of the Lord was *present* to heal them. ⁽Luke 5⁾

³ And they come unto him, bringing one sick of the palsy, which was borne of four, ⁽Mark 2⁾ ² lying on a bed: ⁽Matthew 9⁾ ¹⁸ and they sought *means* to bring him in, and to lay *him* before him. ¹⁹ And when they could not find by what *way* they might bring him in because of the multitude ⁽Luke 5⁾ *[and]* ⁴ they could not come nigh unto him for the press, ⁽Mark 2⁾ ¹⁹ they went upon the housetop, ⁽Luke 5⁾ ⁴ uncovered the roof where he was: and when they had broken *it* up, they let down the bed wherein the sick of the palsy lay, ⁽Mark 2⁾ ¹⁹ through the tiling with *his* couch into the midst before Jesus. ⁽Luke 5⁾

⁵ When Jesus saw their faith, he said unto the sick of the palsy, ⁽Mark 2⁾ ² Son, be of good cheer; your sins be forgiven you. ⁽Matthew 9⁾ ⁶ But there were certain of the scribes ⁽Mark 2⁾ ²¹ and the Pharisees

(Luke 5) 6 sitting there, and reasoning in their hearts, (Mark 2) 21 saying (Luke 5) 3 within themselves, This *man* blasphemes. (Matthew 9) 7 Why does this *man* thus speak blasphemies? (Mark 2) 21 Who is this which speaks blasphemies? Who can forgive sins, but God alone? (Luke 5)

8 And immediately when Jesus perceived in his spirit that they so reasoned within themselves, (Mark 2) 4 knowing their thoughts, (Matthew 9) 22 he answering said unto them, (Luke 5) 8 Why reason you these things in your hearts? (Mark 2) 4 Wherefore think you evil in your hearts? 5 For (Matthew 9) 9 whether is it easier to say to the sick of the palsy, *Your* sins be forgiven you; or to say, Arise, and take up your bed, and walk? 10 But that you may know that the Son of man has power on earth to forgive sins, (Mark 2) 6 (then said he to the sick of the palsy,) (Matthew 9) 24 I say unto you, arise, and take up your couch, (Luke 5) 11 and go your way into your house. (Mark 2)

25 And immediately he rose up before them, and took up that whereon he lay, (Luke 5) 12 the bed, and went forth before them all, (Mark 2) 25 and departed to his own house, glorifying God. (Luke 5) 8 But when the multitudes saw *it*, (Matthew 9) 26 they were all amazed, (Luke 5) 8 they marvelled, and glorified God, which had given such power unto men, (Matthew 9) 26 and were filled with fear, saying, We have seen strange things to day. (Luke 5) 12 We never saw it on this fashion. (Mark 2)

(LUKE 5:12, 15–19, 21–22, 24–26; MARK 1:40–45; 2:1–12;
MATTHEW 8:2, 4; 9:1–6, 8; LUKE 5:22, 24–26)

CHAPTER SIX

Jesus Calls Levi (Matthew)

27 AND after these things, (Luke 5) 9 as Jesus passed forth from thence, (Matthew 9) 13 he went forth again by the sea side; and all the multitude resorted unto him, and he taught them. 14 And as he passed by, he saw (Mark 2) 27 a publican, named Levi (Matthew, Matthew 9.9), (Luke 5) 14 the *son* of Alphaeus, (Mark 2) 27 sitting at the receipt of custom: and he said unto him, Follow me. 28 And he left all, rose up, and followed him. (Luke 5)

29 And Levi made him a great feast in his own house: and there was a great company of publicans and of others that sat down with them. (Luke 5)

15 And it came to pass, that, as Jesus sat at meat in his house, (Mark 2) 10 behold, many publicans and sinners came and sat down (Matthew 9) 15 also together with Jesus and his disciples: for there were many, and they followed him. (Mark 2)

16 And when the scribes and Pharisees saw him eat with publicans and sinners, they (Mark 2) 30 murmured against his disciples, saying, (Luke 5) 16 How is it that (Mark 2) 11 your Master (Matthew 9) *[and]* 30 you eat and drink with publicans and sinners? (Luke 5)

12 But when Jesus heard *that*, he (Matthew 9) 31 answering (Luke 5) 12 said unto them, They that be whole need not a physician, but they that are sick. 13 But go and learn what *that* means, I will have mercy, and not sacrifice: for (Matthew 9) 32 I came not to call the righteous, but sinners to repentance. (Luke 5)

18 And the disciples of John and of the Pharisees used to fast: and they come and say unto him, Why do the disciples of John and of the Pharisees (Mark 2) 33 fast often, and make prayers, (Luke 5) 18 but your disciples fast not; (Mark 2) 33 Yours eat and drink? (Luke 5)

19 And Jesus said unto them, (Mark 2) 34 Can you make the children

of the bridechamber fast; (Luke 5) 15 can the children of the bridechamber mourn, (Matthew 9) 19 while the bridegroom is with them?
As long as they have the bridegroom with them, they cannot fast.
20 But the days will come, when the bridegroom shall be taken
away from them, and then shall they fast in those days. (Mark 2)

36 And he spoke also a parable unto them, (Luke 5) 21 No man also
sews a piece of new cloth on an old garment: else the new piece
that (Mark 2) 16 is put in to fill it up, (Matthew 9) 21 takes away from the old
(Mark 2) 16 garment, (Matthew 9) 21 and the rent is made worse, (Mark 5) 36 and
the piece that was *taken* out of the new agrees not with the old.
(Luke 5) 22 And no man puts new wine into old bottles: (Mark 2) 37 else
the new wine will burst the bottles, (Luke 5) 22 and the wine is spilled,
and the bottles will be marred: (Mark 2) 37 and the bottles shall perish. (Luke 5) 22 But new wine must be put (Mark 2) 17 into new bottles, and
both are preserved. (Matthew 9) 39 No man also having drunk old *wine*
straightway desires new: for he says, The old is better. (Luke 5)

1 After this there was a feast of the Jews; and Jesus went up to
Jerusalem. (John 5)

(LUKE 5:27–34, 36–37, 39; MARK 2:13–16, 18–22;
MATTHEW 9:9–13, 15–17; JOHN 5:1)

Jesus in Jerusalem at the Feast

2 Now there is at Jerusalem by the sheep *market* a pool, which
is called in the Hebrew tongue Bethesda, having five porches.
3 In these lay a great multitude of impotent folk, of blind, halt,
withered, waiting for the moving of the water. 4 For an angel went
down at a certain season into the pool, and troubled the water:
whosoever then first after the troubling of the water stepped in
was made whole of whatsoever disease he had. (John 5)

5 And a certain man was there, which had an infirmity thirty
and eight years. 6 When Jesus saw him lie, and knew that he had
been now a long time *in that case,* he said unto him, Will you
be made whole? 7 The impotent man answered him, Sir, I have

no man, when the water is troubled, to put me into the pool: but while I am coming, another steps down before me. ⁸ Jesus said unto him, Rise, take up your bed, and walk. ⁹ And immediately the man was made whole, and took up his bed, and walked: and on the same day was the sabbath. (John 5)

SABBATH broken

¹⁰ The Jews therefore said unto him that was cured, It is the sabbath day: it is not lawful for you to carry *your* bed· ¹¹ He answered them, He that made me whole, the same said unto me, Take up your bed, and walk. ¹² Then asked they him, What man is that which said unto you, Take up your bed, and walk? ¹³ And he that was healed knew not who it was: for Jesus had conveyed himself away, a multitude being in *that* place. (John 5)

¹⁴ Afterward Jesus found him in the temple, and said unto him, Behold, you are made whole: sin no more, lest a worse thing come unto you. ¹⁵ The man departed, and told the Jews that it was Jesus, which had made him whole. ¹⁶ And therefore did the Jews persecute Jesus, and sought to slay him, because he had done these things on the sabbath day. ¹⁷ But Jesus answered them, My Father works hitherto, and I work. (John 5)

(JOHN 5:2–17)

Verily, Verily, I Say unto You

¹⁸ THEREFORE the Jews sought the more to kill him, because he not only had broken the sabbath, but said also that God was his Father, making himself equal with God. ¹⁹ Then answered Jesus and said unto them, Verily, verily, I say unto you, the Son can do nothing of himself, but what he sees the Father do: for what things soever he does, these also does the Son likewise. ²⁰ For the Father loves the Son, and shows him all things that himself does: and he will show him greater works than these, that you may marvel. ²¹ For as the Father raises up the dead, and quickens *them*; even so the Son quickens whom he will. ²² For the Father judges no man, but has committed all judgment unto the Son: ²³ that all

men should honour the Son, even as they honour the Father. He that honours not the Son honours not the Father which has sent him. (John 5)

24 Verily, verily, I say unto you, he that hears my word, and believes on him that sent me, has everlasting life, and shall not come into condemnation; but is passed from death unto life. 25 Verily, verily, I say unto you, the hour is coming, and now is, when the dead shall hear the voice of the Son of God: and they that hear shall live. 26 For as the Father has life in himself; so has he given to the Son to have life in himself; 27 and has given him authority to execute judgment also, because he is the Son of man. (John 5)

28 Marvel not at this: for the hour is coming, in the which all that are in the graves shall hear his voice, 29 and shall come forth; they that have done good, unto the resurrection of life; and they that have done evil, unto the resurrection of damnation. 30 I can of my own self do nothing: as I hear, I judge: and my judgment is just; because I seek not my own will, but the will of the Father which has sent me. (John 5)

31 If I bear witness of myself, my witness is not true. 32 There is another that bears witness of me; and I know that the witness which he witnesses of me is true. 33 You sent unto John, and he bore witness unto the truth. 34 But I receive not testimony from man: but these things I say, that you might be saved. 35 He was a burning and a shining light: and you were willing for a season to rejoice in his light. 36 But I have greater witness than *that* of John: for the works which the Father has given me to finish, the same works that I do, bear witness of me, that the Father has sent me. 37 And the Father himself, which has sent me, has borne witness of me. You have neither heard his voice at any time, nor seen his shape. 38 And you have not his word abiding in you: for whom he has sent, him you believe not. (John 5)

39 Search the scriptures; for in them you think you have eternal life: and they are they which testify of me. 40 And you will not come to me, that you might have life. 41 I receive not honour from men. 42 But I know you, that you have not the love of God in you. (John 5)

⁴³ I am come in my Father's name, and you receive me not: if another shall come in his own name, him you will receive. ⁴⁴ How can you believe, which receive honour one of another, and seek not the honour that *comes* from God only? ⁴⁵ Do not think that I will accuse you to the Father: there is *one* that accuses you, *even* Moses, in whom you trust. ⁴⁶ For had you believed Moses, you would have believed me: for he wrote of me. ⁴⁷ But if you believe not his writings, how shall you believe my words? ^(John 5)

MOSES

JESUS

(JOHN 5:18–47)

p19, 23, 30

Jesus in the Corn Fields

Second ABBATH broken

¹ AND it came to pass on the second sabbath after the first, that ^{(Luke 6) 1} Jesus ^{(Matthew 12) 1} went through the corn fields; and his disciples ^{(Luke 6) 1} were hungry, and ^{(Matthew 12) 23} began, as they went, to pluck ^{(Mark 2) 1} the ears of corn, and did eat, rubbing *them* in *their* hands. ^{(Luke 6) 2} But when ^{(Matthew 12) 2} certain of the Pharisees ^{(Luke 6) 2} saw *it*, they said unto him, Behold, ^{(Matthew 12) 24} why do ^{(Mark 2) 2} your disciples do that which is not lawful to do ^{(Matthew 12) 2} on the sabbath days? ^(Luke 6)

³ And Jesus answering them said, ^{(Luke 6) 25} Have you never read ^{(Mark 2) 3} so much as this, what David did, ^{(Luke 6) 25} when he had need, and was hungry, he ^{(Mark 2) 3} himself, ^{(Luke 6) 25} and they that were with him? ²⁶ How he went into the house of God in the days of Abiathar the high priest, ^{(Mark 2) 4} and did take and eat the showbread, and gave also to them that were with him; ^{(Luke 6) 4} which was not lawful for him to eat, neither for them which were with him, but only for the priests? ^(Matthew 12)

⁵ Or have you not read in the law, how that on the sabbath days the priests in the temple profane the sabbath, and are blameless? ⁶ But I say unto you, that in this place is *one* greater than the temple. ⁷ But if you had known what *this* means, I will have mercy, and not sacrifice, you would not have condemned the guiltless. ^(Matthew 12)

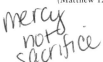

mercy not sacrifice

²⁷ And he said unto them, The sabbath was made for man, and not man for the sabbath: ²⁸ therefore the Son of man is Lord also ^(Mark 2) 8 even of the sabbath day. ^(Matthew 12)

(LUKE 6:1–4; MATTHEW 12:1–2, 4–8; MARK 2:23–28)

Jesus in the Synagogue on Another Sabbath

SABBATH broken

⁹ AND when he was departed thence, ^(Matthew 12) ⁶ it came to pass also on another sabbath, that he entered into the synagogue and taught. ^(Luke 6) ¹⁰ And, behold, ^(Matthew 12) ¹ there was a man there, ^(Mark 3) ⁶ whose right hand was withered. ⁷ And the scribes and Pharisees watched him, whether he would heal ^(Luke 6) ² him ^(Mark 3) ⁷ on the sabbath day; that they might find an accusation against him. ^(Luke 6) ¹⁰ And they asked him, saying, Is it lawful to heal on the sabbath days? That they might accuse him. ^(Matthew 12)

⁸ But he knew their thoughts, and said to the man which had the withered hand, Rise up, and stand forth in the midst. And he arose and stood forth. ⁹ Then said Jesus unto them, I will ask you one thing; Is it lawful on the sabbath days to do good, or to do evil? To save life, or to destroy *it*? ^(Luke 6) ¹¹ What man shall there be among you, that shall have one sheep, and if it fall into a pit on the sabbath day, will he not lay hold on it, and lift *it* out? ¹² How much then is a man better than a sheep? Wherefore it is lawful to do well on the sabbath days. ^(Matthew 12) ⁴ But they held their peace. ^(Mark 3)

⁵ And when he had looked round about ^(Mark 3) ¹⁰ upon them all, ^(Luke 6) ⁵ with anger, being grieved for the hardness of their hearts, he said unto the man, Stretch forth your hand. ^(Mark 3) ¹⁰ And he did so: ^(Luke 6) ⁵ and he stretched *it* out: and his hand was restored whole, ^(Mark 3) ¹³ like as the other. ¹⁴ Then the Pharisees went out, ^(Matthew 12) ¹¹ and they were filled with madness; and communed one with another what they might do to Jesus, ^(Luke 6) ⁶ and straightway ^(Mark 3) ¹⁴ held a council ^(Matthew 12) ⁶ with the Herodians against him, how they might destroy him. ^(Mark 3)

(MATTHEW 12:9–14; MARK 3:1–2, 4–6; LUKE 6:6–11)

Multitudes Come To Be Healed and Delivered

15 BUT when Jesus knew *it*, he withdrew himself (Matthew 12) 7 with his disciples (Mark 3) 15 from thence (Matthew 12) 7 to the sea: and a great multitude from Galilee followed him, and from Judaea, 8 and from Jerusalem, and from Idumaea, and *from* beyond Jordan; and they about Tyre and Sidon, a great multitude, when they had heard what great things he did, came unto him (Mark 3) 15 and he healed them all. (Matthew 12)

9 And he spoke to his disciples, that a small ship should wait on him because of the multitude, lest they should throng him. 10 For he had healed many; insomuch that they pressed upon him for to touch him, as many as had plagues. 11 And unclean spirits, when they saw him, fell down before him, and cried, saying, You are the Son of God. 12 And he straitly charged them that they should not make him known. (Mark 3) *[All this happened]* 17 That it might be fulfilled which was spoken by Esaias the prophet, saying, 18 Behold my servant, whom I have chosen; my beloved, in whom my soul is well pleased: I will put my spirit upon him, and he shall show judgment to the Gentiles. 19 He shall not strive, nor cry; neither shall any man hear his voice in the streets. 20 A bruised reed shall he not break, and smoking flax shall he not quench, till he send forth judgment unto victory. 21 And in his name shall the Gentiles trust.ᵃ
(Matthew 12)

Jesus came gentle + meek (MATTHEW 12:15, 17–21; MARK 3:7–12)
not with political + military power

---

a. O.T. prophecy in Isaiah 42:1–4.

CHAPTER SEVEN

Jesus Ordains Twelve Apostles

¹² AND it came to pass in those days, that he went out into a mountain to pray, and continued all night in prayer to God. (Luke 6)

¹³ And when it was day, he (Luke 6) ¹³ called *unto him* whom he would: and they came unto him. (Mark 3) ¹³ He called *unto him* his disciples: and of them he chose twelve, (Luke 6) ¹⁴ and he ordained twelve, (Mark 3) ¹³ whom also he named apostles; (Luke 6) ¹⁴ that they should be with him, and that he might send them forth to preach, ¹⁵ and to have power to heal sicknesses, and to cast out devils: (Mark 3) ¹ he gave them power *against* unclean spirits, to cast them out, and to heal all manner of sickness and all manner of disease. (Matthew 10)

² Now the names of the twelve apostles are these; The first, Simon, (Matthew 10) ¹⁴ (whom he also (Luke 6) ¹⁶ surnamed (Mark 3) ¹⁴ Peter,) (Luke 6) ² and Andrew his brother; James *the son* of Zebedee, and John his brother; (Matthew 10) ¹⁷ and he surnamed them Boanerges, which is, The sons of thunder: (Mark 3) ³ Philip, and Bartholomew; Thomas, and Matthew the publican; James *the son* of Alphaeus, and Lebbaeus, whose surname was Thaddaeus; (Judas *the brother* of James, Luke 6:16) ⁴ Simon the Canaanite, (Matthew 10) ¹⁵ called Zelotes, (Luke 6) ⁴ and Judas Iscariot, who also betrayed him. (Matthew 10)

¹⁹ And they went into an house. (Mark 3) ¹⁷ And he came down with them, and stood in the plain, and the company of his disciples, and a great multitude of people out of all Judaea and Jerusalem, and from the sea coast of Tyre and Sidon, which came to hear him, and to be healed of their diseases; ¹⁸ and they that were vexed with unclean spirits: and they were healed. ¹⁹ And the whole multitude sought to touch him: for there went virtue out of him, and healed *them* all. (Luke 6)

(LUKE 6:12–19; MARK 3:13–17, 19; MATTHEW 10:1–4)

Jesus' Teachings — Beatitudes

[1] AND seeing the multitudes, he went up into a mountain: and when he was set, his disciples came unto him. (Matthew 5) [20] And he lifted up his eyes on his disciples, (Luke 6) [2] and he opened his mouth, and taught them, saying, [3] Blessed *are* the poor in spirit: for theirs is the kingdom of heaven. (Matthew 5) [20] Blessed *be you* poor: for yours is the kingdom of God. (Luke 6) [4] Blessed *are* they that mourn: for they shall be comforted. (Matthew 5) [21] Blessed *are you* that hunger now: for you shall be filled. Blessed *are you* that weep now: for you shall laugh. (Luke 6) [5] Blessed *are* the meek: for they shall inherit the earth. [6] Blessed *are* they which do hunger and thirst after righteousness: for they shall be filled. [7] Blessed *are* the merciful: for they shall obtain mercy. [8] Blessed *are* the pure in heart: for they shall see God. [9] Blessed *are* the peacemakers: for they shall be called the children of God. [10] Blessed *are* they which are persecuted for righteousness' sake: for theirs is the kingdom of heaven. (Matthew 5) [22] Blessed are you, when men shall hate you, and when they shall separate you *from their company,* and shall reproach *you,* and cast out your name as evil, (Luke 6) [11] revile you, and persecute *you,* and shall say all manner of evil against you falsely, for my sake, (Matthew 5) [22] for the Son of man's sake. [23] Rejoice in that day, and leap for joy: (Luke 6) [12] and be exceeding glad: (Matthew 5) [23] for, behold, your reward *is* great in heaven: for in the like manner did their fathers unto the prophets. (Luke 6) [12] So persecuted they the prophets which were before you. (Matthew 5)

(MATTHEW 5:1–12; LUKE 6:20–23)

Jesus' Teachings — Similitudes

[24] BUT woe unto you that are rich! For you have received your consolation. [25] Woe unto you that are full! For you shall hunger. Woe unto you that laugh now! For you shall mourn and weep. [26] Woe unto you, when all men shall speak well of you! For so did their fathers to the false prophets. (Luke 6)

SALT r LIGHT

¹³ You are the salt of the earth: but if the salt have lost his savour, wherewith shall it be salted? It is thenceforth good for nothing, but to be cast out, and to be trodden under foot of men. ¹⁴ You are the light of the world. A city that is set on an hill cannot be hid. ^{(Matthew 5) 33} No man, when he has lighted a candle, puts *it* in a secret place, neither under a bushel, but on a candlestick, that they which come in may see the light, ^{(Luke 11) 15} and it gives light unto all that are in the house. ¹⁶ Let your light so shine before men, that they may see your good works, and glorify your Father which is in heaven. ^(Matthew 5)

(LUKE 6:24–26; MATTHEW 5:13–16; LUKE 11:33)

Jesus' Teachings — Law

¹⁷ THINK not that I am come to destroy the law, or the prophets: I am not come to destroy, but to fulfil. ¹⁸ For verily I say unto you, till heaven and earth pass, one jot or one tittle shall in no wise pass from the law, till all be fulfilled. ¹⁹ Whosoever therefore shall break one of these least commandments, and shall teach men so, he shall be called the least in the kingdom of heaven: but whosoever shall do and teach *them*, the same shall be called great in the kingdom of heaven. ²⁰ For I say unto you, that except your righteousness shall exceed *the righteousness* of the scribes and Pharisees, you shall in no case enter into the kingdom of heaven. ^(Matthew 5)

(MATTHEW 5:17–20)

Cannot be outward showing must be spiritual - inner man - pure in heart

Jesus' Teachings — Murder

²¹ YOU have heard that it was said by them of old time, You shall not kill; and whosoever shall kill shall be in danger of the judgment: ²² but I say unto you, That whosoever is angry with his brother without a cause shall be in danger of the judgment: and whosoever shall say to his brother, Raca, shall be in danger of the

council: but whosoever shall say, You fool, shall be in danger of hell fire. ²³ Therefore if you bring your gift to the altar, and there remember that your brother has ought against you; ²⁴ leave there your gift before the altar, and go your way; first be reconciled to your brother, and then come and offer your gift. ²⁵ Agree with your adversary quickly, while you are in the way with him; lest at any time the adversary deliver you to the judge, and the judge deliver you to the officer, and you be cast into prison. ²⁶ Verily I say unto you, you shall by no means come out thence, till you have paid the uttermost farthing. (Matthew 5)

First... then [handwritten margin note]

(MATTHEW 5:21–26)

Jesus' Teachings—Adultery

²⁷ You have heard that it was said by them of old time, You shall not commit adultery: ²⁸ but I say unto you, that whosoever looks on a woman to lust after her has committed adultery with her already in his heart. ²⁹ And if your right eye offend you, pluck it out, and cast *it* from you: for it is profitable for you that one of your members should perish, and not *that* your whole body should be cast into hell. ³⁰ And if your right hand offend you, cut it off, and cast *it* from you: for it is profitable for you that one of your members should perish, and not *that* your whole body should be cast into hell. (Matthew 5)

Cut sin cast away temptation [handwritten margin note]

³¹ It has been said, Whosoever shall put away his wife, let him give her a writing of divorcement: ³² but I say unto you, that whosoever shall put away his wife, saving for the cause of fornication, causes her to commit adultery: and whosoever shall marry her that is divorced commits adultery. (Matthew 5)

(MATTHEW 5:27–32)

Jesus' Teachings—Swear Not

³³ AGAIN, you have heard that it has been said by them of old time, You shall not forswear yourself, but shall perform unto the Lord your oaths: ³⁴ but I say unto you, swear not at all; neither by heaven; for it is God's throne: ³⁵ nor by the earth; for it is his footstool: neither by Jerusalem; for it is the city of the great King. ³⁶ Neither shall you swear by your head, because you can not make one hair white or black. ³⁷ But let your communication be, Yea, yea; Nay, nay: for whatsoever is more than these comes of evil. ^(Matthew 5)

(MATTHEW 5:33–37)

Jesus' Teachings— Love Your Enemies

³⁸ YOU have heard that it has been said, An eye for an eye, and a tooth for a tooth: ³⁹ but I say unto you, that you resist not evil: but whosoever shall smite you on your right cheek, turn to him the other also, ^{(Matthew 5) 29} and him that takes away your cloak forbid not *to take your* coat also. ^{(Luke 6) 40} And if any man will sue you at the law, and take away your coat, let him have *your* cloak also. ⁴¹ And whosoever shall compel you to go a mile, go with him twain. ^{(Matthew 5) 30} Give to every man that asks of you; ^{(Luke 6) 42} and from him that would borrow of you turn not you away, ^(Matthew 5) ³⁰ and of him that takes away your goods ask *them* not again. ^(Luke 6)

⁴³ You have heard that it has been said, You shall love your neighbor, and hate your enemy. ⁴⁴ But I say unto you ^(Matthew 5) ²⁷ which hear, ^{(Luke 6) 44} love your enemies, bless them that curse you, do good to them that hate you, and pray for them which despitefully use you, and persecute you; ⁴⁵ that you may be the children of your Father which is in heaven: for he makes his sun to rise on the evil and on the good, and sends rain on the just and on the unjust. ⁴⁶ For if you love them which love you, what reward have you? ^{(Matthew 5) 32} What thank have you? ^{(Luke 6) 46} Do not even the publicans the same? ^{(Matthew 5) 32} For sinners also love those that love them. ^(Luke 6)

[33] And if you do good to them which do good to you, what thank have you? For sinners also do even the same. [(Luke 6)] [47] And if you salute your brethren only, what do you more *than* others? Do not even the publicans so? [(Matthew 5)] [34] And if you lend *to them* of whom you hope to receive, what thank have you? For sinners also lend to sinners, to receive as much again. [35] But love your enemies, and do good, and lend, hoping for nothing again; and your reward shall be great, and you shall be the children of the Highest: for he is kind unto the unthankful and *to* the evil. [36] Be you therefore merciful, as your Father also is merciful. [(Luke 6)] [48] Be you therefore perfect, even as your Father which is in heaven is perfect. [(Matthew 5)]

reward *Highes*

(MATTHEW 5:38–48; LUKE 6:27, 29–30, 32–36)

Jesus' Teachings — Giving, Prayer, Forgiveness

No reward

[1] TAKE heed that you do not your alms before men, to be seen of them: otherwise you have no reward of your Father which is in heaven. [2] Therefore when you do *your* alms, do not sound a trumpet before you, as the hypocrites do in the synagogues and in the streets, that they may have glory of men. Verily I say unto you, they have their reward. [3] But when you do alms, let not your left hand know what your right hand does: [4] that your alms may be in secret: and your Father which sees in secret himself shall reward you openly. [5] And when you pray, you shall not be as the hypocrites *are*: for they love to pray standing in the synagogues and in the corners of the streets, that they may be seen of men. Verily I say unto you, they have their reward. [6] But you, when you pray, enter into your closet, and when you have shut your door, pray to your Father which is in secret; and your Father which sees in secret shall reward you openly. [(Matthew 6)]

[7] But when you pray, use not vain repetitions, as the heathen *do*: for they think that they shall be heard for their much speaking. [8] Be not therefore like unto them: for your Father knows what things you have need of, before you ask him. [9] After this manner

He knows my needs before I ask.

LORD's Prayer

therefore pray: Our Father who is in heaven, Hallowed be your name. [10] Your kingdom come, Your will be done, in earth, as *it is* in heaven. [11] Give us this day our daily bread. [12] And forgive us our debts, as we forgive our debtors. [13] And lead us not into temptation, but deliver us from evil: For yours is the kingdom, and the power, and the glory, for ever. Amen. (Matthew 6)

[14] For if you forgive men their trespasses, your heavenly Father will also forgive you: [15] but if you forgive not men their trespasses, neither will your Father forgive your trespasses. [16] Moreover when you fast, be not, as the hypocrites, of a sad countenance: for they disfigure their faces, that they may appear unto men to fast. Verily I say unto you, they have their reward. [17] But you, when you fast, anoint your head, and wash your face; [18] that you appear not unto men to fast, but unto your Father which is in secret: and your Father, which sees in secret, shall reward you openly. (Matthew 6)

(MATTHEW 6:1–18)

Jesus' Teachings—Faith

where is my heart? on earth or in heaven?

[19] LAY not up for yourselves treasures upon earth, where moth and rust do corrupt, and where thieves break through and steal: [20] but lay up for yourselves treasures in heaven, where neither moth nor rust does corrupt, and where thieves do not break through nor steal: [21] for where your treasure is, there will your heart be also. (Matthew 6)

[22] The light of the body is the eye: if therefore your eye be single, your whole body (Matthew 6) [34] also (Luke 11) [22] shall be full of light. [23] But if your eye be evil, your whole body (Matthew 6) [34] also (Luke 11) [23] shall be full of darkness. If therefore the light that is in you be darkness, how great *is* that darkness! (Matthew 6) [35] Take heed therefore that the light which is in you be not darkness. [36] If your whole body therefore *be* full of light, having no part dark, the whole shall be full of light, as when the bright shining of a candle does give you light. (Luke 11) [24] No man can serve two masters: for either he will hate the

Superficial earthly religion that leaves the heart dark

one, and love the other; or else he will hold to the one, and despise the other. You cannot serve God and mammon. (Matthew 6)

25 Therefore I say unto you, take no thought for your life, what you shall eat, or what you shall drink; nor yet for your body, what you shall put on. Is not the life more than meat, and the body than raiment? 26 Behold the fowls of the air: for they sow not, neither do they reap, nor gather into barns; yet your heavenly Father feeds them. Are you not much better than they? 27 Which of you by taking thought can add one cubit unto his stature? 28 And why take you thought for raiment? Consider the lilies of the field, how they grow; they toil not, neither do they spin: 29 and yet I say unto you, that even Solomon in all his glory was not arrayed like one of these. (Matthew 6)

30 Wherefore, if God so clothe the grass of the field, which to day is, and to morrow is cast into the oven, *shall he* not much more *clothe* you, O you of little faith? 31 Therefore take no thought, saying, What shall we eat? Or, What shall we drink? Or, Wherewithal shall we be clothed? 32 (For after all these things do the Gentiles seek:) for your heavenly Father knows that you have need of all these things. 33 But seek first the kingdom of God, and his righteousness; and all these things shall be added unto you. 34 Take therefore no thought for the morrow: for the morrow shall take thought for the things of itself. Sufficient unto the day *is* the evil thereof. (Matthew 6)

1 Judge not, that you be not judged, (Matthew 7) 37 and you shall not be judged: condemn not, and you shall not be condemned: forgive, and you shall be forgiven: 38 give, and it shall be given unto you; good measure, pressed down, and shaken together, and running over, shall men give into your bosom. (Luke 6) 2 For with what judgment you judge, you shall be judged. (Matthew 7) 38 For with the same measure that you mete withal it shall be measured to you again. (Luke 6)

(MATTHEW 6:19–34; 7:1–2; LUKE 11:34–36; 6:37–38)

[handwritten margin notes: "what do I seek?"; "• judge not • condemn not • forgive • give"]

[handwritten notes at bottom: "Your Heavenly Father knows your needs"; "SEEK GOD – RETURN TO HIM – TO INTIMACY TO PURITY OF HEART + OBEDIENCE OUT OF LOVE"]

CHAPTER EIGHT

Jesus Teaches in Parables

³⁹ AND he spoke a parable unto them, Can the blind lead the blind? Shall they not both fall into the ditch? ⁴⁰ The disciple is not above his master: but every one that is perfect shall be as his master. ⁴¹ And why behold you the mote that is in your brother's eye, but perceive ⁽Luke 6⁾ *[and]* ³ consider not the beam that is in your own eye? ⁽Matthew 7⁾ ⁴² Either how can you say to your brother, Brother, let me pull out the mote that is in your eye, when you yourself behold not the beam that is in your own eye? You hypocrite, cast out first the beam out of your own eye, and then shall you see clearly to pull out the mote that is in your brother's eye. ⁽Luke 6⁾

⁶ Give not that which is holy unto the dogs, neither cast you your pearls before swine, lest they trample them under their feet, and turn again and rend you. ⁷ Ask, and it shall be given you; seek, and you shall find; knock, and it shall be opened unto you: ⁸ for every one that asks receives; and he that seeks finds; and to him that knocks it shall be opened. ⁹ Or what man is there of you, whom if his son ask bread, will he give him a stone? ¹⁰ Or if he ask a fish, will he give him a serpent? ¹¹ If you then, being evil, know how to give good gifts unto your children, how much more shall your Father which is in heaven give good things to them that ask him? ⁽Matthew 7⁾

¹² Therefore all things whatsoever you would that men should do to you, do even so to them: for this is the law and the prophets. ¹³ Enter in at the strait gate: for wide *is* the gate, and broad *is* the way, that leads to destruction, and many there be which go in thereat: ¹⁴ because strait *is* the gate, and narrow *is* the way, which leads unto life, and few there be that find it. ⁽Matthew 7⁾

(LUKE 6:39–42; MATTHEW 7:3, 6–14)

Parable of the Fruit

[15] BEWARE of false prophets, which come to you in sheep's clothing, but inwardly they are ravening wolves. [16] You shall know them by their fruits. Do men gather grapes of thorns, or figs of thistles? [17] Even so every good tree brings forth good fruit; but a corrupt tree brings forth evil fruit. (Matthew 7) [43] For (Luke 6) [18] a good tree cannot bring forth evil fruit, neither *can* a corrupt tree bring forth good fruit. (Matthew 7)

[44] For every tree is known by his own fruit. For of thorns men do not gather figs, nor of a bramble bush gather they grapes. (Luke 6) [19] Every tree that brings not forth good fruit is hewn down, and cast into the fire. [20] Wherefore by their fruits you shall know them. (Matthew 7) [45] A good man out of the good treasure of his heart brings forth that which is good; and an evil man out of the evil treasure of his heart brings forth that which is evil: for of the abundance of the heart his mouth speaks. (Luke 6)

[21] Not every one that says unto me, Lord, Lord, shall enter into the kingdom of heaven; but he that does the will of my Father which is in heaven. (Matthew 7) [46] And why call you me, Lord, Lord, and do not the things which I say? (Luke 6) [22] Many will say to me in that day, Lord, Lord, have we not prophesied in your name? And in your name have cast out devils? And in your name done many wonderful works? [23] And then will I profess unto them, I never knew you: depart from me, you that work iniquity. (Matthew 7)

(MATTHEW 7:15–23; LUKE 6:43–46)

Parable of the House

[24] THEREFORE whosoever (Matthew 7) [47] comes to me, and (Luke 6) [24] hears these sayings of mine, and does them, (Matthew 7) [47] I will show you to whom he is like. (Luke 6) [24] I will liken him unto a wise man, (Matthew 7) [48] which built (Luke 6) [24] his house (Matthew 7) [48] and digged deep, and laid the foundation on a rock. (Luke 6) [25] And the rain descended, and the

floods came, and the winds blew. (Matthew 7) 48 And when the flood arose, the stream beat vehemently upon that house, and could not shake it: (Luke 6) 25 and it fell not: for it was founded upon a rock. (Matthew 7)

isobey

26 And every one that hears these sayings of mine, and does them not, shall be likened unto a foolish man, (Matthew 7) 49 that without a foundation (Luke 6) 26 built his house upon the sand: 27 and the rain descended, and the floods came, and the winds blew, and beat upon that house, (Matthew 7) 49 against which the stream did beat vehemently, and immediately it fell; (Luke 6) 27 and great was the fall of it. (Matthew 7) 49 And the ruin of that house was great. (Luke 6)

28 And it came to pass, when Jesus had ended these sayings, the people were astonished at his doctrine: 29 for he taught them as *one* having authority, and not as the scribes. (Matthew 7)

1 When he was come down from the mountain, great multitudes followed him. (Matthew 8)

(MATTHEW 7:24–29; 8:1; LUKE 6:47–49)

Jesus Heals the Centurion's Servant

1 Now when he had ended all his sayings in the audience of the people, he entered into Capernaum. 2 And a certain centurion's servant, who was dear unto him, was sick, and ready to die. 3 And when he heard of Jesus, he sent unto him the elders of the Jews, beseeching him that he would come and heal his servant. (Luke 7) 6 And saying, Lord, my servant lies at home sick of the palsy, grievously tormented. (Matthew 8)

4 And when they came to Jesus, they besought him instantly, saying, That he was worthy for whom he should do this: 5 for he loves our nation, and he has built us a synagogue. (Luke 7) 7 And Jesus said unto him, I will come and heal him. (Matthew 8) 6 Then Jesus went with them. And when he was now not far from the house, the centurion sent friends to him, saying unto him, Lord, trouble not yourself: for I am not worthy that you should enter under my roof:

fear of the Lord
faith
wisdom

wherefore neither thought I myself worthy to come unto you: but say in a word (but speak the word only, ^{Matthew 8:8}), and my servant shall be healed. ⁸ For I also am a man set under authority, having under me soldiers, and I say unto one, Go, and he goes; and to another, Come, and he comes; and to my servant, Do this, and he does *it*. ^(Luke 7)

⁹ When Jesus heard these things, he marvelled at him, and turned him about, and said unto the people that followed him, ^(Luke 7) ¹⁰ Verily I say unto you, I have not found so great faith, no, not in Israel. ¹¹ And I say unto you, that many shall come from the east and west, and shall sit down with Abraham, and Isaac, and Jacob, in the kingdom of heaven. ¹² But the children of the [*unbelieving*] kingdom shall be cast out into outer darkness: there shall be weeping and gnashing of teeth. ¹³ And Jesus said unto the centurion, Go your way; and as you have believed, *so* be it done unto you. And his servant was healed in the selfsame hour. ^(Matthew 8) ¹⁰ And they that were sent, returning to the house, found the servant whole that had been sick. ^(Luke 7)

(LUKE 7:1–10; MATTHEW 8:6–8, 10–13)

Jesus Awakes the Dead Young Man

¹¹ AND it came to pass the day after, that he went into a city called Nain; and many of his disciples went with him, and much people. ¹² Now when he came nigh to the gate of the city, behold, there was a dead man carried out, the only son of his mother, and she was a widow: and much people of the city was with her. ^(Luke 7)

¹³ And when the Lord saw her, he had compassion on her, and said unto her, Weep not. ¹⁴ And he came and touched the bier: and they that bore *him* stood still. And he said, Young man, I say unto you, arise. ¹⁵ And he that was dead sat up, and began to speak. And he delivered him to his mother. ¹⁶ And there came a fear on all: and they glorified God, saying, That a great prophet is risen up among us; and, That God has visited his people. ¹⁷ And this

rumour of him went forth throughout all Judaea, and throughout all the region round about. (Luke 7)

(LUKE 7:11–17)

Jesus Speaks of John the Baptist

¹⁸ AND the disciples of John showed him of all these things. (Luke 7) ² Now when John had heard in the prison the works of Christ, (Matthew 11) ¹⁹ John calling *unto him* two of his disciples sent *them* to Jesus, saying, Are you he that should come? (Luke 7) ³ Or do we look for another? (Matthew 11) ²⁰ When the men were come unto him, they said, John Baptist has sent us unto you, saying, Are you he that should come? Or look we for another? (Luke 7)

²¹ And in that same hour he cured many of *their* infirmities and plagues, and of evil spirits; and unto many *that were* blind he gave sight. ²² Then Jesus answering said unto them, Go your way, and tell John what things you have seen and heard; how that the blind see, the lame walk, the lepers are cleansed, the deaf hear, the dead are raised, to the poor the gospel is preached. ²³ And blessed is *he*, whosoever shall not be offended in me. (Luke 7)

²⁴ And when the messengers of John were departed, (Luke 7) ⁷ Jesus began to say unto the multitudes concerning John, What went you out into the wilderness (Matthew 11) ²⁴ for to see? (Luke 7) ⁷ A reed shaken with the wind? ⁸ But what went you out for to see? A man clothed in soft raiment? (Matthew 11) ²⁵ Behold, they which are gorgeously apparelled, (Luke 7) ⁸ they that wear soft *clothing*, (Matthew 11) ²⁵ and live delicately, are in kings' courts. ²⁶ But what went you out for to see? A prophet? Yea, I say unto you, and much more than a prophet. (Luke 7)

¹⁰ For this is *he*, of whom it is written, Behold, I send my messenger before your face, which shall prepare your way before you. (Matthew 11) ²⁸ For (Luke 7) ¹¹ verily I say unto you, (Matthew 11) ²⁸ among those that are born of women (Luke 7) ¹¹ there has not risen (Matthew 11) ²⁸ a greater prophet (Luke 7) ¹¹ than John the Baptist: notwithstanding he

that is least in the kingdom of heaven is greater than he. [12] And from the days of John the Baptist until now the kingdom of heaven suffers violence, and the violent take it by force. [13] For all the prophets and the law prophesied until John. [14] And if you will receive *it,* this is Elias, which was for to come. [15] He that has ears to hear, let him hear. (Matthew 11)

[29] And all the people that heard *him,* and the publicans, justified God, being baptized with the baptism of John. [30] But the Pharisees and lawyers rejected the counsel of God against themselves, being not baptized of him. (Luke 7)

[31] And the Lord said, Whereunto then shall I liken the men of this generation? And to what are they like? [32] They are like unto children sitting in the marketplace, and calling one to another, (Luke 7) [16] unto their fellows, (Matthew 11) [32] and saying, We have piped unto you, and you have not danced; we have mourned to you, and you have not wept. [33] For John the Baptist came neither eating bread nor drinking wine; and you say, He has a devil. [34] The Son of man is come eating and drinking; and you say, Behold a gluttonous man, and a winebibber, a friend of publicans and sinners! [35] But wisdom is justified of all her children. (Luke 7)

(LUKE 7:18–26, 28–35; MATTHEW 11:2–3, 7–8, 10–16)

CHAPTER NINE

The Alabaster Box of Ointment

³⁶ AND one of the Pharisees desired him that he would eat with him. And he went into the Pharisee's house, and sat down to meat. (Luke 7)

³⁷ And, behold, a woman in the city, which was a sinner, when she knew that *Jesus* sat at meat in the Pharisee's house, brought an alabaster box of ointment, ³⁸ and stood at his feet behind *him* weeping, and began to wash his feet with tears, and did wipe *them* with the hairs of her head, and kissed his feet, and anointed *them* with the ointment. (Luke 7)

³⁹ Now when the Pharisee which had bidden him saw *it,* he spoke within himself, saying, This man, if he were a prophet, would have known who and what manner of woman *this is* that touches him: for she is a sinner. (Luke 7)

⁴⁰ And Jesus answering said unto him, Simon, I have somewhat to say unto you. And he said, Master, say on. ⁴¹ There was a certain creditor which had two debtors: the one owed five hundred pence, and the other fifty. ⁴² And when they had nothing to pay, he frankly forgave them both. Tell me therefore, which of them will love him most? (Luke 7)

⁴³ Simon answered and said, I suppose that *he,* to whom he forgave most. And he said unto him, You have rightly judged. ⁴⁴ And he turned to the woman, and said unto Simon, See you this woman? I entered into your house, you gave me no water for my feet: but she has washed my feet with tears, and wiped *them* with the hairs of her head. ⁴⁵ You gave me no kiss: but this woman since the time I came in has not ceased to kiss my feet. ⁴⁶ My head with oil you did not anoint: but this woman has anointed my feet with ointment. ⁴⁷ Wherefore I say unto you, her sins, which are many, are forgiven;

for she loved much: but to whom little is forgiven, *the same* loves little. ⁴⁸ And he said unto her, Your sins are forgiven.^(Luke 7)

⁴⁹ And they that sat at meat with him began to say within themselves, Who is this that forgives sins also? ⁵⁰ And he said to the woman, Your faith has saved you; go in peace. ^(Luke 7)

¹ And it came to pass afterward, that he went throughout every city and village, preaching and showing the glad tidings of the kingdom of God: and the twelve *were* with him, ² and certain women, which had been healed of evil spirits and infirmities, Mary called Magdalene, out of whom went seven devils, ³ and Joanna the wife of Chuza Herod's steward, and Susanna, and many others, which ministered unto him of their substance. ^(Luke 8)

(LUKE 7:36–50; 8:1–3)

Jesus Delivers One Possessed with a Devil

²⁰ AND the multitude came together again, so that they could not so much as eat bread. ²¹ And when his friends heard *of it,* they went out to lay hold on him: for they said, He is beside himself. ^(Mark 3)

²² Then was brought unto him one possessed with a devil, blind, and dumb: and he healed him, insomuch that ^(Matthew 12) ¹⁴ when the devil was gone out, ^(Luke 11) ²² the blind and dumb both spoke and saw. ²³ And all the people were amazed, ^(Matthew 12) ¹⁵ wondered, ^(Luke 11) ²³ and said, Is not this the son of David? ²⁴ But when the Pharisees ^(Matthew 12) ²² and the scribes which came down from Jerusalem ^(Mark 3) ²⁴ heard *it,* they said, This *fellow* ^(Matthew 12) ²² has Beelzebub, and by the prince of the devils casts he out devils. ^(Mark 3) ¹⁶ And others, tempting *him,* sought of him a sign from heaven. ^(Luke 11)

²⁵ And Jesus, ^(Matthew 12) ¹⁷ knowing their thoughts, ^(Luke 11) ²³ called them *unto him,* and said unto them in parables, How can Satan cast out Satan? ^(Mark 3) ²⁵ Every kingdom divided against itself is brought to desolation. ^(Matthew 12) ²⁴ And if a kingdom be divided against itself, that kingdom cannot stand. ²⁵ And if a house be divided against itself, that house cannot stand ^(Mark 3) ²⁵ and every city

or house divided against itself shall not stand (Matthew 12) 17 and a house *divided* against a house falls. (Luke 11) 26 And if Satan rise up against himself, and be divided, he cannot stand, but has an end. (Mark 3) 26 And if Satan cast out Satan, he is divided against himself; how shall then his kingdom stand? (Matthew 12) 18 Because you say that I cast out devils through Beelzebub. (Luke 11) 27 And if I by Beelzebub cast out devils, by whom do your children cast *them* out? Therefore they shall be your judges. (Matthew 12) 20 But if I with the finger of God cast out devils, (Luke 11) 28 if I cast out devils by the Spirit of God, then (Matthew 12) 20 no doubt (Luke 11) 28 the kingdom of God is come (Matthew 12) 20 upon you. (Luke 11)

27 No man can enter into a strong man's house, and spoil his goods, except he will first bind the strong man; and then he will spoil his house. (Mark 3) 21 When a strong man armed keeps his palace, his goods are in peace: 22 but when a stronger than he shall come upon him, and overcome him, he takes from him all his armour wherein he trusted, and divides his spoils. 23 He that is not with me is against me: and he that gathers not with me scatters (Luke 11) 30 abroad. (Matthew 12)

24 When the unclean spirit is gone out of a man, he walks through dry places, seeking rest; and finding none, (Luke 11) 44 then he says, I will return into my house from whence I came out; and when he is come, he finds *it* empty, swept, and garnished. 45 Then goes he, and takes with himself seven other spirits more wicked than himself, and they enter in, and dwell there: and the last *state* of that man is worse than the first. Even so shall it be also unto this wicked generation. (Matthew 12)

(MARK 3:20–27; LUKE 11:14, 16–18, 20–24; MATTHEW 12:22–28, 30, 44–45)

Blasphemy against the Holy Ghost

28 VERILY I say unto you, (Mark 3) 31 all manner of (Matthew 12) 28 sins shall be forgiven unto the sons of men, and blasphemies wherewith

soever they shall blaspheme: [29] but he that shall blaspheme against the Holy Ghost has never forgiveness, but is in danger of eternal damnation: (Mark 3) [31] the blasphemy *against* the *Holy* Ghost shall not be forgiven unto men. [32] And whosoever speaks a word against the Son of man, it shall be forgiven him: but whosoever speaks against the Holy Ghost, it shall not be forgiven him, neither in this world, neither in the *world* to come. (Matthew 12) [30] Because they said, He has an unclean spirit. (Mark 3)

good fruit

good heart

good speech

[33] Either make the tree good, and his fruit good; or else make the tree corrupt, and his fruit corrupt: for the tree is known by *his* fruit. [34] O generation of vipers, how can you, being evil, speak good things? For out of the abundance of the heart the mouth speaks. [35] A good man out of the good treasure of the heart brings forth good things: and an evil man out of the evil treasure brings forth evil things. [36] But I say unto you, that every idle word that men shall speak, they shall give account thereof in the day of judgment. [37] For by your words you shall be justified, and by your words you shall be condemned. (Matthew 12)

[27] And it came to pass, as he spoke these things, a certain woman of the company lifted up her voice, and said unto him, Blessed *is* the womb that bore you, and the paps which you have sucked. [28] But he said, Yea rather, blessed *are* they that hear the word of God, and keep it. (Luke 11)

hear obey

(MARK 3:28–30; MATTHEW 12:31–37; LUKE 11:27–28)

Signs of Jonas and the Queen of the South

[29] AND when the people were gathered thick together, (Luke 11) [38] certain of the scribes and of the Pharisees answered, saying, Master, we would see a sign from you. [39] But he answered and said unto them, (Matthew 12) [29] This is (Luke 11) [39] an evil and adulterous (Matthew 12) [29] generation: they seek a sign; and there shall no sign be given (Luke 11) [39] to it, (Matthew 12) [29] but the sign of Jonas the prophet. (Luke 11) [40] For as Jonas was three days and three nights in the whale's belly;

so shall the Son of man be three days and three nights in the heart of the earth. (Matthew 12) 30 For as Jonas was a sign unto the Ninevites, so shall also the Son of man be to this generation. (Luke 11)

31 The queen of the south *[Sheba]* shall rise up in the judgment with the men of this generation, (Luke 11) 42 and shall condemn (Matthew 12) 31 them: (Luke 11) 42 for she came from the uttermost parts of the earth to hear the wisdom of Solomon; and, behold, a greater than Solomon *is* here. (Matthew 12)

32 The men of Nineve shall rise up in the judgment with this generation, and shall condemn it: for they repented at the preaching of Jonas; and, behold, a greater than Jonas *is* here. (Luke 11)

(LUKE 11:29–32; MATTHEW 12:38–40, 42)

Mary Desires To Speak to Jesus

46 WHILE he yet talked to the people, (Matthew 12) 32 and the multitude sat about him, (Mark 3) 46 behold, *his* mother and his brethren stood without, desiring to speak with him. (Matthew 12) 19 *[They]* could not come at him for the press, (Luke 8) 31 and, standing without, sent unto him, calling him. (Mark 3) 20 And it was told him *by certain* which said, (Luke 8) 47 Behold, your mother and your brethren stand without (Matthew 12) *[and]* 32 seek for you, (Mark 3) 20 desiring to see you (Luke 8) *[and]* 47 to speak with you. 48 But he answered and said unto him that told him, Who is my mother? And who are my brethren? (Matthew 12)

34 And he looked round about on them which sat about him, (Mark 3) 49 and he stretched forth his hand toward his disciples, and said, Behold my mother and my brethren! (Matthew 12) 21 My mother and my brethren are these which hear the word of God, and do it. (Luke 8) 50 For whosoever shall do the will of my Father which is in heaven, (Matthew 12) 35 whosoever shall do the will of God, the same is my brother, and my sister, and mother. (Mark 3)

(MATTHEW 12:46–50; MARK 3:31–32, 34–35; LUKE 8:19–21)

CHAPTER TEN

Parable of the Sower and His Seed

¹ THE same day went Jesus out of the house, and sat by the sea side. (Matthew 13)

² And great multitudes were gathered together unto him, (Matthew 13) 4 and were come to him out of every city, (Luke 8) 1 so that he entered into a ship, and sat in the sea; (Mark 4) 2 and the whole multitude stood on the shore. (Matthew 13)

¹ And he began again to teach by the sea side: (Mark 4) 3 and he spoke many things unto them in parables. (Matthew 13) 2 And he taught them many things by parables, and said unto them in his doctrine, ³ Hearken; Behold, there went out a sower to sow (Mark 4) 5 his seed. (Luke 8)

⁴ And it came to pass, as he sowed, some fell by the way side, (Mark 4) 5 and it was trodden down, (Luke 8) 4 and the fowls of the air came and devoured it up. ⁵ And some fell on stony ground, (Mark 4) 6 upon a rock, (Luke 8) 5 where it had not much earth; and immediately it sprang up, because it had (Mark 4) 5 no deepness of earth. (Matthew 13) 6 But when the sun was up, it was scorched; and because it had no root, (Mark 4) 6 and because it lacked moisture, (Luke 8) 6 it withered away. (Mark 4)

⁷ And some fell among thorns; (Matthew 13) 7 and the thorns grew up, (Mark 4) 7 sprang up with it, and choked it, (Luke 8) 7 and it yielded no fruit. (Mark 4) 8 But other fell into good ground, (Matthew 13) 8 and did yield fruit that sprang up and increased; and brought forth, (Mark 4) 8 some an hundredfold, some sixtyfold, some thirtyfold. (Matthew 13) 8 And when he had said these things, he cried, He that has ears to hear, let him hear. (Luke 8)

(MATTHEW 13:1–8; MARK 4:1–8; LUKE 8:4–8)

71

Disciples Ask about the Parable of the Sower

[10] AND when he was alone, they that were about him with the twelve asked of him the parable, [(Mark 4) 9] saying, What might this parable be? [(Luke 8) 10] Why speak you unto them in parables? [(Matthew 13)]

[11] He answered and said unto them, Because it is given unto you to know the mysteries of the kingdom of heaven, [(Matthew 13) 11] but unto them that are without, [(Mark 4) 11] it is not given. [12] For whosoever has, to him shall be given, and he shall have more abundance: but whosoever has not, from him shall be taken away even that he has. [13] Therefore speak I to them in parables: because they seeing see not; and hearing they hear not, neither do they understand. [(Matthew 13)]

what have I been given?

[14] And in them is fulfilled the prophecy of Esaias, which says, By hearing you shall hear, and shall not understand; and seeing you shall see, and shall not perceive: [15] for this people's heart is waxed gross, and *their* ears are dull of hearing, and their eyes they have closed; lest at any time they should see with *their* eyes and hear with *their* ears, and should understand with *their* heart, and should be converted, [(Matthew 13) 12] and *their* sins should be forgiven them, [(Mark 4) 15] and I should heal them.[a] [(Matthew 13)]

[16] But blessed *are* your eyes, for they see: and your ears, for they hear. [17] For verily I say unto you, that many prophets and righteous *men* have desired to see *those things* which you see, and have not seen *them*; and to hear *those things* which you hear, and have not heard *them*. [(Matthew 13)]

[13] And he said unto them, Know you not this parable? And how then will you know all parables? [(Mark 4) 18] Hear you therefore the parable of the sower. [(Matthew 13) 11] Now the parable is this: [(Luke 8) 14] the sower sows the word. [(Mark 4) 11] The seed is the word of God. [(Luke 8)] [19] When any one hears the word of the kingdom, and understands it not, then [(Matthew 13) 15] immediately [(Mark 4) 19] comes the wicked *one*, [(Matthew 13) 15] Satan, [(Mark 4) 12] the devil, [(Luke 8) 15] and takes away the word [(Mark 4) 19] which was sown in his heart, [(Matthew 13) 12] lest they should

a. O.T. prophecy in Isaiah 6:9–10; see also John 12:39–40 and Acts 28:25–27.

believe and be saved. (Luke 8) 19 This is he which received seed by the way side. (Matthew 13)

20 But he that received the seed into stony places, (Matthew 13) 13 on the rock, (Luke 8) 20 the same is he that hears the word, and anon [soon] with joy receives it; 21 yet has he not root in himself, (Matthew 13) 17 and so endure[s] but for a time: (Mark 4) 13 which for a while believe[s], and in time of temptation, (Luke 8) 21 when tribulation, (Matthew 13) 17 affliction or persecution arises for the word's sake, immediately (Mark 4) 21 he is offended (Matthew 13) [and] 13 fall[s] away. (Luke 8)

22 He also that received seed among the thorns is he that hears the word; (Matthew 13) 14 go[es] forth, (Luke 8) 19 and the cares of this world, and the deceitfulness of riches, and the lusts of other things, (Mark 4) 14 pleasures of *this* life, (Luke 8) 19 entering in, choke the word, and it becomes unfruitful. (Mark 4) 14 *[And such people, being]* choked with *[all these things]*, bring no fruit to perfection. (Luke 8)

23 But he that received seed into the good ground is he that hears the word, (Matthew 13) 15 which in an honest and good heart, having heard the word, (Luke 8) 20 *[they]* receive *it*, (Mark 4) 15 keep *it*, (Luke 8) 23 and understand *it*; which also bear fruit, (Matthew 13) 15 with patience, (Luke 8) 23 and bring forth, some an hundredfold, some sixty, some thirty. (Matthew 13)

(MARK 4:10–15, 17, 19–20; MATTHEW 13:10–23; LUKE 8:9, 11–15)

Parables of the Kingdom of God

21 AND he said unto them, Is a candle brought to be put under a bushel, or under a bed? And not to be set on a candlestick? (Mark 4) 16 No man, when he has lighted a candle, covers it with a vessel, or puts *it* under a bed; but sets *it* on a candlestick, that they which enter in may see the light. 17 For nothing is secret, that shall not be made manifest; neither *any thing* hid, that shall not be known and come abroad. (Luke 8)

23 If any man has ears to hear, let him hear. 24 And he said unto them, (Mark 4) 18 Take heed therefore (Luke 8) 24 what you hear; with what measure you mete, it shall be measured to you: and unto you that

hear) shall more be given. [25] For he that has, to him shall be given: and he that has not, from him shall be taken even that which [(Mark 4)] [18] he seems to have. [(Luke 8)]

[26] And he said, So is the kingdom of God, as if a man should cast seed into the ground; [27] and should sleep, and rise night and day, and the seed should spring and grow up, he knows not how. [28] For the earth brings forth fruit of herself; first the blade, then the ear, after that the full corn in the ear. [29] But when the fruit is brought forth, immediately he puts in the sickle, because the harvest is come. [(Mark 4)]

[24] Another parable put he forth unto them, saying, The kingdom of heaven is likened unto a man which sowed good seed in his field: [25] but while men slept, his enemy came and sowed tares among the wheat, and went his way. [26] But when the blade was sprung up, and brought forth fruit, then appeared the tares also. [(Matthew 13)]

[27] So the servants of the householder came and said unto him, Sir, did not you sow good seed in your field? From whence then has it tares? [28] He said unto them, An enemy has done this. The servants said unto him, Will you then that we go and gather them up? [29] But he said, Nay; lest while you gather up the tares, you root up also the wheat with them. [30] Let both grow together until the harvest: and in the time of harvest I will say to the reapers, Gather together first the tares, and bind them in bundles to burn them: but gather the wheat into my barn. [(Matthew 13)]

[31] Another parable put he forth unto them, saying, [(Matthew 13)] [30] Whereunto shall we liken the kingdom of God? Or with what comparison shall we compare it? [(Mark 4)] [18] And whereunto shall I resemble it? [(Luke 13)] [31] It is like a grain of mustard seed, [(Mark 4)] [31] which a man took, and sowed in his field: [(Matthew 13)] [31] which, when it is sown in the earth, [(Mark 4)] [32] indeed is the least of all [(Matthew 13)] [31] the seeds that be in the earth: [32] but when it is sown, it grows up, and becomes greater than all herbs, [(Mark 4)] [32] and becomes [(Matthew 13)] [19] a great tree; [(Luke 13)] [32] and shoots out great branches; [(Mark 4)] [32] so that the birds of the air [(Matthew 13)] [32] may lodge under the shadow of it, [(Mark 4)] [32] in the branches thereof. [(Matthew 13)]

³³ Another parable spoke he unto them; (Matthew 13) 20 and again he said, Whereunto shall I liken the kingdom of God? (Luke 13) 33 The kingdom of heaven is like unto leaven, which a woman took, and hid in three measures of meal, till the whole was leavened. (Matthew 13)

³³ And with many such parables spoke he the word unto them, as they were able to hear *it*. (Mark 4) 34 All these things spoke Jesus unto the multitude in parables; and without a parable spoke he not unto them: (Matthew 13) 34 and when they were alone, he expounded all things to his disciples, (Mark 4) 35 that it might be fulfilled which was spoken by the prophet, saying, I will open my mouth in parables; I will utter things which have been kept secret from the foundation of the world.ᵃ (Matthew 13)

(MARK 4:21, 23–34; MATTHEW 13:24–35; LUKE 8:16–18; 13:18–20)

Jesus Explains the Parable of the Tares

³⁶ THEN Jesus sent the multitude away, and went into the house: and his disciples came unto him, saying, Declare unto us the parable of the tares of the field. ³⁷ He answered and said unto them, He that sows the good seed is the Son of man; ³⁸ the field is the world; the good seed are the children of the kingdom; but the tares are the children of the wicked *one;* ³⁹ the enemy that sowed them is the devil; the harvest is the end of the world; and the reapers are the angels. (Matthew 13)

⁴⁰ As therefore the tares are gathered and burned in the fire; so shall it be in the end of this world. ⁴¹ The Son of man shall send forth his angels, and they shall gather out of his kingdom all things that offend, and them which do iniquity; ⁴² and shall cast them into a furnace of fire: there shall be wailing and gnashing of teeth. ⁴³ Then shall the righteous shine forth as the sun in the kingdom of their Father. Who has ears to hear, let him hear. (Matthew 13)

(MATTHEW 13:36–43)

---

a. O.T. prophecy in Psalm 78:2.

The Kingdom of Heaven

⁴⁴ AGAIN, the kingdom of heaven is like unto treasure hid in a field; the which when a man has found, he hides, and for joy thereof goes and sells all that he has, and buys that field. ⁴⁵ Again, the kingdom of heaven is like unto a merchant man, seeking goodly pearls: ⁴⁶ who, when he had found one pearl of great price, went and sold all that he had, and bought it. (Matthew 13)

⁴⁷ Again, the kingdom of heaven is like unto a net, that was cast into the sea, and gathered of every kind: ⁴⁸ which, when it was full, they drew to shore, and sat down, and gathered the good into vessels, but cast the bad away. ⁴⁹ So shall it be at the end of the world: the angels shall come forth, and sever the wicked from among the just, ⁵⁰ and shall cast them into the furnace of fire: there shall be wailing and gnashing of teeth. (Matthew 13)

⁵¹ Jesus said unto them, Have you understood all these things? They say unto him, Yea, Lord. ⁵² Then said he unto them, Therefore every scribe *which is* instructed unto the kingdom of heaven is like unto a man *that is* an householder, which brings forth out of his treasure *things* new and old. (Matthew 13)

¹⁸ Now when Jesus saw great multitudes about him, he gave commandment to depart unto the other side. ¹⁹ And a certain scribe came, and said unto him, Master, I will follow you whithersoever you go. ²⁰ And Jesus said unto him, The foxes have holes, and the birds of the air *have* nests; but the Son of man has not where to lay *his* head. ²¹ And another of his disciples said unto him, Lord, suffer me first to go and bury my father. ²² But Jesus said unto him, Follow me; and let the dead bury their dead. (Matthew 8)

(MATTHEW 13:44–52; 8:18–22)

Jesus Calms the Sea

³⁵ AND the same day, when the even was come, he said unto them *[his disciples]*, (Mark 4) ²² Let us go over unto the other side of the

lake. (Luke 8) 36 And when they had sent away the multitude, (Mark 4) 22 he went into a ship with his disciples: (Luke 8) 23 his disciples followed him. (Matthew 8) 22 And they launched forth. (Luke 8) 36 And there were also with him other little ships. (Mark 4) 23 But as they sailed he fell asleep. (Luke 8) 24 And, behold, there arose (Matthew 8) 23 and there came down (Luke 8) 37 a great storm of wind (Mark 4) 23 on the lake, (Luke 8) 37 and the waves beat into the ship, (Mark 4) 24 insomuch that the ship was covered with the waves, (Matthew 8) 37 so that it was now full, (Mark 4) 23 and they were filled *with water,* and were in jeopardy. (Luke 8)

38 And he was in the hinder part of the ship, asleep on a pillow. (Mark 4) 25 And his disciples came to *him,* and awoke him, saying, (Matthew 8) 24 Master, master, (Luke 8) 38 care you not that we perish? (Mark 4) 25 Lord, save us: we perish. 26 And he said unto them, Why are you (Matthew 8) 40 so fearful, (Mark 4) 26 O you of little faith? (Matthew 8) 40 How is it that you have no faith? (Mark 4) 25 Where is your faith? (Luke 8)

26 Then he arose, and rebuked the winds, (Matthew 8) 24 and the raging of the water, (Luke 8) 39 and said unto the sea, Peace, be still. And the wind ceased, and there was a great calm. (Mark 4) 27 But the men, (Matthew 8) 25 being afraid (Luke 8) 41 exceedingly, (Mark 4) 25 wondered, saying one to another, What manner of man is this! For he commands even the winds and water, and they obey him. (Luke 8)

(MARK 4:35–41; MATTHEW 8:23–27; LUKE 8:22–25)

fearful / no faith

Holy Spirit,
Instruct me and teach me and show me the way in which I should go; Counsel me with your eye upon me. Help me not to fear; help me to have faith. (Ps 32:8) 2/3/22

CHAPTER ELEVEN

Jesus Delivers a Man of Many Devils

¹ AND they came over unto the other side of the sea. (Mark 5) ²⁶ And they arrived at the country of the Gadarenes, (Luke 8) ²⁸ into the country of the Gergesenes, (Matthew 8) ²⁶ which is over against Galilee. (Luke 8) ² And when he was come out of the ship, (Mark 5) ²⁷ and when he went forth to land, (Luke 8) ² immediately there met him (Mark 5) ²⁸ two possessed with devils, coming out of the tombs, exceeding fierce, so that no man might pass by that way. (Matthew 8) *[One of them was]* ²⁷ out of the city a certain man, (Luke 8) ² with an unclean spirit, (Mark 5) ²⁷ which had devils long time and wore no clothes, neither abode in *any* house, but (Luke 8) ³ who had *his* dwelling among the tombs; and no man could bind him, no, not with chains: ⁴ because that he had been often bound with fetters and chains, and the chains had been plucked asunder by him, and the fetters broken in pieces: neither could any *man* tame him. (Mark 5)

⁵ And always, night and day, he was in the mountains, and in the tombs, crying, and cutting himself with stones. ⁶ But when he saw Jesus afar off, he ran, (Mark 5) ²⁸ he cried out, and fell down before him, (Luke 8) ⁶ and worshipped him, ⁷ and cried with a loud voice, and said, What have I to do with you, Jesus, *you* Son of the most high God? (Mark 5) ²⁹ Are you come hither to torment us before the time? (Matthew 8) ²⁸ I beseech you, (Luke 8) ⁷ I adjure you by God, that you torment me not. (Mark 5)

²⁹ (For he had commanded the unclean spirit to come out of the man.) (Luke 8) ⁸ For he said unto him, Come out of the man, *you* unclean spirit. (Mark 5) ²⁹ (For oftentimes it had caught him: and he was kept bound with chains and in fetters; and he broke the bands, and was driven of the devil into the wilderness.) (Luke 8)

³⁰ And Jesus asked him, saying, What is your name? (Luke 8) ⁹ And

he answered, saying, My name *is* Legion: for we are many. (Mark 5)
^{30} Because many devils were entered into him. (Luke 8) ^{10} And he besought him much that he would (Mark 5) ^{31} not command them to go
out into the deep, (Luke 8) *[and]* ^{10} that he would not send them away
out of the country. (Mark 5)

^{11} Now there was there nigh unto the mountains, (Mark 5) ^{30} a good
way off from them, (Matthew 8) ^{11} a great herd of swine feeding. ^{12} And
all the devils besought him (Mark 5) ^{32} that he would suffer them to
enter into them, (Luke 8) ^{31} saying, If you cast us out, suffer us to go
away into the herd of swine. (Matthew 8) ^{12} Send us into the swine, that
we may enter into them. (Mark 5) ^{32} And he suffered them. (Luke 8) ^{32} And
he said unto them, Go. (Matthew 8) ^{13} And forthwith Jesus gave them
leave. And the unclean spirits went out (Mark 5) ^{33} of the man, and entered into the swine: (Luke 8) ^{32} and, behold, the whole herd of swine
ran violently down a steep place (Matthew 8) ^{13} into the sea, (they were
about two thousand;) and were choked in the sea, (Mark 5) ^{32} and perished in the waters. (Matthew 8)

^{34} When they that fed (Luke 8) ^{14} the swine (Mark 5) ^{34} saw what was
done, they fled, and went (Luke 8) ^{33} their ways, (Matthew 8) ^{34} and told *it* in
the city and in the country. (Luke 8) ^{14} And they went out to see what
it was that was done. ^{15} And they come to Jesus, (Mark 5) ^{35} and found
the man, (Luke 8) ^{15} him that was possessed with the devil, and had
the legion, (Mark 5) ^{35} out of whom the devils were departed, sitting
at the feet of Jesus, clothed, and in his right mind: and they were
afraid. (Luke 8) ^{16} And they that saw *it* told them how it befell to him
that was possessed with the devil, (Mark 5) *[and]* ^{36} by what means he
that was possessed of the devils was healed, (Luke 8) ^{16} and *also* concerning the swine. (Mark 5)

^{34} And, behold, (Matthew 8) ^{37} the whole multitude of the country
of the Gadarenes round about (Luke 8) ^{34} came out to meet Jesus:
and when they saw him, (Matthew 8) *[they]* ^{37} besought him to depart
from them. (Luke 8) ^{17} And they began to pray him to depart out of
their coasts. (Mark 5) ^{37} For they were taken with great fear: and he
went up into the ship, and returned back again. (Luke 8) ^{18} And when
he was come into the ship, he that had been possessed with the

devil, (Mark 5) 38 out of whom the devils were departed, besought him that he might be with him. (Luke 8) 19 Howbeit Jesus suffered him not, (Mark 5) 38 but Jesus sent him away, saying (Luke 8) 19 unto him, <u>Go home</u> to your friends. (Mark 5) 39 <u>Return</u> to your own <u>house,</u> (Luke 8) 19 and tell them how great things the Lord (Mark 5) 39 God (Luke 8) 19 has done for you, and has had compassion on you. 20 And he departed, (Mark 5) 39 and he went his way, (Luke 8) 20 and began to publish (Mark 5) 39 throughout the whole city (Luke 8) [of] 20 Decapolis how great things Jesus had done for him: and all *men* did marvel. (Mark 5)

(MARK 5:1–20; LUKE 8:26–39; MATTHEW 8:28–34)

Jesus Heals the Issue of Blood and Jairus's Daughter

21 AND when Jesus was passed over again by ship unto the other side, much people gathered unto him: and he was nigh unto the sea. (Mark 5) 40 And it came to pass, that, when Jesus was returned, the people *gladly* received him: for they were all waiting for him. (Luke 8)

41 And, behold, there came (Luke 8) 22 one of the rulers of the synagogue, Jairus by name; and when he saw him, (Mark 5) 41 <u>he fell down</u> at Jesus' feet, (Luke 8) 18 <u>and worshipped him,</u> (Matthew 9) 23 and besought him greatly (Mark 5) 41 that he would come into his house: 42 for he had one only daughter, about twelve years of age, and she lay a-dying. (Luke 8) 23 My little daughter lies at the point of death: I *pray*, come and lay your hands on her, that she may be healed; and she shall live. (Mark 5) 19 And Jesus arose, and followed him, and *so did* his disciples. (Matthew 9) 24 And much people followed him, and thronged him. (Mark 5)

20 And, behold, (Matthew 9) 25 a certain woman, (Mark 5) 20 which was diseased with an issue of blood twelve years, (Matthew 9) 26 and had suffered many things of many physicians, and had spent all that she had, (Mark 5) 43 all her living, (Luke 8) 26 and was nothing bettered, (Mark 5) 43 neither could be healed of any, (Luke 8) 26 but rather grew worse, 27 when she had heard of Jesus, came in the press behind (Mark 5) 20 *him*, (Matthew 9) 27 and touched (Mark 5) 44 the border of his garment: (Luke 8) 21 for

she said within herself, (Matthew 9) 28 If I may touch but his clothes, I shall be whole. 29 And straightway the fountain of her blood was dried up; and she felt in *her* body that she was healed of that plague. (Mark 5) 44 And immediately her issue of blood stanched. (Luke 8)

30 And Jesus, immediately knowing in himself that virtue had gone out of him, turned him about in the press, and said, Who touched my clothes? (Mark 5) 45 Who touched me? When all denied, Peter and they that were with him, (Luke 8) 31 his disciples, said unto him, (Mark 5) 45 Master, (Luke 8) 31 you see (Mark 5) 45 the multitude throng you and press *you*, and say you, Who touched me? 46 And Jesus said, Somebody has touched me: for I perceive that virtue is gone out of me. (Luke 8) 32 And he looked round about to see her that had done this thing. (Mark 5)

47 And when the woman saw that she was not hid, she came (Luke 8) 33 fearing and trembling, knowing what was done in her, (Mark 5) 47 and falling down before him, she (Luke 8) 33 told him all the truth, (Mark 5) 47 she declared unto him before all the people for what cause she had touched him, and how she was healed immediately. (Luke 8) 22 And when he saw her, (Matthew 9) 48 he said unto her, (Luke 8) 22 Daughter, be of good comfort; (Matthew 9) 34 your faith has made you whole; go in peace, and be whole of your plague. (Mark 5) 22 And the woman was made whole from that hour. (Matthew 9)

35 While he yet spoke, there came from the ruler of the synagogue's *house certain* which said, Your daughter is dead: why trouble you the Master any further? 36 As soon as Jesus heard the word that was spoken, he said unto the ruler of the synagogue, Be not afraid, only believe, (Mark 5) 50 and she shall be made whole. (Luke 8)

37 And he suffered no man to follow him, save Peter, and James, and John the brother of James. 38 And he came to the house of the ruler of the synagogue, and saw the tumult, (Mark 5) 23 and saw the minstrels and the people making a noise, (Matthew 9) 38 and them that wept and wailed greatly. 39 And when he was come in, he said unto them, Why make you this ado, and weep? (Mark 5) 52 Weep not; (Luke 8) 24 give place: for the maid is not dead, but sleeps. (Matthew 9) 53 And they laughed him to scorn, knowing that she was dead. (Luke 8)

⁴⁰ But when he had put them all out, he takes the father and the mother of the damsel, and them that were with him. (Mark 5) ⁵¹ And when he came into the house, he suffered no man to go in, save Peter, and James, and John, and the father and the mother of the maiden, (Luke 8) ⁴⁰ and entered in where the damsel was lying. ⁴¹ And he took the damsel by the hand, and said unto her, Talitha cumi; which is, being interpreted, Damsel, I say unto you, arise. (Mark 5)

⁵⁵ And her spirit came again, (Luke 8) ⁴² and straightway the damsel arose, and walked; for she was *of the age* of twelve years. (Mark 5) ⁵⁶ And her parents were astonished (Luke 8) ⁴² with a great astonishment, (Mark 5) ⁵⁶ but he charged them (Luke 8) ⁴³ straitly (Mark 5) ⁵⁶ that they should tell no man what was done, (Luke 8) ⁴³ and commanded that something should be given her to eat. (Mark 5) ²⁶ And the fame hereof went abroad into all that land. (Matthew 9)

(MARK 5:21–43; MATTHEW 9:18–24, 26;
LUKE 8:40–48, 50–53, 55–56)

Jesus Heals Two Blind Men and Casts Out a Devil

²⁷ AND when Jesus departed thence, two blind men followed him, crying, and saying, *You* Son of David, have mercy on us. ²⁸ And when he was come into the house, the blind men came to him: and Jesus said unto them, Believe you that I am able to do this? They said unto him, Yea, Lord. (Matthew 9)

²⁹ Then touched he their eyes, saying, According to your faith be it unto you. ³⁰ And their eyes were opened; and Jesus straitly charged them, saying, See *that* no man know *it*. ³¹ But they, when they were departed, spread abroad his fame in all that country. (Matthew 9)

³² As they went out, behold, they brought to him a dumb man possessed with a devil. ³³ And when the devil was cast out, the dumb spoke: and the multitudes marvelled, saying, It was never so seen in Israel. ³⁴ But the Pharisees said, He casts out devils through the prince of the devils. (Matthew 9)

(MATTHEW 9:27–34)

Jesus Comes to His Own Country

¹ AND he went out from thence, and came into his own country; and his disciples follow him. ² And when the sabbath day was come, he began to teach in the synagogue: and many hearing *him* were astonished, saying, From (Mark 6) ⁵⁶ whence then has this *man* all these things? (Matthew 13) ² And what wisdom *is* this which is given unto him, that even such mighty works are wrought by his hands? ³ Is not this the carpenter, (Mark 6) ⁵⁵ the carpenter's son, (Matthew 13) ³ the son of Mary, the brother of James, and Joses, and of Juda, and Simon? And are not his sisters here with us? And they were offended at him. (Mark 6)

⁴ But Jesus said unto them, A prophet is not without honour, but in his own country, and among his own kin, and in his own house. ⁵ And he could there do no mighty work, save that he laid his hands upon a few sick folk, and healed *them*. ⁶ And he marvelled because of their unbelief. (Mark 6)

³⁵ And Jesus went (Matthew 9) ⁶ round (Mark 6) ³⁵ about all the cities and villages, teaching in their synagogues, and preaching the gospel of the kingdom, and healing every sickness and every disease among the people. ³⁶ But when he saw the multitudes, he was moved with compassion on them, because they fainted, and were scattered abroad, as sheep having no shepherd. (Matthew 9)

³⁷ Then said he unto his disciples, The harvest truly *is* plenteous, but the labourers *are* few; ³⁸ pray therefore the Lord of the harvest, that he will send forth labourers into his harvest. (Matthew 9)

(MARK 6:1–6; MATTHEW 13:55; 9:35–38)

CHAPTER TWELVE

Jesus Sends Forth His Twelve Disciples

¹ THEN he called his twelve disciples together, and gave them power and authority over all devils, (Luke 9) 7 unclean spirits; (Mark 6) 1 and to cure diseases. (Luke 9)

⁵ These twelve Jesus (Matthew 10) 7 began to send forth by two and two; (Mark 6) 2 to preach the kingdom of God, and to heal the sick, (Luke 9) 5 and commanded them, saying, Go not into the way of the Gentiles, and into *any* city of the Samaritans enter you not: ⁶ but go rather to the lost sheep of the house of Israel. (Matthew 10)

⁷ And as you go, preach, saying, The kingdom of heaven is at hand. ⁸ Heal the sick, cleanse the lepers, raise the dead, cast out devils: freely you have received, freely give. (Matthew 10) 3 And he said unto them, Take nothing for *your* journey, (Luke 9) 8 save a staff only. (Mark 6) 9 Provide neither gold, nor silver, nor brass in your purses, ¹⁰ nor scrip for *your* journey, neither shoes, nor yet staves; (Matthew 10) 3 neither bread, neither money; (Luke 9) 10 for the workman is worthy of his meat. (Matthew 10) 9 But *be* shod with sandals; and not put on two coats. (Mark 6)

¹⁰ And he said unto them, (Mark 6) 11 And into whatsoever city or town you shall enter, enquire who in it is worthy; and there abide till you go thence. (Matthew 10) 10 In what place soever you enter into an house, there abide till you depart from that place. (Mark 6)

¹² And when you come into an house, salute it. ¹³ And if the house be worthy, let your peace come upon it: but if it be not worthy, let your peace return to you. (Matthew 10)

¹⁴ And whosoever shall not receive you, nor hear your words, when you depart out of that house or city, (Matthew 10) 5 shake off the very dust (Luke 9) 11 under your feet for a testimony against them. Verily I say unto you, it shall be more tolerable for (Mark 6) 15 the land of

Sodom and Gomorrha in the day of judgment, than for that city. (Matthew 10)

¹⁶ Behold, I send you forth as sheep in the midst of wolves: be you therefore wise as serpents, and harmless as doves. ¹⁷ But beware of men: for they will deliver you up to the councils, and they will scourge you in their synagogues; ¹⁸ and you shall be brought before governors and kings for my sake, for a testimony against them and the Gentiles. ¹⁹ But when they deliver you up, take no thought how or what you shall speak: for it shall be given you in that same hour what you shall speak. ²⁰ For it is not you that speak, but the Spirit of your Father which speaks in you. (Matthew 10)

²¹ And the brother shall deliver up the brother to death, and the father the child: and the children shall rise up against *their* parents, and cause them to be put to death. ²² And you shall be hated of all *men* for my name's sake: but he that endures to the end shall be saved. ²³ But when they persecute you in this city, flee you into another: for verily I say unto you, you shall not have gone over the cities of Israel, till the Son of man be come. (Matthew 10)

(LUKE 9:1–3, 5; MATTHEW 10:5–23; MARK 6:7–11)

Jesus Teaches Discipleship

²⁴ THE disciple is not above *his* master, nor the servant above his lord. ²⁵ It is enough for the disciple that he be as his master, and the servant as his lord. If they have called the master of the house Beelzebub, how much more *shall they call* them of his household? ²⁶ Fear them not therefore: for there is nothing covered, that shall not be revealed; and hid, that shall not be known. ²⁷ What I tell you in darkness, *that* speak in light: and what you hear in the ear, *that* preach upon the housetops. (Matthew 10)

²⁸ And fear not them which kill the body, but are not able to kill the soul: but rather fear him which is able to destroy both soul and body in hell. ²⁹ Are not two sparrows sold for a farthing? And one of them shall not fall on the ground without your Father. ³⁰ But the

very hairs of your head are all numbered. [31] Fear you not therefore, you are of more value than many sparrows. (Matthew 10)

[32] Whosoever therefore shall confess me before men, him will I confess also before my Father which is in heaven. [33] But whosoever shall deny me before men, him will I also deny before my Father which is in heaven. [34] Think not that I am come to send peace on earth: I came not to send peace, but a sword. [35] For I am come to set a man at variance against his father, and the daughter against her mother, and the daughter in law against her mother in law. [36] And a man's foes *shall be* they of his own household. (Matthew 10)

[37] He that loves father or mother more than me is not worthy of me: and he that loves son or daughter more than me is not worthy of me. [38] And he that takes not his cross, and follows after me, is not worthy of me. [39] He that finds his life shall lose it: and he that loses his life for my sake shall find it. (Matthew 10) *crucified w/Christ*

[40] He that receives you receives me, and he that receives me receives him that sent me. [41] He that receives a prophet in the name of a prophet shall receive a prophet's reward; and he that receives a righteous man in the name of a righteous man shall receive a righteous man's reward. [42] And whosoever shall give to drink unto one of these little ones a cup of cold *water* only in the name of a disciple, verily I say unto you, he shall in no wise lose his reward. (Matthew 10)

[1] And it came to pass, when Jesus had made an end of commanding his twelve disciples, he departed thence to teach and to preach in their cities. (Matthew 11)

[6] And they departed, and went through the towns, preaching the gospel, (Luke 9) [12] and preached that men should repent. [13] And they cast out many devils, and anointed with oil many that were sick, and healed *them*. (Mark 6)

(MATTHEW 10:24–42; 11:1; LUKE 9:6; MARK 6:12–13)

The Head of John the Baptist

¹ At that time Herod the tetrarch heard of the fame of Jesus, ⁽ᴹᵃᵗ⁻
ᵗʰᵉʷ ¹⁴⁾ ⁷ of all that was done by him: ⁽ᴸᵘᵏᵉ ⁹⁾ ¹⁴ (for his name was spread
abroad:) ⁽ᴹᵃʳᵏ ⁶⁾ ⁷ and he was perplexed, because that it was said of
some, that John was risen from the dead; ⁸ and of some, that Elias
had appeared; and of others, that one of the old prophets was
risen again. ⁽ᴸᵘᵏᵉ ⁹⁾

¹⁶ But when Herod heard *thereof,* he said ⁽ᴹᵃʳᵏ ⁶⁾ ² unto his servants, This is John the Baptist, ⁽ᴹᵃᵗᵗʰᵉʷ ¹⁴⁾ ¹⁶ whom I beheaded: he is
risen from the dead; ⁽ᴹᵃʳᵏ ⁶⁾ ² and therefore mighty works do show
forth themselves in him. ⁽ᴹᵃᵗᵗʰᵉʷ ¹⁴⁾ *[At another time Herod said,]*
⁹ John have I beheaded: but who is this, of whom I hear such
things? And he desired to see him. ⁽ᴸᵘᵏᵉ ⁹⁾ ¹⁷ For Herod himself had
sent forth and laid hold upon John, and bound him, ⁽ᴹᵃʳᵏ ⁶⁾ ³ and
put *him* in prison for Herodias' sake, his brother Philip's wife: ⁽ᴹᵃᵗ⁻
ᵗʰᵉʷ ¹⁴⁾ ¹⁷ for he had married her. ¹⁸ For John had said unto Herod,
It is not lawful for you to have your brother's wife. ¹⁹ Therefore
Herodias had a quarrel against him, and would have killed him;
but she could not: ²⁰ for Herod feared John, knowing that he was
a just man and an holy, and observed him; and when he heard
him, he did many things, and heard him gladly. ⁽ᴹᵃʳᵏ ⁶⁾ ⁵ And when
he would have put him to death, he feared the multitude, because
they counted him as a prophet. ⁽ᴹᵃᵗᵗʰᵉʷ ¹⁴⁾

²¹ And when a convenient day was come, that Herod on his
birthday made a supper to his lords, high captains, and chief *es-
tates* of Galilee; ²² and when the daughter of the said Herodias
came in, and danced ⁽ᴹᵃʳᵏ ⁶⁾ ⁶ before them, ⁽ᴹᵃᵗᵗʰᵉʷ ¹⁴⁾ ²² and pleased
Herod and them that sat with him, the king said unto the damsel, Ask of me whatsoever you will, and I will give *it* you. ²³ And
he swore unto her, Whatsoever you shall ask of me, I will give *it*
you, unto the half of my kingdom. ⁽ᴹᵃʳᵏ ⁶⁾ ⁷ Whereupon he promised
with an oath to give her whatsoever she would ask. ⁽ᴹᵃᵗᵗʰᵉʷ ¹⁴⁾ ²⁴ And
she went forth, and said unto her mother, What shall I ask? And
she said, The head of John the Baptist. ²⁵ And she, ⁽ᴹᵃʳᵏ ⁶⁾ ⁸ being

before instructed of her mother, (Matthew 14) 25 came in straightway with haste unto the king, and asked, saying, I will that you give me by and by in a charger the head of John the Baptist. (Mark 6)

26 And the king was exceeding sorry; *yet* for his oath's sake, and for their sakes, (Mark 6) 9 them which sat with him at meat, (Matthew 14) 26 he would not reject her, (Mark 6) *[but]* 9 he commanded *it* to be given *her.* (Matthew 14) 27 And immediately the king sent an executioner, and commanded his head to be brought: and he went and beheaded (Mark 6) 10 John (Matthew 14) 27 in the prison, 28 and brought his head in a charger, and gave it to the damsel: and the damsel gave it to her mother. 29 And when his disciples heard *of it,* they came and took up his corpse, and laid it in a tomb, (Mark 6) 12 and went and told Jesus. (Matthew 14)

(MATTHEW 14:1–3, 5–10, 12; MARK 6:14, 16–29; LUKE 9:7–9)

Five Barley Loaves and Two Small Fishes

10 AND the apostles, when they were returned, (Luke 9) 30 gathered themselves together unto Jesus, and told him all things, both what they had done, and what they had taught. 31 And he said unto them, Come you yourselves apart into a desert place, and rest a while: for there were many coming and going, and they had no leisure so much as to eat. (Mark 6) 10 And he took them, (Luke 9) 32 and they departed into a desert place by ship privately; (Mark 6) 10 a desert place belonging to the city called Bethsaida, (Luke 9) 1 over the sea of Galilee, which is *the sea* of Tiberias. (John 6)

33 And the people saw them departing, and many knew him, and ran afoot thither out of all cities, and outwent them, and came together unto him. (Mark 6) 2 And a great multitude followed him, because they saw his miracles which he did on them that were diseased. (John 6) 34 And Jesus, when he came out, saw much people, (Mark 6) 11 and he received them, (Luke 9) 34 and was moved with compassion toward them, because they were as sheep not having a shepherd. (Mark 6) 3 And Jesus went up into a mountain, and there he sat

with his disciples. (John 6) 34 And he began to teach them many things (Mark 6) 11 and spoke unto them of the kingdom of God, and healed them that had need of healing. (Luke 9) 4 And the passover, a feast of the Jews, was nigh. (John 6)

35 And when the day was now far spent, (Mark 6) 15 and when it was evening, (Matthew 14) 35 his disciples came unto him, and said, This is a desert place, and now the time is far passed. (Mark 6) 12 Send the multitude away, that they may go into the towns and country round about, (Luke 9) 36 and into the villages, (Mark 6) 12 and lodge, (Luke 9) 36 and buy themselves bread: (Mark 6) 12 for we are here in a desert place, (Luke 9) [and] 36 they have nothing to eat. (Mark 6) 16 But Jesus (Matthew 14) 37 answered and said unto them, (Mark 6) 16 They need not depart; give you them to eat. (Matthew 14) 37 And they say unto him, Shall we go and buy two hundred pennyworth of bread, and give them to eat? (Mark 6)

5 When Jesus then lifted up his eyes, and saw a great company come unto him, he said unto Philip, Whence shall we buy bread, that these may eat? 6 And this he said to prove him: for he himself knew what he would do. 7 Philip answered him, Two hundred pennyworth of bread is not sufficient for them, that every one of them may take a little. (John 6) 38 He said unto them, How many loaves have you? Go and see. (Mark 6)

38 And when they knew, (Mark 6) 8 one of his disciples, Andrew, Simon Peter's brother, said unto him, 9 There is a lad here, which has five barley loaves, and two small fishes: but what are they among so many? (John 6) 13 We have no more but five loaves and two fishes; except we should go and buy meat for all this people. (Luke 9) 18 He said, Bring them hither to me. (Matthew 14) 39 And he commanded them to make all sit down by companies upon the green grass. (Mark 6) 10 And Jesus said (John 6) 14 to his disciples, (Luke 9) 10 Make the men sit down (John 6) 14 by fifties in a company. (Luke 9) 10 Now there was much grass in the place. (John 6)

15 And they did so, and made them all sit down. (Luke 9) 10 So the men sat down, (John 6) 40 in ranks, by hundreds, and by fifties, (Mark 6) 10 in number about five thousand. (John 6) 41 And when he had taken

the five loaves and the two fishes, he looked up to heaven, (Mark 6) ¹¹ and when he had given thanks, (John 6) *[he]* ⁴¹ blessed, and broke the loaves, and gave *them* to his disciples to set (Mark 6) ¹⁶ before the multitude (Luke 9) ¹¹ that were set down; (John 6) ⁴¹ and the two fishes divided he among them all, (Mark 6) ¹¹ as much as they would. (John 6)

⁴² And they did all eat, and were (Mark 6) ¹⁷ all filled. (Luke 9) ¹² When they were filled, he said unto his disciples, Gather up the fragments that remain, that nothing be lost. ¹³ Therefore they gathered *them* together, and filled twelve baskets with the fragments of the five barley loaves, (John 6) ⁴³ and of the fishes, (Mark 6) ¹³ which remained over and above unto them that had eaten. (John 6) ²¹ And they that had eaten (Matthew 14) ⁴⁴ of the loaves (Mark 6) ²¹ were about five thousand men, beside women and children. (Matthew 14)

¹⁴ Then those men, when they had seen the miracle that Jesus *Prophet* did, said, This is of a truth that prophet that should come into the world. ¹⁵ When Jesus therefore perceived that they would come and take him by force, to make him a king, he departed again into a mountain himself alone. (John 6)

(LUKE 9:10–17; MARK 6:30–44; JOHN 6:1–15;
MATTHEW 14:15–16, 18, 21)

CHAPTER THIRTEEN

Jesus Walks on the Sea

[16] AND when even was *now* come, (John 6) [45] straightway (Mark 6) [22] Jesus constrained his disciples to get (Matthew 14) [45] into the ship, (Mark 6) [22] and to go before him (Matthew 14) [45] to the other side before unto Bethsaida, while he sent away the people. (Mark 6)

[So,] [16] his disciples went down unto the sea, [17] and entered into a ship and went over the sea toward Capernaum. And it was now dark, and Jesus was not come to them. (John 6) [23] And when he had sent the multitudes away, he went up into a mountain apart to pray: and when the evening was come, he was there alone. (Matthew 14)

[24] But the ship was now in the midst of the sea, tossed with waves: for the wind was contrary. (Matthew 14) [18] And the sea arose by reason of a great wind that blew. (John 6) [47] And he *[Jesus was]* alone on the land. [48] And he saw them toiling in rowing; for the wind was contrary unto them: and about the fourth watch of the night, (Mark 6) [19] when they had rowed about five and twenty or thirty furlongs, (John 6) [25] Jesus (Matthew 14) [48] came unto them, walking upon the sea, and would have passed by them. (Mark 6)

[26] And when the disciples (Matthew 14) [49] saw him walking upon the sea, (Mark 6) [19] and drawing nigh unto the ship: (John 6) [49] they supposed it had been a spirit, and cried out: [50] for they all saw him, and were troubled. (Mark 6) [19] And they were afraid, (John 6) [26] saying, It is a spirit; and they cried out for fear. (Matthew 14) [50] And immediately (Mark 6) [27] Jesus (Matthew 14) [50] talked with them, and said unto them, Be of good cheer: it is I; be not afraid. (Mark 6)   *It is 'I AM'. Do not fear*

[28] And Peter answered him and said, Lord, if it be you, bid me come unto you on the water. [29] And he said, Come. And when Peter was come down out of the ship, he walked on the water, to go to Jesus. [30] But when he saw the wind boisterous, he was afraid;

and beginning to sink, he cried, saying, Lord, save me. [31] And immediately Jesus stretched forth *his* hand, and caught him, and said unto him, O you of little faith, wherefore did you doubt? (Matthew 14)

[32] And when they were come into the ship, the wind ceased. [33] Then they that were in the ship came and worshipped him, saying, Of a truth you are the Son of God. (Matthew 14) [51] And they were sore amazed in themselves beyond measure, and wondered. [52] For they considered not *the miracle* of the loaves: for their heart was hardened. (Mark 6)

[21] Then they willingly received him into the ship: and immediately the ship was at the land whither they went. (John 6) [53] And when they had passed over, they came into the land of Gennesaret, and drew to the shore. [54] And when they were come out of the ship, straightway they knew him. (Mark 6) [35] And when the men of that place had knowledge of him, they sent out into all that country round about, (Matthew 14) [55] and began to carry about in beds those that were sick, where they heard he was. [56] And whithersoever he entered, into villages, or cities, or country, they laid the sick in the streets, and besought him that they might touch if it were but the border of his garment: and as many as touched him were made (Mark 6) [36] perfectly whole. (Matthew 14)

(JOHN 6:16–19, 21; MARK 6:45, 47–56; MATTHEW 14:22–33, 35–36)

Jesus the Bread of Life

[22] THE day following, when the people which stood on the other side of the sea saw that there was none other boat there, save that one whereinto his disciples were entered, and that Jesus went not with his disciples into the boat, but *that* his disciples were gone away alone; [23] (Howbeit there came other boats from Tiberias nigh unto the place where they did eat bread, after that the Lord had given thanks:) (John 6)

[24] When the people therefore saw that Jesus was not there, neither his disciples, they also took shipping, and came to Capernaum,

seeking for Jesus. [25] And when they had found him on the other side of the sea, they said unto him, Rabbi, when came you hither? [26] Jesus answered them and said, Verily, verily, I say unto you, you seek me, not because you saw the miracles, but because you did eat of the loaves, and were filled. [27] Labour not for the meat which perishes, but for that meat which endures unto everlasting life, which the Son of man shall give unto you: for him has God the Father sealed. (John 6)

[28] Then said they unto him, What shall we do, that we might work the works of God? [29] Jesus answered and said unto them, This is the work of God, that you believe on him whom he has sent. [30] They said therefore unto him, What sign show you then, that we may see, and believe you? What do you work? [31] Our fathers did eat manna in the desert; as it is written, He gave them bread from heaven to eat. [32] Then Jesus said unto them, Verily, verily, I say unto you, Moses gave you not that bread from heaven; but my Father gives you the true bread from heaven. [33] For the bread of God is he which comes down from heaven, and gives life unto the world. (John 6)

[34] Then said they unto him, Lord, evermore give us this bread. [35] And Jesus said unto them, I am the bread of life: he that comes to me shall never hunger; and he that believes on me shall never thirst. [36] But I said unto you, that you also have seen me, and believe not. [37] All that the Father gives me shall come to me; and him that comes to me I will in no wise cast out. [38] For I came down from heaven, not to do my own will, but the will of him that sent me. [39] And this is the Father's will which has sent me, that of all which he has given me I should lose nothing, but should raise it up again at the last day. [40] And this is the will of him that sent me, that every one which sees the Son, and believes on him, may have everlasting life: and I will raise him up at the last day. (John 6)

(JOHN 6:22–40)

Many of Jesus' Disciples Go Back

[41] THE Jews then murmured at him, because he said, I am the bread which came down from heaven. [42] And they said, Is not this Jesus, the son of Joseph, whose father and mother we know? How is it then that he says, I came down from heaven? (John 6)

[43] Jesus therefore answered and said unto them, Murmur not among yourselves. [44] No man can come to me, except the Father which has sent me draw him: and I will raise him up at the last day. [45] It is written in the prophets, And they shall be all taught of God.[a] Every man therefore that has heard, and has learned of the Father, comes unto me. [46] Not that any man has seen the Father, save he which is of God, he has seen the Father. (John 6)

[47] Verily, verily, I say unto you, he that believes on me has everlasting life. [48] I am that bread of life. [49] Your fathers did eat manna in the wilderness, and are dead. [50] This is the bread which comes down from heaven, that a man may eat thereof, and not die. [51] I am the living bread which came down from heaven: if any man eat of this bread, he shall live for ever: and the bread that I will give is my flesh, which I will give for the life of the world. (John 6)

[52] The Jews therefore strove among themselves, saying, How can this man give us *his* flesh to eat? [53] Then Jesus said unto them, Verily, verily, I say unto you, except you eat the flesh of the Son of man, and drink his blood, you have no life in you. [54] Whoso eats my flesh, and drinks my blood, has eternal life; and I will raise him up at the last day. [55] For my flesh is meat indeed, and my blood is drink indeed. [56] He that eats my flesh, and drinks my blood, dwells in me, and I in him. [57] As the living Father has sent me, and I live by the Father: so he that eats me, even he shall live by me. [58] This is that bread which came down from heaven: not as your fathers did eat manna, and are dead: he that eats of this bread shall live for ever. (John 6)

[59] These things said he in the synagogue, as he taught in Capernaum. [60] Many therefore of his disciples, when they had heard *this*,

---

a. O.T. prophecy in Isaiah 54:13.

said, This is a hard saying; who can hear it? [61] When Jesus knew in himself that his disciples murmured at it, he said unto them, Does this offend you? [62] *What* and if you shall see the Son of man ascend up where he was before? [63] It is the spirit that quickens; the flesh profits nothing: the words that I speak unto you, *they* are spirit, and *they* are life. [64] But there are some of you that believe not. For Jesus knew from the beginning who they were that believed not, and who should betray him. [65] And he said, Therefore said I unto you, that no man can come unto me, except it were given unto him of my Father. (John 6)

[66] From that *time* many of his disciples went back, and walked no more with him. [67] Then said Jesus unto the twelve, Will you also go away? [68] Then Simon Peter answered him, Lord, to whom shall we go? You have the words of eternal life. [69] And we believe and are sure that you are that Christ, the Son of the living God. [70] Jesus answered them, Have not I chosen you twelve, and one of you is a devil? [71] He spoke of Judas Iscariot *the son* of Simon: for he it was that should betray him, being one of the twelve. (John 6)

[1] After these things Jesus walked in Galilee: for he would not walk in Jewry, because the Jews sought to kill him. (John 7)

(JOHN 6:41–71; 7:1)

What Defiles a Man?

[1] THEN came together unto (Mark 7) [1] Jesus (Matthew 15) [1] the Pharisees, and certain of the scribes, which came from Jerusalem. [2] And when they saw some of his disciples eat bread with defiled, that is to say, with unwashed, hands, they found fault. (Mark 7)

[3] For the Pharisees, and all the Jews, except they wash *their* hands oft, eat not, holding the tradition of the elders. [4] And *when they come* from the market, except they wash, they eat not. And many other things there be, which they have received to hold, *as* the washing of cups, and pots, brasen vessels, and of tables. [5] Then the Pharisees and scribes asked him, (Mark 7) [1] saying, [2] Why do your

disciples transgress the tradition of the elders? For they wash not their hands when they eat bread. (Matthew 15)

³ But he answered and said unto them, Why do you also transgress the commandment of God by your tradition? (Matthew 15) 6 Well has Esaias prophesied of you hypocrites, as it is written, (Mark 7) ⁸ This people draw nigh unto me with their mouth[s], and honour me with *their* lips; but their heart is far from me. ⁹ But in vain they do worship me, teaching *for* doctrines the commandments of men.^a (Matthew 15) 8 For laying aside the commandment of God, you hold the tradition of men, *as* the washing of pots and cups: and many other such like things you do. (Mark 7)

⁹ And he said unto them, Full well you reject the commandment of God, that you may keep your own tradition. (Mark 7) 4 For God commanded, *[through Moses]* saying, (Matthew 15) 10 Honour your father and your mother; and, Whoso curses father or mother, let him die the death: ¹¹ but you say, If a man shall say to his father or mother, *It is* Corban, that is to say, a gift, by whatsoever you might be profited by me; (Mark 7) 6 and honour not his father or his mother, *he shall be free.* (Matthew 15) 12 And you suffer him no more to do ought for his father or his mother. (Mark 7) 6 Thus have you made the commandment of God, (Matthew 15) 13 the word of God of none effect through your tradition, which you have delivered: and many such like things do you. (Mark 7)

¹⁴ And when he had called all the people *unto him,* he said unto them, Hearken unto me every one *of you,* (Mark 7) 10 hear, and understand: (Matthew 15) 15 there is nothing from without a man, that entering into him can defile him: but the things which come out of him, those are they that defile the man. (Mark 7) 11 Not that which goes into the mouth defiles a man; but that which comes out of the mouth, this defiles a man. (Matthew 15) 16 If any man have ears to hear, let him hear. (Mark 7)

¹⁷ And when he was entered into the house from the people, his disciples asked him concerning the parable, (Mark 7) 12 and said unto him, Know you that the Pharisees were offended, after they heard

---

a. O.T. prophecy in Isaiah 29:13.

this saying? ¹³ But he answered and said, Every plant, which my heavenly Father has not planted, shall be rooted up. ¹⁴ Let them alone: they be blind leaders of the blind. And if the blind lead the blind, both shall fall into the ditch. ^(Matthew 15)

¹⁵ Then answered Peter and said unto him, Declare unto us this parable. ¹⁶ And Jesus said, Are you also yet without understanding? ¹⁷ Do not you yet understand, ^(Matthew 15) ¹⁸ that whatsoever thing from without enters into the man, ^(Mark 7) ¹⁷ enters in at the mouth [and] goes into the belly, and is cast out into the draught? ^(Matthew 15) ¹⁸ It cannot defile him; ¹⁹ because it enters not into his heart, but into the belly, and goes out into the draught, purging all meats? ²⁰ And he said, That which comes out of the man, that defiles the man. ^(Mark 7) ¹⁸ But those things which proceed out of the mouth come forth from the heart; and they defile the man. ^(Matthew 15) ²¹ For from within, out of the heart of men, proceed evil thoughts, adulteries, fornications, murders, ²² thefts, covetousness, wickedness, deceit, lasciviousness, an evil eye, blasphemy, pride, foolishness, ^(Mark 7) ¹⁹ false witness. ^(Matthew 15) ²³ All these evil things come from within, and defile the man. ^(Mark 7) ²⁰ These are *the things* which defile a man: but to eat with unwashed hands defiles not a man. ^(Matthew 15)

(MARK 7:1–6, 8–23; MATTHEW 15:1–4, 6, 8–20)

CHAPTER FOURTEEN

Jesus at Tyre and Sidon

24 AND from thence he arose, (Mark 7) 21 went thence, and departed into the coasts (Matthew 15) 24 of Tyre and Sidon, and entered into an house, and would have no man know *it:* but he could not be hid. 25 For a *certain* woman (Mark 7) 22 of Canaan, (Matthew 15) 25 whose young daughter had an unclean spirit, heard of him, and came (Mark 7) 22 out of the same coasts. (Matthew 15) 26 The woman was a Greek, a Syrophenician by nation; and she besought him that he would cast forth the devil out of her daughter, (Mark 7) 22 and cried unto him, saying, Have mercy on me, O Lord, *you* son of David; my daughter is grievously vexed with a devil. 23 But he answered her not a word. (Matthew 15)

23 And his disciples came and besought him, saying, Send her away; for she cries after us. 24 But he answered and said, I am not sent but unto the lost sheep of the house of Israel. 25 Then came she (Matthew 15) 25 and fell at his feet: (Mark 7) 25 and worshipped him, saying, Lord, help me. (Matthew 15) 27 But Jesus (Mark 7) 26 answered and (Matthew 15) 27 said unto her, Let the children first be filled: for it is not meet to take the children's bread, and to cast *it* unto the dogs. 28 And she answered and said unto him, Yes, (Mark 7) 27 Truth, (Matthew 15) 28 Lord: yet the dogs under the table eat of the children's crumbs (Mark 7) 27 which fall from their masters' table. (Matthew 15)

28 Then Jesus answered and said unto her, O woman, great *is* your faith: be it unto you even as you will. (Matthew 15) 29 For this saying go your way; the devil is gone out of your daughter. (Mark 7) 28 And her daughter was made whole from that very hour. (Matthew 15) 30 And when she was come to her house, she found the devil gone out, and her daughter laid upon the bed. (Mark 7)

29 And Jesus (Matthew 15) 31 departing from the coasts of Tyre and

Sidon, (Mark 7) 29 came nigh (Matthew 15) 31 unto the sea of Galilee, through the midst of the coasts of Decapolis, (Mark 7) 29 and went up into a mountain, and sat down there. 30 And great multitudes came unto him, having with them *those that were* lame, blind, dumb, maimed, and many others, and cast them down at Jesus' feet; and he healed them. (Matthew 15)

32 And they bring unto him one that was deaf, and had an impediment in his speech; and they beseech him to put his hand upon him. 33 And he took him aside from the multitude, and put his fingers into his ears, and he spit, and touched his tongue. (Mark 7)

34 And looking up to heaven, he sighed, and said unto him, Ephphatha, that is, Be opened. 35 And straightway his ears were opened, and the string of his tongue was loosed, and he spoke plain. 36 And he charged them that they should tell no man: but the more he charged them, so much the more a great deal they published *it;* 37 and were beyond measure astonished, (Mark 7) 31 insomuch that the multitude wondered, when they saw the dumb to speak, the maimed to be whole, the lame to walk, and the blind to see: and they glorified the God of Israel, (Matthew 15) 37 saying, He has done all things well: he makes both the deaf to hear, and the dumb to speak. (Mark 7)

(MARK 7:24–37; MATTHEW 15:21–31)

Seven Loaves and a Few Small Fish

32 THEN (Matthew 15) 1 in those days the multitude being very great, and having nothing to eat, Jesus called his disciples *unto him,* and said unto them, 2 I have compassion on the multitude, because they have now been with me three days, and have nothing to eat: 3 and if I send them away fasting to their own houses, they will faint by the way: for divers of them came from far. 4 And his disciples answered him, From whence can a man satisfy these *men* with bread here in the wilderness? (Mark 8) 33 Whence should we have so much bread in the wilderness, as to fill so great a multitude? 34 And Jesus (Matthew 15)

⁵ asked them, How many loaves have you? ^(Mark 8) ³⁴ And they said, Seven, and a few little fishes. ^(Matthew 15) ⁶ And he commanded ^(Mark 8) ³⁵ the multitude ^(Matthew 15) ⁶ to sit down on the ground: and he took the seven loaves, and gave thanks, and broke ^(Mark 8) ³⁶ *them,* ^(Matthew 15) ⁶ and gave to his disciples to set before *them;* and they did set *them* before the people. ⁷ And they had a few small fishes: and he blessed, and commanded to set them also before *them.* ^(Mark 8)

³⁷ And they did all eat, and were filled: and they took up of the broken *meat* that was left seven baskets full. ^(Matthew 15) ⁹ And they that had eaten were about ^(Mark 8) ³⁸ four thousand men, beside women and children. ³⁹ And he sent away the multitude. ^(Matthew 15) ¹⁰ And straightway he entered into a ship with his disciples, and came into the parts of Dalmanutha ^(Mark 8) ³⁹ into the coasts of Magdala. ^(Matthew 15)

(MATTHEW 15:32–39; MARK 8:1–7, 9–10)

The Pharisees and Sadducees Question Jesus

¹¹ AND the Pharisees ^(Mark 8) ¹ also with the Sadducees ^(Matthew 16) ¹¹ came forth, and began to question with him, seeking of him ^(Mark 8) ¹ that he would show them a sign from heaven, ^(Matthew 16) ¹¹ tempting him. ¹² And he sighed deeply in his spirit, and ^(Mark 8) ² he answered and said unto them, When it is evening, you say, *It will be* fair weather: for the sky is red. ³ And in the morning, *It will be* foul weather to day: for the sky is red and lowering. O *you* hypocrites, you can discern the face of the sky; but can you not *discern* the signs of the times? ^(Matthew 16) ¹² Why does this ^(Mark 8) ⁴ wicked and adulterous ^(Matthew 16) ¹² generation seek after a sign? Verily I say unto you, there shall no sign be given unto this generation, ^(Mark 8) ⁴ but the sign of the prophet Jonas. ^(Matthew 16) ¹³ And he left them, and entering into the ship again departed to the other side. ^(Mark 8)

¹⁴ Now *the disciples* had forgotten to take bread, neither had they in the ship with them more than one loaf. ^(Mark 8) ⁵ And when his disciples were come to the other side, ⁶ Jesus ^(Matthew 16) ¹⁵ charged

them, saying, (Mark 8) 6 Take heed and beware of the leaven of the Pharisees and of the Sadducees, (Matthew 16) 15 and *of* the leaven of Herod. (Mark 8) 7 And they reasoned among themselves, saying, *It is* because we have taken no bread. 8 *Which* when Jesus perceived, he said unto them, O you of little faith, why reason you among yourselves, because you have brought no bread? (Matthew 16) 17 Perceive you not yet, neither understand? Have you your heart yet hardened? 18 Having eyes, see you not? And having ears, hear you not? And do you not remember? 19 When I broke the five loaves among five thousand, how many baskets full of fragments took you up? They say unto him, Twelve. 20 And when the seven among the four thousand, how many baskets full of fragments took you up? And they said, Seven. (Mark 8)

21 And he said unto them, How is it that you do not understand (Mark 8) 11 that I spoke *it* not to you concerning bread, that you should beware of the leaven of the Pharisees and of the Sadducees? 12 Then understood they how that he bade *them* not beware of the leaven of bread, but of the doctrine of the Pharisees and of the Sadducees. (Matthew 16)

22 And he came to Bethsaida; and they bring a blind man unto him, and besought him to touch him. 23 And he took the blind man by the hand, and led him out of the town; and when he had spit on his eyes, and put his hands upon him, he asked him if he saw ought. 24 And he looked up, and said, I see men as trees, walking. 25 After that he put *his* hands again upon his eyes, and made him look up: and he was restored, and saw every man clearly. 26 And he sent him away to his house, saying, Neither go into the town, nor tell *it* to any in the town. (Mark 8)

(MARK 8:11–15, 17–26; MATTHEW 16:1–8, 11–12)

Whom Do People Say That I Am?

27 AND Jesus went out, and his disciples. (Mark 8) 13 Jesus came into the coasts (Matthew 16) *[and]* 27 the towns of Caesarea Philippi: and by

the way, (Mark 8) 18 it came to pass, as he was alone praying, his disciples were with him: and he asked them, (Luke 9) 27 saying unto them, (Mark 8) 13 Whom do men say that I the Son of man am? (Matthew 16)

28 And they (Mark 8) 19 answering said, (Luke 9) 14 Some say *that you are* John the Baptist: (Matthew 16) 28 but some *say,* Elias; and others, (Mark 8) 14 Jeremias, (Matthew 16) 19 and others *say,* that one of the old prophets is risen again. (Luke 9) 29 And he said unto them, But whom say you that I am? (Mark 8) 16 And Simon Peter answered and said, (Matthew 16) 20 The Christ of God. (Luke 9) 16 You are the Christ, the Son of the living God. (Matthew 16)

17 And Jesus answered and said unto him, Blessed are you, Simon Barjona: for flesh and blood has not revealed *it* unto you, but my Father which is in heaven. 18 And I say also unto you, that you are Peter, and upon this rock I will build my church; and the gates of hell shall not prevail against it. 19 And I will give unto you the keys of the kingdom of heaven: and whatsoever you shall bind on earth shall be bound in heaven: and whatsoever you shall loose on earth shall be loosed in heaven. 20 Then (Matthew 16) 21 he straitly charged (Luke 9) 20 his disciples, (Matthew 16) 21 and commanded *them* (Luke 9) 30 that they should tell no man of him, (Mark 8) 20 that he was Jesus the Christ. (Matthew 16)

(MARK 8:27–30; MATTHEW 16:13–14, 16–20; LUKE 9:18–21)

Jesus Rebukes Peter

21 FROM that time forth began Jesus to show unto his disciples, (Matthew 16) *[and]* 31 to teach them (Mark 8) 21 how that he, (Matthew 16) 31 the Son of man, (Mark 8) 21 must go unto Jerusalem, and suffer many things, (Matthew 16) 31 and be rejected of the elders, and *of* the chief priests, and scribes, and be killed, and after three days rise again. 32 And he spoke that saying openly. (Mark 8)

22 Then Peter took him, and began to rebuke him, saying, Be it far from you, Lord: this shall not be unto you. (Matthew 16) 33 But when he had turned about and looked on his disciples, he rebuked Peter,

saying, Get behind me, Satan: (Mark 8) 23 you are an offence unto me: for you savour not the things that be of God, (Matthew 16) 33 but the things that be of men. (Mark 8)

34 And when he had called the people *unto him* with his disciples also, (Mark 8) 23 he said to *them* all, If any *man* will come after me, let him deny himself, and take up his cross daily, and follow me. (Luke 9) 35 For whosoever will save his life shall lose it; but whosoever shall lose his life for my sake and the gospel's, the same shall (Mark 8) 25 find it (Matthew 16) *[and]* 35 save it. 36 For what shall it profit a man, if he shall gain the whole world, and lose his own soul (Mark 8) 25 and lose himself, or be cast away? (Luke 9) 37 Or what shall a man give in exchange for his soul? (Mark 8)

38 Whosoever therefore shall be ashamed of me and of my words in this adulterous and sinful generation; of him also shall the Son of man be ashamed, (Mark 8) 26 when he shall come in his own glory, and *in his* Father's, and of the holy angels. (Luke 9) 27 For the Son of man shall come in the glory of his Father with his angels; and then he shall reward every man according to his works. (Matthew 16)

1 And he said unto them, (Mark 9) 27 But I tell you of a truth, there be some standing here, which shall not taste of death, (Luke 9) 28 till they see the Son of man coming in his kingdom, (Matthew 16) 1 till they have seen the kingdom of God come with power. (Mark 9)

(MATTHEW 16:21–23, 25, 27–28; MARK 8:31–38; 9:1; LUKE 9:23, 25–27)

CHAPTER FIFTEEN

Elias and Moses Talk to Jesus

² AND after six days Jesus took *with him* Peter, and James, ^(Mark 9) ¹ and John his brother, ^(Matthew 17) ² and led them up into an high mountain apart by themselves ^(Mark 9) ²⁸ to pray: ^(Luke 9) ² and he was transfigured before them. ^(Mark 9) ²⁹ And as he prayed, the fashion of his countenance was altered, ^(Luke 9) ² and his face did shine as the sun. ^(Matthew 17) ³ And his raiment became shining, exceeding white as snow; ^(Mark 9) ²⁹ *and* glistering ^(Luke 9) ² as the light; ^(Matthew 17) ³ so as no fuller on earth can white them. ^(Mark 9)

³ And, behold, ^(Matthew 17) ⁴ there appeared unto them ^(Mark 9) ³⁰ two men, which were Moses and Elias: ³¹ who appeared in glory, ^(Luke 9) ⁴ and they were talking with Jesus, ^(Mark 9) ³¹ and spoke of his decease which he should accomplish at Jerusalem. ³² But Peter and they that were with him were heavy with sleep: and when they were awake, they saw his glory, and the two men that stood with him. ³³ And it came to pass, as they departed from him, Peter said unto Jesus, Master, it is good for us to be here: ^(Luke 9) ⁵ and ^(Mark 9) ⁴ if you will, let us make here three tabernacles; ^(Matthew 17) ³³ one for you, and one for Moses, and one for Elias: not knowing what he said. ^(Luke 9) ⁶ For he knew not what to say; for they were sore afraid. ^(Mark 9)

⁵ While he yet ^(Matthew 17) ³⁴ thus ^(Luke 9) ⁵ spoke, behold, ^(Matthew 17) ³⁴ there came ^(Luke 9) ⁵ a bright cloud ^(Matthew 17) ³⁴ and overshadowed them: and they feared as they entered into the cloud. ^(Luke 9) ⁵ And behold, ^(Matthew 17) ³⁵ there came a voice out of the cloud, saying, ^(Luke 9) ⁵ This is my beloved Son, in whom I am well pleased; hear him. ^(Matthew 17) ³⁶ And when the voice was past, ^(Luke 9) ⁶ and when the disciples heard *it*, they fell on their face, and were sore afraid. ⁷ And Jesus came and touched them, and said, Arise, and be not afraid. ^(Matthew 17) ⁸ And suddenly, when they had ^(Mark 9) ⁸ lifted up

their eyes (Matthew 17) [and] 8 looked round about, they saw no man any more, save Jesus only with themselves. (Mark 9)

9 And as they came down from the mountain, (Mark 9) 9 Jesus (Matthew 17) 9 charged them that they should tell no man what things they had seen, (Mark 9) 9 the vision, (Matthew 17) 9 till the Son of man were risen (Mark 9) 9 again (Matthew 17) 9 from the dead. 10 And they kept that saying with themselves, (Mark 9) 36 and told no man in those days any of those things which they had seen, (Luke 9) 10 questioning one with another what the rising from the dead should mean. (Mark 9)

10 And his disciples asked him, saying, Why then say the scribes that Elias must first come? 11 And Jesus answered and said unto them, (Matthew 17) 12 Elias verily comes first, and restores all things; and how it is written of the Son of man, that he must suffer many things, and be set at nought. 13 But I say unto you, that Elias is indeed come (Mark 9) 12 already, and they knew him not, but have done unto him whatsoever they wanted, (Matthew 17) 13 as it is written of him. (Mark 9) 12 Likewise shall also the Son of man suffer of them. 13 Then the disciples understood that he spoke unto them of John the Baptist. (Matthew 17)

(MARK 9:2–6, 8–10, 12–13; MATTHEW 17:1–13; LUKE 9:28–36)

This Spirit Goes Only by Prayer and Fasting

37 AND it came to pass, that on the next day, when they were come down from the hill, much people met him. (Luke 9) 14 And when he came to *his* disciples, he saw a great multitude about them, and the scribes questioning with them. 15 And straightway all the people, when they beheld him, were greatly amazed, and running to *him* saluted him. (Mark 9)

16 And he asked the scribes, What question you with them? (Mark 9) 38 And, behold, a man of the company, (Luke 9) 14 kneeling down to him, (Matthew 17) 38 cried out, saying, (Luke 9) 17 Master, I have brought unto you my son, which has a dumb spirit. (Mark 9) 38 Master, I beseech you, look upon my son: for he is my only child. (Luke 9) 15 Lord, have mercy

on my son: for he is lunatick, and sore vexed: for oftentimes he falls into the fire, and oft into the water. (Matthew 17) 39 And, lo, a spirit takes him, (Luke 9) 18 and wheresoever he takes him, he tears him: and he foams, and gnashes with his teeth, and pines away. (Mark 9) 39 And he suddenly cries out; and it tears him that he foams again, and bruising him hardly departs from him. (Luke 9) 16 And I brought him to your disciples, (Matthew 17) 18 and I spoke to your disciples that they should cast him out. (Mark 9) 40 And I besought your disciples to cast him out; and they could not (Luke 9) 16 cure him. (Matthew 17)

17 Then Jesus answered and said, (Matthew 17) 41 O faithless and perverse generation, how long shall I be with you, and (Luke 9) 19 how long shall I suffer you? (Mark 9) 41 Bring your son hither (Luke 9) 17 to me. (Matthew 17) 20 And they brought him unto him: and when he saw him, (Mark 9) 42 and as he was yet a-coming, (Luke 9) 20 straightway the spirit (Mark 9) 42 threw him down, and tore *him*, (Luke 9) 20 and he fell on the ground, and wallowed foaming. (Mark 9)

21 And he asked his father, How long is it ago since this came unto him? And he said, Of a child. 22 And oftentimes it has cast him into the fire, and into the waters, to destroy him: but if you can do any thing, have compassion on us, and help us. 23 Jesus said unto him, If you can believe, all things *are* possible to him that believes. 24 And straightway the father of the child cried out, and said with tears, Lord, I believe; help my unbelief. (Mark 9)

25 When Jesus saw that the people came running together, he rebuked the foul spirit, saying unto him, *You* dumb and deaf spirit, I charge you, come out of him, and enter no more into him. 26 And *the spirit* cried, and rent him sore, and came out of him: and he was as one dead; insomuch that many said, He is dead. 27 But Jesus took him by the hand, and lifted him up; and he arose. (Mark 9) 42 And *[Jesus]* healed the child, and delivered him again to his father, (Luke 9) 18 and the child was cured from that very hour. (Matthew 17)

28 And when he was come into the house, his disciples asked him privately, Why could not we cast him out? (Mark 9) 20 And Jesus said unto them, Because of your unbelief: for verily I say unto you, if you have faith as a grain of mustard seed, you shall say unto this

mountain, Remove hence to yonder place; and it shall remove; and nothing shall be impossible unto you. [21] Howbeit this kind goes not out but by prayer and fasting. (Matthew 17)

[43] And they were all amazed at the mighty power of God. (Luke 9) [30] And they departed thence, and passed through Galilee; and he would not that any man should know *it*. (Mark 9) [22] And while they abode in Galilee (Matthew 17) *[and]* [43] while they wondered every one at all things which Jesus did, (Luke 9) [31] he taught his disciples, and said unto them, (Mark 9) [44] Let these sayings sink down into your ears: for the Son of man (Luke 9) [22] shall be betrayed (Matthew 17) *[and]* [44] delivered into the hands of men, (Luke 9) [31] and they shall kill him; and after that he is killed, he shall rise (Mark 9) [23] again (Matthew 17) [31] the third day. (Mark 9) [23] And they were exceeding sorry. (Matthew 17) [45] But they understood not this saying, and it was hid from them, that they perceived it not: and they feared to ask him of that saying. (Luke 9)

(LUKE 9:37–45; MARK 9:14–28, 30–31; MATTHEW 17:14–18, 20–23)

Who Is the Greatest in the Kingdom of Heaven?

[33] AND he came to Capernaum. (Mark 9) [24] And when they were come to Capernaum, they that received tribute *money* came to Peter, and said, Does not your master pay tribute? [25] He said, Yes. And when he was come into the house, Jesus prevented him, saying, What think you, Simon? Of whom do the kings of the earth take custom or tribute? Of their own children, or of strangers? [26] Peter said unto him, Of strangers. Jesus said unto him, Then are the children free. [27] Notwithstanding, lest we should offend them, go to the sea, and cast an hook, and take up the fish that first comes up; and when you have opened his mouth, you shall find a piece of money: that take, and give unto them for me and you. (Matthew 17)

[33] And being in the house he asked them, What was it that you disputed among yourselves by the way? [34] But they held their peace: for by the way they had disputed among themselves, who *should be* the greatest. (Mark 9)

⁴⁷ And Jesus, perceiving the thought of their heart, ⁽Luke 9⁾ ³⁵ sat down, and called the twelve, and said unto them, If any man desire to be first, *the same* shall be last of all, and servant of all. ⁽Mark 9⁾ 2 And Jesus called a little child unto him, ⁽Matthew 18⁾ ⁴⁷ and set him by him, ⁽Luke 9⁾ ³⁶ in the midst of them: and when he had taken him in his arms, he said unto them, ⁽Mark 9⁾ 3 Verily I say unto you, except you be converted, and become as little children, you shall not enter into the kingdom of heaven. ⁴ Whosoever therefore shall humble himself as this little child, the same is greatest in the kingdom of heaven. ⁵ And whoso shall receive one such little child in my name receives me. ⁽Matthew 18⁾ ³⁷ And whosoever shall receive me, receives not me, but him that sent me: ⁽Mark 9⁾ ⁴⁸ for he that is least among you all, the same shall be great. ⁽Luke 9⁾

(MARK 9:33–37; 17:24–27; 18:2–5; LUKE 9:47–48)

Spiritual Insight from Jesus

³⁸ AND John answered him, saying, Master, we saw one casting out devils in your name, and he follows not us: and we forbad him, because he follows ⁽Mark 9⁾ ⁴⁹ not with us. ⁽Luke 9⁾ 39 But Jesus said ⁽Mark 9⁾ ⁵⁰ unto him, ⁽Luke 9⁾ 39 Forbid him not: for there is no man which shall do a miracle in my name, that can lightly speak evil of me. ⁴⁰ For he that is not against us is on our part. ⁴¹ For whosoever shall give you a cup of water to drink in my name, because you belong to Christ, verily I say unto you, he shall not lose his reward. ⁽Mark 9⁾

⁶ But whoso shall offend one of these little ones which believe in me, it were better for him that a millstone were hanged about his neck, and *that* he ⁽Matthew 18⁾ ⁴² were cast into the sea ⁽Mark 9⁾ *[and]* ⁶ drowned in the depth of the sea. ⁷ Woe unto the world because of offences! For it must needs be that offences come; but woe to that man by whom the offence comes! ⁽Matthew 18⁾

⁸ Wherefore if your hand or your foot offend you, cut them off, and cast *them* from you: it is better for you to enter into life halt or maimed, rather than having two hands or two feet to be cast

into everlasting fire, (Matthew 18) 43 to go into hell, into the fire that never shall be quenched: 44 where their worm dies not, and the fire is not quenched. 47 And if your eye offend you, (Mark 9) 9 pluck it out, and cast *it* from you: (Matthew 18) 47 it is better for you to enter into the kingdom of God, (Mark 9) 9 into life with one eye, rather (Matthew 18) 47 than having two eyes to be cast into hell fire: 48 where their worm dies not, and the fire is not quenched. (Mark 9)

49 For every one shall be salted with fire, and every sacrifice shall be salted with salt. 50 Salt *is* good: but if the salt have lost his saltness, wherewith will you season it? Have salt in yourselves, and have peace one with another. (Mark 9) 10 Take heed that you despise not one of these little ones; for I say unto you, that in heaven their angels do always behold the face of my Father which is in heaven. 11 For the Son of man is come to save that which was lost. (Matthew 18)

12 How think you? If a man have an hundred sheep, and one of them be gone astray, does he not leave the ninety and nine, and go into the mountains, and seek that which is gone astray? 13 And if so be that he find it, verily I say unto you, he rejoices more of that *sheep,* than of the ninety and nine which went not astray. 14 Even so it is not the will of your Father which is in heaven, that one of these little ones should perish. (Matthew 18)

15 Moreover if your brother shall trespass against you, go and tell him his fault between you and him alone: if he shall hear you, you have gained your brother. 16 But if he will not hear *you, then* take with you one or two more, that in the mouth of two or three witnesses every word may be established. 17 And if he shall neglect to hear them, tell *it* unto the church: but if he neglect to hear the church, let him be unto you as an heathen man and a publican. (Matthew 18)

18 Verily I say unto you, whatsoever you shall bind on earth shall be bound in heaven: and whatsoever you shall loose on earth shall be loosed in heaven. 19 Again I say unto you, that if two of you shall agree on earth as touching any thing that they shall ask, it shall be done for them of my Father which is in heaven. 20 For where two or three are gathered together in my name, there am I

in the midst of them. (Matthew 18)

²¹ Then came Peter to him, and said, Lord, how oft shall my brother sin against me, and I forgive him? Till seven times? ²² Jesus said unto him, I say not unto you, Until seven times: but, Until seventy times seven. (Matthew 18)

(MARK 9:38–44, 47–50; LUKE 9:49–50; MATTHEW 18:6–22)

The Kingdom of Heaven Is Like a Certain King

²³ THEREFORE is the kingdom of heaven likened unto a certain king, which would take account of his servants. ²⁴ And when he had begun to reckon, one was brought unto him, which owed him ten thousand talents. ²⁵ But forasmuch as he had not to pay, his lord commanded him to be sold, and his wife, and children, and all that he had, and payment to be made. ²⁶ The servant therefore fell down, and worshipped him, saying, Lord, have patience with me, and I will pay you all. (Matthew 18)

²⁷ Then the lord of that servant was moved with compassion, and loosed him, and forgave him the debt. ²⁸ But the same servant went out, and found one of his fellowservants, which owed him an hundred pence: and he laid hands on him, and took *him* by the throat, saying, Pay me that you owe. ²⁹ And his fellowservant fell down at his feet, and besought him, saying, Have patience with me, and I will pay you all. ³⁰ And he would not: but went and cast him into prison, till he should pay the debt. (Matthew 18)

³¹ So when his fellowservants saw what was done, they were very sorry, and came and told unto their lord all that was done. ³² Then his lord, after that he had called him, said unto him, O you wicked servant, I forgave you all that debt, because you desired me: ³³ should not you also have had compassion on your fellowservant, even as I had pity on you? ³⁴ And his lord was wroth, and delivered him to the tormentors, till he should pay all that was due unto him. ³⁵ So likewise shall my heavenly Father do also unto

you, if you from your hearts forgive not every one his brother their trespasses. (Matthew 18)

(MATTHEW 18:23–35)

CHAPTER SIXTEEN

Jesus Goes to the Feast of Tabernacles

² Now the Jew's <u>feast of tabernacles</u> was at hand. ³ His brethren therefore said unto him, Depart hence, and go into Judaea, that your disciples also may see the works that you do. ⁴ For *there is* no man *that* does any thing in secret, and he himself seeks to be known openly. If you do these things, show yourself to the world. ⁵ For neither did his brethren believe in him. (John 7)

⁶ Then Jesus said unto them, My time is not yet come: but your time is alway ready. ⁷ The world cannot hate you; but me it hates, because I testify of it, that the works thereof are evil. ⁸ Go up unto this feast: I go not up yet unto this feast; for my time is not yet full come. ⁹ When he had said these words unto them, he abode *still* in Galilee. (John 7)

¹⁰ But when his brethren were gone up, then went he also up unto the feast, not openly, but as it were in secret. ¹¹ Then the Jews sought him at the feast, and said, Where is he? ¹² And there was much murmuring among the people concerning him: for some said, He is a good man: others said, Nay; but he deceives the people. ¹³ Howbeit no man spoke openly of him for fear of the Jews. (John 7)

(JOHN 7:2–13)

Midway through the Feast Jesus Teaches at the Temple

¹⁴ Now about the <u>midst of the feast</u> Jesus went up into the temple, and taught. ¹⁵ And the Jews marvelled, saying, How knows this man letters, having never learned? ¹⁶ Jesus answered them, and said, My doctrine is not mine, <u>but his that sent me.</u> ¹⁷ If any man

will do his will, he shall know of the doctrine, whether it be of God, or *whether* I speak of myself. ¹⁸ He that speaks of himself seeks his own glory: but he that seeks his glory that sent him, the same is true, and no unrighteousness is in him. (John 7)

¹⁹ Did not Moses give you the law, and *yet* none of you keeps the law? Why go you about to kill me? ²⁰ The people answered and said, You have a devil: who goes about to kill you? ²¹ Jesus answered and said unto them, I have done one work, and you all marvel. ²² Moses therefore gave unto you circumcision; (not because it is of Moses, but of the fathers;) and you on the sabbath day circumcise a man. ²³ If a man on the sabbath day receive circumcision, that the law of Moses should not be broken; are you angry at me, because I have made a man every whit whole on the sabbath day? ²⁴ Judge not according to the appearance, but judge righteous judgment. (John 7)

²⁵ Then said some of them of Jerusalem, Is not this he, whom they seek to kill? ²⁶ But, lo, he speaks boldly, and they say nothing unto him. Do the rulers know indeed that this is the very Christ? ²⁷ Howbeit we know this man whence he is: but when Christ comes, no man knows whence he is. (John 7)

²⁸ Then cried Jesus in the temple as he taught, saying, You both know me, and you know whence I am: and I am not come of myself, but he that sent me is true, whom you know not. ²⁹ But I know him: for I am from him, and he has sent me. (John 7)

³⁰ Then they sought to take him: but no man laid hands on him, because his hour was not yet come. ³¹ And many of the people believed on him, and said, When Christ comes, will he do more miracles than these which this *man* has done? ³² The Pharisees heard that the people murmured such things concerning him; and the Pharisees and the chief priests sent officers to take him. (John 7)

³³ Then said Jesus unto them, Yet a little while am I with you, and *then* I go unto him that sent me. ³⁴ You shall seek me, and shall not find *me*: and where I am, *thither* you cannot come. ³⁵ Then said the Jews among themselves, Whither will he go, that we shall not find him? Will he go unto the dispersed among the Gentiles, and

teach the Gentiles? ³⁶ What *manner of* saying is this that he said, You shall seek me, and shall not find *me:* and where I am, *thither* you cannot come? ^(John 7)

(JOHN 7:14–36)

The Last Day of the Feast of Tabernacles

³⁷ IN the last day, that great *day* of the feast, Jesus stood and cried, saying, If any man thirst, let him come unto me, and drink. ³⁸ He that believes on me, as the scripture has said, out of his belly shall flow rivers of living water. ³⁹ (But this spoke he of the Spirit, which they that believe on him should receive: for the Holy Ghost was not yet *given;* because that Jesus was not yet glorified.) ^(John 7)

⁴⁰ Many of the people therefore, when they heard this saying, said, Of a truth this is the Prophet. ⁴¹ Others said, This is the Christ. But some said, Shall Christ come out of Galilee? ⁴² Has not the scripture said, that Christ comes of the seed of David, and out of the town of Bethlehem, where David was?^a ⁴³ So there was a division among the people because of him. ⁴⁴ And some of them would have taken him; but no man laid hands on him. ^(John 7)

⁴⁵ Then came the officers to the chief priests and Pharisees; and they said unto them, Why have you not brought him? ⁴⁶ The officers answered, Never man spoke like this man. ⁴⁷ Then answered them the Pharisees, Are you also deceived? ⁴⁸ Have any of the rulers or of the Pharisees believed on him? ⁴⁹ But this people who know not the law are cursed. ^(John 7)

⁵⁰ Nicodemus said unto them, (he that came to Jesus by night, being one of them,) ⁵¹ Does our law judge *any* man, before it hear him, and know what he does? ⁵² They answered and said unto him, Are you also of Galilee? Search, and look: for out of Galilee arises no prophet. ⁵³ And every man went unto his own house. ^(John 7)

(JOHN 7:37–53)

---

a. O.T. prophecy in Isaiah 11:1, 10; Jeremiah 23:5; Micah 5:1–2.

A Woman Taken in Adultery

[1] JESUS went unto the mount of Olives. [2] And early in the morning he came again into the temple, and all the people came unto him; and he sat down, and taught them. [3] And the scribes and Pharisees brought unto him a woman taken in adultery; and when they had set her in the midst, [4] they say unto him, Master, this woman was taken in adultery, in the very act. [5] Now Moses in the law commanded us, that such should be stoned: but what say you? [6] This they said, tempting him, that they might have to accuse him. But Jesus stooped down, and with *his* finger wrote on the ground, *as though he heard them not.* (John 8)

[7] So when they continued asking him, he lifted up himself, and said unto them, He that is without sin among you, let him first cast a stone at her. [8] And again he stooped down, and wrote on the ground. [9] And they which heard *it,* being convicted by *their own* conscience, went out one by one, beginning at the eldest, *even* unto the last: and Jesus was left alone, and the woman standing in the midst. [10] When Jesus had lifted up himself, and saw none but the woman, he said unto her, Woman, where are those your accusers? Has no man condemned you? [11] She said, No man, Lord. And Jesus said unto her, Neither do I condemn you: go, and sin no more. (John 8)

(JOHN 8:1–11)

Jesus, the Light of the World

[12] THEN spoke Jesus again unto them, saying, I am the light of the world: he that follows me shall not walk in darkness, but shall have the light of life. [13] The Pharisees therefore said unto him, You bear record of yourself; your record is not true. [14] Jesus answered and said unto them, Though I bear record of myself, *yet* my record is true: for I know whence I came, and whither I go; but you cannot tell whence I come, and whither I go. [15] You judge after the

flesh; I judge no man. ¹⁶ And yet if I judge, my judgment is true: for I am not alone, but I and the Father that sent me. ¹⁷ It is also written in your law, that the testimony of two men is true. ¹⁸ I am one that bear witness of myself, and the Father that sent me bears witness of me. ¹⁹ Then said they unto him, Where is your Father? Jesus answered, You neither know me, nor my Father: if you had known me, you should have known my Father also. ⁽John 8⁾

²⁰ These words spoke Jesus in the treasury, as he taught in the temple: and no man laid hands on him; for his hour was not yet come. ²¹ Then said Jesus again unto them, I go my way, and you shall seek me, and shall die in your sins: whither I go, you cannot come. ²² Then said the Jews, Will he kill himself? Because he said, Whither I go, you cannot come. ⁽John 8⁾

²³ And he said unto them, You are from beneath; I am from above: you are of this world; I am not of this world. ²⁴ I said therefore unto you, that you shall die in your sins: for if you believe not that I am *he,* you shall die in your sins. ²⁵ Then said they unto him, Who are you? And Jesus said unto them, Even *the same* that I said unto you from the beginning. ²⁶ I have many things to say and to judge of you: but he that sent me is true; and I speak to the world those things which I have heard of him. ⁽John 8⁾

²⁷ They understood not that he spoke to them of the Father. ²⁸ Then said Jesus unto them, When you have lifted up the Son of man, then shall you know that I am *he,* and *that* I do nothing of myself; but as my Father has taught me, I speak these things. ²⁹ And he that sent me is with me: the Father has not left me alone; for I do always those things that please him. ⁽John 8⁾

³⁰ As he spoke these words, many believed on him. ³¹ Then said Jesus to those Jews which believed on him, If you continue in my word, *then* are you my disciples indeed; ³² and you shall know the truth, and the truth shall make you free. ⁽John 8⁾

(JOHN 8:12–32)

We Are Abraham's Seed

³³ THEY answered him, We be Abraham's seed, and were never in bondage to any man: how say you, You shall be made free? ³⁴ Jesus answered them, Verily, verily, I say unto you, whosoever commits sin is the servant of sin. ³⁵ And the servant abides not in the house for ever: *but* the Son abides ever. ³⁶ If the Son therefore shall make you free, you shall be free indeed. ³⁷ I know that you are Abraham's seed; but you seek to kill me, because my word has no place in you. ³⁸ I speak that which I have seen with my Father: and you do that which you have seen with your father. (John 8)

³⁹ They answered and said unto him, Abraham is our father. Jesus said unto them, If you were Abraham's children, you would do the works of Abraham. ⁴⁰ But now you seek to kill me, a man that has told you the truth, which I have heard of God: this did not Abraham. ⁴¹ You do the deeds of your father. Then said they to him, We be not born of fornication; we have one Father, *even* God. (John 8)

⁴² Jesus said unto them, If God were your Father, you would love me: for I proceeded forth and came from God; neither came I of myself, but he sent me. ⁴³ Why do you not understand my speech? *Even* because you cannot hear my word. ⁴⁴ You are of *your* father the devil, and the lusts of your father you will do. He was a murderer from the beginning, and abode not in the truth, because there is no truth in him. When he speaks a lie, he speaks of his own: for he is a liar, and the father of it. ⁴⁵ And because I tell *you* the truth, you believe me not. ⁴⁶ Which of you convinces me of sin? And if I say the truth, why do you not believe me? ⁴⁷ He that is of God hears God's words: you therefore hear *them* not, because you are not of God. (John 8)

⁴⁸ Then answered the Jews, and said unto him, Say we not well that you are a Samaritan, and have a devil? ⁴⁹ Jesus answered, I have not a devil; but I honour my Father, and you do dishonour me. ⁵⁰ And I seek not my own glory: there is one that seeks and judges. ⁵¹ Verily, verily, I say unto you, if a man keep my saying, he shall never see death. (John 8)

⁵² Then said the Jews unto him, Now we know that you have a devil. Abraham is dead, and the prophets; and you say, If a man keep my saying, he shall never taste of death. ⁵³ Are you greater than our father Abraham, which is dead? And the prophets are dead: whom make you yourself? (John 8)

⁵⁴ Jesus answered, If I honour myself, my honour is nothing: it is my Father that honours me; of whom you say, that he is your God: ⁵⁵ yet you have not known him; but I know him: and if I should say, I know him not, I shall be a liar like unto you: but I know him, and keep his saying. ⁵⁶ Your father Abraham rejoiced to see my day: and he saw *it,* and was glad. (John 8)

⁵⁷ Then said the Jews unto him, You are not yet fifty years old, and have you seen Abraham? ⁵⁸ Jesus said unto them, Verily, verily, I say unto you, before Abraham was, I am. ⁵⁹ Then took they up stones to cast at him: but Jesus hid himself, and went out of the temple, going through the midst of them, and so passed by. (John 8)

(JOHN 8:33–59)

.

CHAPTER SEVENTEEN

Who Did Sin, This Man or His Parents?

¹ AND as *Jesus* passed by, he saw a man which was blind from *his* birth. ² And his disciples asked him, saying, Master, who did sin, this man, or his parents, that he was born blind? ³ Jesus answered, Neither has this man sinned, nor his parents: but that the works of God should be made manifest in him. ⁴ I must work the works of him that sent me, while it is day: the night comes, when no man can work. ⁵ As long as I am in the world, I am the light of the world. (John 9)

⁶ When he had thus spoken, he spat on the ground, and made clay of the spittle, and he anointed the eyes of the blind man with the clay, ⁷ and said unto him, Go, wash in the pool of Siloam, (which is by interpretation, Sent.) He went his way therefore, and washed, and came seeing. (John 9)

⁸ The neighbours therefore, and they which before had seen him that he was blind, said, Is not this he that sat and begged? ⁹ Some said, This is he: others *said*, He is like him: *but* he said, I am *he.* ¹⁰ Therefore said they unto him, How were your eyes opened? ¹¹ He answered and said, A man that is called Jesus made clay, and anointed my eyes, and said unto me, Go to the pool of Siloam, and wash: and I went and washed, and I received sight. ¹² Then said they unto him, Where is he? He said, I know not. (John 9)

¹³ They brought to the Pharisees him that aforetime was blind. ¹⁴ And it was the sabbath day when Jesus made the clay, and opened his eyes. ¹⁵ Then again the Pharisees also asked him how he had received his sight. He said unto them, He put clay upon my eyes, and I washed, and do see. ¹⁶ Therefore said some of the Pharisees, This man is not of God, because he keeps not the sabbath day. Others said, How can a man that is a sinner do such miracles? And there

was a division among them. (John 9)

¹⁷ They say unto the blind man again, What say you of him, that he has opened your eyes? He said, He is a prophet. ¹⁸ But the Jews did not believe concerning him, that he had been blind, and received his sight, until they called the parents of him that had received his sight. ¹⁹ And they asked them, saying, Is this your son, who you say was born blind? How then does he now see? ²⁰ His parents answered them and said, We know that this is our son, and that he was born blind: ²¹ But by what means he now sees, we know not; or who has opened his eyes, we know not: he is of age; ask him: he shall speak for himself. (John 9)

²² These *words* spoke his parents, because they feared the Jews: for the Jews had agreed already, that if any man did confess that he was Christ, he should be put out of the synagogue. ²³ Therefore said his parents, He is of age; ask him. (John 9)

²⁴ Then again called they the man that was blind, and said unto him, Give God the praise: we know that this man is a sinner. ²⁵ He answered and said, Whether he be a sinner *or no*, I know not: one thing I know, that, whereas I was blind, now I see. ²⁶ Then said they to him again, What did he to you? How opened he your eyes? ²⁷ He answered them, I have told you already, and you did not hear: wherefore would you hear *it* again? Will you also be his disciples? (John 9)

²⁸ Then they reviled him, and said, You are his disciple; but we are Moses' disciples. ²⁹ We know that God spoke unto Moses: *as for* this *fellow*, we know not from whence he is. ³⁰ The man answered and said unto them, Why herein is a marvellous thing, that you know not from whence he is, and *yet* he has opened my eyes. ³¹ Now we know that God hears not sinners: but if any man be a worshipper of God, and does his will, him he hears. ³² Since the world began was it not heard that any man opened the eyes of one that was born blind. ³³ If this man were not of God, he could do nothing. ³⁴ They answered and said unto him, You were altogether born in sins, and do you teach us? And they cast him out. (John 9)

³⁵ Jesus heard that they had cast him out; and when he had found him, he said unto him, Do you believe on the Son of God?

³⁶ He answered and said, Who is he, Lord, that I might believe on him? ³⁷ And Jesus said unto him, You have both seen him, and it is he that talks with you. ³⁸ And he said, Lord, I believe. And he worshipped him. ³⁹ And Jesus said, For judgment I am come into this world, that they which see not might see; and that they which see might be made blind. (John 9)

⁴⁰ And *some* of the Pharisees which were with him heard these words, and said unto him, Are we blind also? ⁴¹ Jesus said unto them, If you were blind, you should have no sin: but now you say, We see; therefore your sin remains. (John 9)

¹ Verily, verily, I say unto you, he that enters not by the door into the sheepfold, but climbs up some other way, the same is a thief and a robber. ² But he that enters in by the door is the shepherd of the sheep. ³ To him the porter opens; and the sheep hear his voice: and he calls his own sheep by name, and leads them out. ⁴ And when he puts forth his own sheep, he goes before them, and the sheep follow him: for they know his voice. ⁵ And a stranger will they not follow, but will flee from him: for they know not the voice of strangers. (John 10)

(JOHN 9:1–41; 10:1–5)

Jesus, the Good Shepherd

⁶ THIS parable spoke Jesus unto them: but they understood not what things they were which he spoke unto them. ⁷ Then said Jesus unto them again, Verily, verily, I say unto you, I am the door of the sheep. ⁸ All that ever came before me are thieves and robbers: but the sheep did not hear them. ⁹ I am the door: by me if any man enter in, he shall be saved, and shall go in and out, and find pasture. ¹⁰ The thief comes not, but for to steal, and to kill, and to destroy: I am come that they might have life, and that they might have *it* more abundantly. (John 10)

¹¹ I am the good shepherd: the good shepherd gives his life for the sheep. ¹² But he that is an hireling, and not the shepherd, whose

own the sheep are not, sees the wolf coming, and leaves the sheep, and flees: and the wolf catches them, and scatters the sheep. [13] The hireling flees, because he is an hireling, and cares not for the sheep. (John 10)

[14] I am the good shepherd, and know my *sheep,* and am known of mine. [15] As the Father knows me, even so know I the Father: and I lay down my life for the sheep. [16] And other sheep I have, which are not of this fold: them also I must bring, and they shall hear my voice; and there shall be one fold, *and* one shepherd. (John 10)

[17] Therefore does my Father love me, because I lay down my life, that I might take it again. [18] No man takes it from me, but I lay it down of myself. I have power to lay it down, and I have power to take it again. This commandment have I received of my Father. (John 10)

[19] There was a division therefore again among the Jews for these sayings. [20] And many of them said, He has a devil, and is mad; why hear you him? [21] Others said, These are not the words of him that has a devil. Can a devil open the eyes of the blind? (John 10)

(JOHN 10:6–21)

Jesus Sets His Face to Jerusalem

[51] AND it came to pass, when the time was come that he should be received up, he stedfastly set his face to go to Jerusalem, [52] and sent messengers before his face: and they went, and entered into a village of the Samaritans, to make ready for him. [53] And they did not receive him, because his face was as though he would go to Jerusalem. (Luke 9)

[54] And when his disciples James and John saw *this,* they said, Lord, will you that we command fire to come down from heaven, and consume them, even as Elias did? [55] But he turned, and rebuked them, and said, You know not what manner of spirit you are of. [56] For the Son of man is not come to destroy men's lives, but to save *them.* (Luke 9)

[56] And they went to another village. [57] And it came to pass, that,

as they went in the way, a certain *man* said unto him, Lord, I will follow you whithersoever you go. ⁵⁸ And Jesus said unto him, Foxes have holes, and birds of the air *have* nests; but the Son of man has not where to lay *his* head. ⁵⁹ And he said unto another, Follow me. (Luke 9)

⁵⁹ But he said, Lord, suffer me first to go and bury my father. ⁶⁰ Jesus said unto him, Let the dead bury their dead: but go and preach the kingdom of God. ⁶¹ And another also said, Lord, I will follow you; but let me first go bid them farewell, which are at home at my house. ⁶² And Jesus said unto him, No man, having put his hand to the plough, and looking back, is fit for the kingdom of God. (Luke 9)

(LUKE 9:51–62)

Jesus Sends Out the Seventy

appointed TO

MOSES JESUS

¹ AFTER these things the Lord appointed other seventy also, and sent them two and two before his face into every city and place, whither he himself would come. ² Therefore said he unto them, The harvest truly *is* great, but the labourers *are* few: pray therefore the Lord of the harvest, that he would send forth labourers into his harvest. ³ Go your ways: behold, I send you forth as lambs among wolves. (Luke 10)

⁴ Carry neither purse, nor scrip, nor shoes: and salute no man by the way. ⁵ And into whatsoever house you enter, first say, Peace *be* to this house. ⁶ And if the son of peace be there, your peace shall rest upon it: if not, it shall turn to you again. ⁷ And in the same house remain, eating and drinking such things as they give: for the labourer is worthy of his hire. Go not from house to house. (Luke 10)

⁸ And into whatsoever city you enter, and they receive you, eat such things as are set before you: ⁹ and heal the sick that are therein, and say unto them, The kingdom of God is come nigh unto you. ¹⁰ But into whatsoever city you enter, and they receive you not, go your ways out into the streets of the same, and say, ¹¹ Even the

very dust of your city, which cleaves on us, we do wipe off against you: notwithstanding be you sure of this, that the kingdom of God is come nigh unto you. ¹² But I say unto you, that it shall be more tolerable in that day for Sodom, than for that city. ^(Luke 10)

²⁰ Then began he to upbraid the cities wherein most of his mighty works were done, because they repented not: ²¹ Woe unto you, Chorazin! Woe unto you, Bethsaida! For if the mighty works, which were done in you, had been done in Tyre and Sidon, they would have repented long ago, ^(Matthew 11) ¹³ sitting in sackcloth and ashes. ^(Luke 10) ²² But I say unto you, it shall be more tolerable for Tyre and Sidon at the day of judgment, than for you. ^(Matthew 11)

²³ And you, Capernaum, which are exalted unto heaven, shall be brought down to hell: for if the mighty works, which have been done in you, had been done in Sodom, it would have remained until this day. ²⁴ But I say unto you, that it shall be more tolerable for the land of Sodom in the day of judgment, than for you. ^(Matthew 11)

¹⁶ He that hears you hears me; and he that despises you despises me; and he that despises me despises him that sent me. ^(Luke 10)

¹⁷ And the seventy returned again with joy, saying, Lord, even the devils are subject unto us through your name. ¹⁸ And he said unto them, I beheld Satan as lightning fall from heaven. ¹⁹ Behold, I give unto you power to tread on serpents and scorpions, and over all the power of the enemy: and nothing shall by any means hurt you. ²⁰ Notwithstanding in this rejoice not, that the spirits are subject unto you; but rather rejoice, because your names are written in heaven. ^(Luke 10)

²¹ In that hour Jesus rejoiced in spirit, and said, I thank you, O Father, Lord of heaven and earth, that you have hidden these things from the wise and prudent, and have revealed them unto babes: even so, Father; for so it seemed good in your sight. ²² All things are delivered to me of my Father: and no man knows who the Son is, but the Father; and who the Father is, but the Son, and *he* to whom the Son will reveal *him*. ^(Luke 10)

²⁸ Come unto me, all *you* that labour and are heavy laden, and I will give you rest. ²⁹ Take my yoke upon you, and learn of me;

for I am meek and lowly in heart: and you shall find rest unto your souls. ³⁰ For my yoke *is* easy, and my burden is light. (Matthew 11) ²³ And he turned him unto *his* disciples, and said privately, Blessed *are* the eyes which see the things that you see: ²⁴ for I tell you, that many prophets and kings have desired to see those things which you see, and have not seen *them;* and to hear those things which you hear, and have not heard *them.* (Luke 10)

(LUKE 10:1–13, 16–24; MATTHEW 11:20–24, 28–30)

The Parable of the Good Samaritan

²⁵ AND, behold, a certain lawyer stood up, and tempted him, saying, Master, what shall I do to inherit eternal life? ²⁶ He said unto him, What is written in the law? How read you? ²⁷ And he answering said, You shall love the Lord your God with all your heart, and with all your soul, and with all your strength, and with all your mind; and your neighbour as yourself. ²⁸ And he said unto him, You have answered right: this do, and you shall live. ²⁹ But he, willing to justify himself, said unto Jesus, And who is my neighbour? (Luke 10)

³⁰ And Jesus answering said, A certain *man* went down from Jerusalem to Jericho, and fell among thieves, which stripped him of his raiment, and wounded *him,* and departed, leaving *him* half dead. ³¹ And by chance there came down a certain priest that way: and when he saw him, he passed by on the other side. ³² And likewise a Levite, when he was at the place, came and looked *on him,* and passed by on the other side. (Luke 10)

³³ But a certain Samaritan, as he journeyed, came where he was: and when he saw him, he had compassion *on him,* ³⁴ and went to *him,* and bound up his wounds, pouring in oil and wine, and set him on his own beast, and brought him to an inn, and took care of him. ³⁵ And on the morrow when he departed, he took out two pence, and gave *them* to the host, and said unto him, Take care of him; and whatsoever you spend more, when I come again, I

will repay you. ³⁶ Which now of these three, think you, was neigh-bour unto him that fell among the thieves? ³⁷ And he said, He that showed mercy on him. Then said Jesus unto him, Go, and do like-wise. (Luke 10)

(LUKE 10:25–37)

CHAPTER EIGHTEEN

The Lord's Prayer

¹ AND it came to pass, that, as he was praying in a certain place, when he ceased, one of his disciples said unto him, Lord, teach us to pray, as John also taught his disciples. (Luke 11)

² And he said unto them, When you pray, say, Our Father who is in heaven, Hallowed be your name. Your kingdom come. Your will be done, as in heaven, so in earth. ³ Give us day by day our daily bread. ⁴ And forgive us our sins; for we also forgive every one that is indebted to us. And lead us not into temptation; but deliver us from evil. (Luke 11)

⁵ And he said unto them, Which of you shall have a friend, and shall go unto him at midnight, and say unto him, Friend, lend me three loaves; ⁶ for a friend of mine in his journey is come to me, and I have nothing to set before him? ⁷ And he from within shall answer and say, Trouble me not: the door is now shut, and my children are with me in bed; I cannot rise and give you. (Luke 11)

⁸ I say unto you, though he will not rise and give him, because he is his friend, yet because of his importunity he will rise and give him as many as he needs. (Luke 11)

⁹ And I say unto you, ask, and it shall be given you; seek, and you shall find; knock, and it shall be opened unto you. ¹⁰ For every one that asks receives; and he that seeks finds; and to him that knocks it shall be opened. (Luke 11)

¹¹ If a son shall ask bread of any of you that is a father, will he give him a stone? Or if *he ask* a fish, will he for a fish give him a serpent? ¹² Or if he shall ask an egg, will he offer him a scorpion? ¹³ If you then, being evil, know how to give good gifts unto your children: how much more shall *your* heavenly Father give the Holy Spirit to them that ask him? (Luke 11)

(LUKE 11:1–13)

Woe unto You Pharisees

37 And as he spoke, a certain Pharisee besought him to dine with him: and he went in, and sat down to meat. 38 And when the Pharisee saw *it*, he marvelled that he had not first washed before dinner. 39 And the Lord said unto him, Now do you Pharisees make clean the outside of the cup and the platter; but your inward part is full of ravening and wickedness. 40 *You* fools, did not he that made that which is without make that which is within also? 41 But rather give alms of such things as you have; and, behold, all things are clean unto you. (Luke 11)

42 But woe unto you, Pharisees! For you tithe mint and rue and all manner of herbs, and pass over judgment and the love of God: these ought you to have done, and not to leave the other undone. 43 Woe unto you, Pharisees! For you love the uppermost seats in the synagogues, and greetings in the markets. 44 Woe unto you, scribes and Pharisees, hypocrites! For you are as graves which appear not, and the men that walk over *them* are not aware of *them*. (Luke 11)

(Luke 11:37–44)

Woe unto You Lawyers

45 Then answered one of the lawyers, and said unto him, Master, thus saying you reproach us also. 46 And he said, Woe unto you also, *you* lawyers! For you load men with burdens grievous to be borne, and you yourselves touch not the burdens with one of your fingers. 47 Woe unto you! For you build the sepulchres of the prophets, and your fathers killed them. 48 Truly you bear witness that you allow the deeds of your fathers: for they indeed killed them, and you build their sepulchres. (Luke 11)

49 Therefore also said the wisdom of God, I will send them prophets and apostles, and *some* of them they shall slay and persecute: 50 that the blood of all the prophets, which was shed from the foundation of the world, may be required of this generation;

⁵¹ from the blood of Abel unto the blood of Zacharias, which perished between the altar and the temple: verily I say unto you, it shall be required of this generation. (Luke 11)

⁵² Woe unto you, lawyers! For you have taken away the key of knowledge: you entered not in yourselves, and them that were entering in you hindered. ⁵³ And as he said these things unto them, the scribes and the Pharisees began to urge *him* vehemently, and to provoke him to speak of many things: ⁵⁴ laying wait for him, and seeking to catch something out of his mouth, that they might accuse him. (Luke 11)

(LUKE 11:45–54)

Whosoever Shall Confess Me before Men

¹ IN the mean time, when there were gathered together an innumerable multitude of people, insomuch that they trod one upon another, he began to say unto his disciples first of all, Beware of the leaven of the Pharisees, which is hypocrisy. ² For there is nothing covered, that shall not be revealed; neither hid, that shall not be known. ³ Therefore whatsoever you have spoken in darkness shall be heard in the light; and that which you have spoken in the ear in closets shall be proclaimed upon the housetops. (Luke 12)

⁴ And I say unto you my friends, be not afraid of them that kill the body, and after that have no more that they can do. ⁵ But I will forewarn you whom you shall fear: Fear him, which after he has killed has power to cast into hell; yea, I say unto you, fear him. (Luke 12)

⁶ Are not five sparrows sold for two farthings, and not one of them is forgotten before God? ⁷ But even the very hairs of your head are all numbered. Fear not therefore: you are of more value than many sparrows. (Luke 12)

⁸ Also I say unto you, whosoever shall confess me before men, him shall the Son of man also confess before the angels of God: ⁹ but he that denies me before men shall be denied before the angels of God. ¹⁰ And whosoever shall speak a word against the Son

of man, it shall be forgiven him: but unto him that blasphemes against the Holy Ghost it shall not be forgiven. (Luke 12)

¹¹ And when they bring you unto the synagogues, and *unto* magistrates, and powers, take you no thought how or what thing you shall answer, or what you shall say: ¹² for the Holy Ghost shall teach you in the same hour what you ought to say. (Luke 12)

(LUKE 12:1–12)

Parable of a Certain Rich Man

¹³ AND one of the company said unto him, Master, speak to my brother, that he divide the inheritance with me. ¹⁴ And he said unto him, Man, who made me a judge or a divider over you? ¹⁵ And he said unto them, Take heed, and beware of covetousness: for a man's life consists not in the abundance of the things which he possesses. (Luke 12)

Beware of. Coveting

¹⁶ And he spoke a parable unto them, saying, The ground of a certain rich man brought forth plentifully: ¹⁷ and he thought with-in himself, saying, What shall I do, because I have no room where to bestow my fruits? ¹⁸ And he said, This will I do: I will pull down my barns, and build greater; and there will I bestow all my fruits and my goods. ¹⁹ And I will say to my soul, Soul, you have much goods laid up for many years; take your ease, eat, drink, *and* be merry. ²⁰ But God said unto him, *You* fool, this night your soul shall be required of you: then whose shall those things be, which you have provided? (Luke 12)

²¹ So *is* he that lays up treasure for himself, and is not rich to-ward God. ²² And he said unto his disciples, Therefore I say unto you, take no thought for your life, what you shall eat; neither for the body, what you shall put on. ²³ The life is more than meat, and the body *is more* than raiment. ²⁴ Consider the ravens: for they neither sow nor reap; which neither have storehouse nor barn; and God feeds them: how much more are you better than the fowls? ²⁵ And which of you with taking thought can add to his stature

one cubit? [26] If you then be not able to do that thing which is least, why take you thought for the rest? (Luke 12)

[27] Consider the lilies how they grow: they toil not, they spin not; and yet I say unto you, that Solomon in all his glory was not arrayed like one of these. [28] If then God so clothe the grass, which is to day in the field, and to morrow is cast into the oven; how much more *will he clothe* you, O you of little faith? [29] And seek not you what you shall eat, or what you shall drink, neither be you of doubtful mind. [30] For all these things do the nations of the world seek after: and your Father knows that you have need of these things. [31] But rather seek the kingdom of God; and all these things shall be added unto you. [32] Fear not, little flock; for it is your Father's good pleasure to give you the kingdom. (Luke 12)

[33] Sell that you have, and give alms; provide yourselves bags which wax not old, a treasure in the heavens that fails not, where no thief approaches, neither moth corrupts. [34] For where your treasure is, there will your heart be also. [35] Let your loins be girded about, and *your* lights burning. (Luke 12)

[49] I am come to send fire on the earth; and what will I, if it be already kindled? [50] But I have a baptism to be baptized with; and how am I straitened till it be accomplished! [51] Suppose you that I am come to give peace on earth? I tell you, Nay; but rather division: [52] for from henceforth there shall be five in one house divided, three against two, and two against three. [53] The father shall be divided against the son, and the son against the father; the mother against the daughter, and the daughter against the mother; the mother in law against her daughter in law, and the daughter in law against her mother in law. (Luke 12)

(LUKE 12:13–35, 49–53)

Parable of the Man and the Fig Tree

[54] AND he said also to the people, When you see a cloud rise out of the west, straightway you say, There comes a shower; and so it

is. ⁵⁵ And when *you see* the south wind blow, you say, There will be heat; and it comes to pass. ⁵⁶ *You* hypocrites, you can discern the face of the sky and of the earth; but how is it that you do not discern this time? ⁵⁷ Yea, and why even of yourselves judge you not what is right? ⁵⁸ When you go with your adversary to the magistrate, *as you are* in the way, give diligence that you may be delivered from him; lest he hale you to the judge, and the judge deliver you to the officer, and the officer cast you into prison. ⁵⁹ I tell you, you shall not depart thence, till you have paid the very last mite. (Luke 12)

¹ There were present at that season some that told him of the Galilaeans, whose blood Pilate had mingled with their sacrifices. ² And Jesus answering said unto them, Suppose you that these Galilaeans were sinners above all the Galilaeans, because they suffered such things? ³ I tell you, Nay: but, except you repent, you shall all likewise perish. ⁴ Or those eighteen, upon whom the tower in Siloam fell, and slew them, think you that they were sinners above all men that dwelt in Jerusalem? ⁵ I tell you, Nay: but, except you repent, you shall all likewise perish. (Luke 13)

⁶ He spoke also this parable; A certain *man* had a fig tree planted in his vineyard; and he came and sought fruit thereon, and found none. ⁷ Then said he unto the dresser of his vineyard, Behold, these three years I come seeking fruit on this fig tree, and find none: cut it down; why cumbers it the ground? ⁸ And he answering said unto him, Lord, let it alone this year also, till I shall dig about it, and dung *it:* ⁹ and if it bear fruit, *well:* and if not, *then* after that you shall cut it down. (Luke 13)

(LUKE 12:54–59; 13:1–9)

CHAPTER NINETEEN

Woman Loosed from a Spirit of Infirmity

abbath [10] AND he was teaching in one of the synagogues on the sabbath. [11] And, behold, there was a woman which had a spirit of infirmity eighteen years, and was bowed together, and could in no wise lift up *herself.* [12] And when Jesus saw her, he called *her to him,* and said unto her, Woman, you are loosed from your infirmity. [13] And he laid *his* hands on her: and immediately she was made straight, and glorified God. (Luke 13)

[14] And the ruler of the synagogue answered with indignation, because that Jesus had healed on the sabbath day, and said unto the people, There are six days in which men ought to work: in them therefore come and be healed, and not on the sabbath day. (Luke 13)

[15] The Lord then answered him, and said, *You* hypocrite, does not each one of you on the sabbath loose his ox or *his* ass from the stall, and lead *him* away to watering? [16] And ought not this woman, being a daughter of Abraham, whom Satan has bound, lo, these eighteen years, be loosed from this bond on the sabbath day? [17] And when he had said these things, all his adversaries were ashamed: and all the people rejoiced for all the glorious things that were done by him. (Luke 13)

(LUKE 13:10–17)

Jesus Journeys through Jerusalem

[22] AND he went through the cities and villages, teaching, and journeying toward Jerusalem. [23] Then said one unto him, Lord, are there few that be saved? And he said unto them, [24] Strive to enter in at the strait gate: for many, I say unto you, will seek to enter in, and shall

137

not be able. ²⁵ When once the master of the house is risen up, and has shut to the door, and you begin to stand without, and to knock at the door, saying, Lord, Lord, open unto us; and he shall answer and say unto you, I know you not whence you are. (Luke 13)

²⁶ Then shall you begin to say, We have eaten and drunk in your presence, and you have taught in our streets. ²⁷ But he shall say, I tell you, I know you not whence you are; depart from me, all *you* workers of iniquity. ²⁸ There shall be weeping and gnashing of teeth, when you shall see Abraham, and Isaac, and Jacob, and all the prophets, in the kingdom of God, and you *yourselves* thrust out. ²⁹ And they shall come from the east, and *from* the west, and from the north, and *from* the south, and shall sit down in the kingdom of God. ³⁰ And, behold, there are last which shall be first, and there are first which shall be last. (Luke 13)

³¹ The same day there came certain of the Pharisees, saying unto him, Get out, and depart hence: for Herod will kill you. ³² And he said unto them, Go, and tell that fox, Behold, I cast out devils, and I do cures to day and to morrow, and the third *day* I shall be perfected. ³³ Nevertheless I must walk to day, and to morrow, and the day following: for it cannot be that a prophet perish out of Jerusalem. (Luke 13)

³⁴ O Jerusalem, Jerusalem, which kills the prophets, and stones them that are sent unto you; how often would I have gathered your children together, as a hen *does gather* her brood under *her* wings, and you would not! ³⁵ Behold, your house is left unto you desolate: and verily I say unto you, you shall not see me, until *the time* come when you shall say, Blessed is he that comes in the name of the Lord. (Luke 13)

(LUKE 13:22–35)

Winter—the Feast of Dedication

²² AND it was at Jerusalem the feast of the dedication, and it was winter. ²³ And Jesus walked in the temple in Solomon's porch.

²⁴ Then came the Jews round about him, and said unto him, How long do you make us to doubt? If you be the Christ, tell us plainly. (John 10)

²⁵ Jesus answered them, I told you, and you believed not: the works that I do in my Father's name, they bear witness of me. ²⁶ But you believe not, because you are not of my sheep, as I said unto you. ²⁷ My sheep hear my voice, and I know them, and they follow me: ²⁸ and I give unto them eternal life; and they shall never perish, neither shall any *man* pluck them out of my hand. ²⁹ My Father, which gave *them* me, is greater than all; and no *man* is able to pluck *them* out of my Father's hand. ³⁰ I and *my* Father are one. ³¹ Then the Jews took up stones again to stone him. (John 10)

³² Jesus answered them, Many good works have I shown you from my Father; for which of those works do you stone me? ³³ The Jews answered him, saying, For a good work we stone you not; but for blasphemy; and because that you, being a man, make yourself God. ³⁴ Jesus answered them, Is it not written in your law, I said, You are gods? ³⁵ If he called them gods, unto whom the word of God came, and the scripture cannot be broken; ³⁶ say you of him, whom the Father has sanctified, and sent into the world, You blaspheme; because I said, I am the Son of God? ³⁷ If I do not the works of my Father, believe me not. ³⁸ But if I do, though you believe not me, believe the works: that you may know, and believe, that the Father *is* in me, and I in him. (John 10)

³⁹ Therefore they sought again to take him: but he escaped out of their hand, ⁴⁰ and went away again beyond Jordan into the place where John at first baptized; and there he abode. ⁴¹ And many resorted unto him, and said, John did no miracle: but all things that John spoke of this man were true. ⁴² And many believed on him there. (John 10)

³⁸ Now it came to pass, as they went, that he entered into a certain village: and a certain woman named Martha received him into her house. ³⁹ And she had a sister called Mary, which also sat at Jesus' feet, and heard his word. ⁴⁰ But Martha was cumbered about much serving, and came to him, and said, Lord, do you not

care that my sister has left me to serve alone? Bid her therefore that she help me. [41] And Jesus answered and said unto her, Martha, Martha, you are careful and troubled about many things: [42] but one thing is needful: and Mary has chosen that good part, which shall not be taken away from her. (Luke 10)

(John 10:22–42; Luke 10:38–42)

Jesus Heals a Man with Dropsy on the Sabbath

[1] And it came to pass, as he went into the house of one of the chief Pharisees to eat bread on the sabbath day, that they watched him. [2] And, behold, there was a certain man before him which had the dropsy. [3] And Jesus answering spoke unto the lawyers and Pharisees, saying, Is it lawful to heal on the sabbath day? [4] And they held their peace. And he took *him*, and healed him, and let him go; [5] and answered them, saying, Which of you shall have an ass or an ox fallen into a pit, and will not straightway pull him out on the sabbath day? [6] And they could not answer him again to these things. (Luke 14)

[7] And he put forth a parable to those which were bidden, when he marked how they chose out the chief rooms; saying unto them. [8] When you are bidden of any *man* to a wedding, sit not down in the highest room; lest a more honourable man than you be bidden of him; [9] and he that bade you and him come and say to you, Give this man place; and you begin with shame to take the lowest room. [10] But when you are bidden, go and sit down in the lowest room; that when he that bade you come, he may say unto you, Friend, go up higher: then shall you have worship in the presence of them that sit at meat with you. (Luke 14)

[11] For whosoever exalts himself shall be abased; and he that humbles himself shall be exalted. [12] Then said he also to him that bade him, When you make a dinner or a supper, call not your friends, nor your brethren, neither your kinsmen, nor *your* rich neighbours; lest they also bid you again, and a recompence be

made you. ¹³ But when you make a feast, call the poor, the maimed, the lame, the blind: ¹⁴ and you shall be blessed; for they cannot rec-ompense you: for you shall be recompensed at the resurrection of the just. ¹⁵ And when one of them that sat at meat with him heard these things, he said unto him, Blessed *is* he that shall eat bread in the kingdom of God. (Luke 14)

(LUKE 14:1–15)

Parable of the Great Supper

¹⁶ THEN said he unto him, A certain man made a great supper, and bade many: ¹⁷ and sent his servant at supper time to say to them that were bidden, Come; for all things are now ready. ¹⁸ And they all with one *consent* began to make excuse. The first said unto him, I have bought a piece of ground, and I must go and see it: I pray you have me excused. ¹⁹ And another said, I have bought five yoke of oxen, and I go to prove them: I pray you have me excused. ²⁰ And another said, I have married a wife, and therefore I cannot come. (Luke 14)

²¹ So that servant came, and showed his lord these things. Then the master of the house being angry said to his servant, Go out quickly into the streets and lanes of the city, and bring in hither the poor, and the maimed, and the halt, and the blind. ²² And the servant said, Lord, it is done as you have commanded, and yet there is room. ²³ And the lord said unto the servant, Go out into the highways and hedges, and compel *them* to come in, that my house may be filled. ²⁴ For I say unto you, that none of those men which were bidden shall taste of my supper. (Luke 14)

(LUKE 14:16–24)

Counting the Cost

²⁵ AND there went great multitudes with him: and he turned, and

said unto them, ²⁶ If any *man* come to me, and hate not his father, and mother, and wife, and children, and brethren, and sisters, yea, and his own life also, he cannot be my disciple. ²⁷ And whosoever does not bear his cross, and come after me, cannot be my disciple. (Luke 14)

²⁸ For which of you, intending to build a tower, sits not down first, and counts the cost, whether he have *sufficient* to finish *it*? ²⁹ Lest haply, after he has laid the foundation, and is not able to finish *it,* all that behold *it* begin to mock him, ³⁰ saying, This man began to build, and was not able to finish. (Luke 14)

³¹ Or what king, going to make war against another king, sits not down first, and consults whether he be able with ten thousand to meet him that comes against him with twenty thousand? ³² Or else, while the other is yet a great way off, he sends an ambassage, and desires conditions of peace. ³³ So likewise, whosoever he be of you that forsakes not all that he has, he cannot be my disciple. (Luke 14)

³⁴ Salt *is* good: but if the salt have lost his savour, wherewith shall it be seasoned? ³⁵ It is neither fit for the land, nor yet for the dunghill; *but* men cast it out. He that has ears to hear, let him hear. (Luke 14)

(LUKE 14:25–35)

Parable of the Lost Sheep

¹ THEN drew near unto him all the publicans and sinners for to hear him. ² And the Pharisees and scribes murmured, saying, This man receives sinners, and eats with them. (Luke 15)

³ And he spoke this parable unto them, saying, ⁴ What man of you, having an hundred sheep, if he lose one of them, does not leave the ninety and nine in the wilderness, and go after that which is lost, until he find it? ⁵ And when he has found *it,* he lays *it* on his shoulders, rejoicing. ⁶ And when he comes home, he calls together *his* friends and neighbours, saying unto them, Rejoice with me; for I have found my sheep which was lost. (Luke 15)

[7] I say unto you, that likewise joy shall be in heaven over one sinner that repents, more than over ninety and nine just persons, which need no repentance. [8] Either what woman having ten pieces of silver, if she lose one piece, does not light a candle, and sweep the house, and seek diligently till she find *it*? [9] And when she has found *it*, she calls *her* friends and *her* neighbours together, saying, Rejoice with me; for I have found the piece which I had lost. [10] Likewise, I say unto you, there is joy in the presence of the angels of God over one sinner that repents. (Luke 15)

(LUKE 15:1–10)

prayer: that many might come
to know you as Savior

CHAPTER TWENTY

Parable of the Prodigal Son

[11] AND he said, A certain man had two sons: [12] and the younger of them said to *his* father, Father, give me the portion of goods that falls *to me.* And he divided unto them *his* living. (Luke 15)

[13] And not many days after the younger son gathered all together, and took his journey into a far country, and there wasted his substance with riotous living. [14] And when he had spent all, there arose a mighty famine in that land; and he began to be in want. [15] And he went and joined himself to a citizen of that country; and he sent him into his fields to feed swine. [16] And he would gladly have filled his belly with the husks that the swine did eat: and no man gave unto him. (Luke 15)

[17] And when he came to himself, he said, How many hired servants of my father's have bread enough and to spare, and I perish with hunger! [18] I will arise and go to my father, and will say unto him, Father, I have sinned against heaven, and before you, [19] and am no more worthy to be called your son: make me as one of your hired servants. (Luke 15)

[20] And he arose, and came to his father. But when he was yet a great way off, his father saw him, and had compassion, and ran, and fell on his neck, and kissed him. (Luke 15)

[21] And the son said unto him, Father, I have sinned against heaven, and in your sight, and am no more worthy to be called your son. [22] But the father said to his servants, Bring forth the best robe, and put *it* on him; and put a ring on his hand, and shoes on *his* feet: [23] and bring hither the fatted calf, and kill *it;* and let us eat, and be merry: [24] for this my son was dead, and is alive again; he was lost, and is found. And they began to be merry. (Luke 15)

[25] Now his elder son was in the field: and as he came and drew

nigh to the house, he heard musick and dancing. [26] And he called one of the servants, and asked what these things meant. [27] And he said unto him, Your brother is come; and your father has killed the fatted calf, because he has received him safe and sound. (Luke 15)

[28] And he was angry, and would not go in: therefore came his father out, and intreated him. [29] And he answering said to *his* father, Lo, these many years do I serve you, neither transgressed I at any time your commandment: and yet you never gave me a kid, that I might make merry with my friends: [30] but as soon as this your son was come, which has devoured your living with harlots, you have killed for him the fatted calf. [31] And he said unto him, Son, you are ever with me, and all that I have is yours. [32] It was meet that we should make merry, and be glad: for this your brother was dead, and is alive again; and was lost, and is found. (Luke 15)

(LUKE 15:11–32)

Parable of the Steward and Unrighteous Mammon

[1] AND he said also unto his disciples, There was a certain rich man, which had a steward; and the same was accused unto him that he had wasted his goods. [2] And he called him, and said unto him, How is it that I hear this of you? Give an account of your stewardship; for you may be no longer steward. [3] Then the steward said within himself, What shall I do? For my lord takes away from me the stewardship: I cannot dig; to beg I am ashamed. [4] I am resolved what to do, that, when I am put out of the stewardship, they may receive me into their houses. (Luke 16)

[5] So he called every one of his lord's debtors *unto him,* and said unto the first, How much owe you unto my lord? [6] And he said, An hundred measures of oil. And he said unto him, Take your bill, and sit down quickly, and write fifty. [7] Then said he to another, And how much owe you? And he said, An hundred measures of wheat. And he said unto him, Take your bill, and write fourscore *[eighty].* (Luke 16)

⁸ And the lord commended the unjust steward, because he had done wisely: for the children of this world are in their generation wiser than the children of light. ⁹ And I say unto you, make to yourselves friends of the mammon of unrighteousness; that, when you fail, they may receive you into everlasting habitations. (Luke 16)

¹⁰ He that is faithful in that which is least is faithful also in much: and he that is unjust in the least is unjust also in much. ¹¹ If therefore you have not been faithful in the unrighteous mammon, who will commit to your trust the true *riches?* ¹² And if you have not been faithful in that which is another man's, who shall give you that which is your own? (Luke 16)

¹³ No servant can serve two masters: for either he will hate the one, and love the other; or else he will hold to the one, and despise the other. You cannot serve God and mammon. ¹⁴ And the Pharisees also, who were covetous, heard all these things: and they derided him. ¹⁵ And he said unto them, You are they which justify yourselves before men; but God knows your hearts: for that which is highly esteemed among men is abomination in the sight of God. (Luke 16)

¹⁶ The law and the prophets *were* until John: since that time the kingdom of God is preached, and every man presses into it. ¹⁷ And it is easier for heaven and earth to pass, than one tittle of the law to fail. ¹⁸ Whosoever puts away his wife, and marries another, commits adultery: and whosoever marries her that is put away from her husband commits adultery. (Luke 16)

(LUKE 16:1–18)

Lazarus and the Rich Man

¹⁹ THERE was a certain rich man, which was clothed in purple and fine linen, and fared sumptuously every day: ²⁰ and there was a certain beggar named Lazarus, which was laid at his gate, full of sores, ²¹ and desiring to be fed with the crumbs which fell from the rich man's table: moreover the dogs came and licked his sores. (Luke 16)

²² And it came to pass, that the beggar died, and was carried by the angels into Abraham's bosom: the rich man also died, and was buried; ²³ and in hell he lifts up his eyes, being in torments, and sees Abraham afar off, and Lazarus in his bosom. ²⁴ And he cried and said, Father Abraham, have mercy on me, and send Lazarus, that he may dip the tip of his finger in water, and cool my tongue; for I am tormented in this flame. (Luke 16)

²⁵ But Abraham said, Son, remember that you in your lifetime received your good things, and likewise Lazarus evil things: but now he is comforted, and you are tormented. ²⁶ And beside all this, between us and you there is a great gulf fixed: so that they which would pass from hence to you cannot; neither can they pass to us, that *would come* from thence. (Luke 16)

²⁷ Then he said, I pray therefore, father, that you would send him to my father's house: ²⁸ for I have five brethren; that he may testify unto them, lest they also come into this place of torment. ²⁹ Abraham said unto him, They have Moses and the prophets; let them hear them. ³⁰ And he said, Nay, father Abraham: but if one went unto them from the dead, they will repent. ³¹ And he said unto him, If they hear not Moses and the prophets, neither will they be persuaded, though one rose from the dead. (Luke 16)

(LUKE 16:19–31)

Faith as a Grain of a Mustard Seed

¹ THEN said he unto the disciples, It is impossible but that offences will come: but woe *unto him,* through whom they come! ² It were better for him that a millstone were hanged about his neck, and he cast into the sea, than that he should offend one of these little ones. (Luke 17)

³ Take heed to yourselves: If your brother trespass against you, rebuke him; and if he repent, forgive him. ⁴ And if he trespass against you seven times in a day, and seven times in a day turn again to you, saying, I repent: you shall forgive him. (Luke 17)

⁵ And the apostles said unto the <u>Lord, Increase our faith.</u> ⁶ And the Lord said, If you had faith as a grain of mustard seed, you might say unto this sycamine tree, Be you plucked up by the root, and be you planted in the sea; and it should obey you. ⁷ But which of you, having a servant plowing or feeding cattle, will say unto him by and by, when he is come from the field, Go and sit down to meat? ⁸ And will not rather say unto him, Make ready wherewith I may sup, and gird yourself, and serve me, till I have eaten and drunken; and afterward you shall eat and drink? ⁹ Does he thank that servant because he did the things that were commanded him? I think not. ¹⁰ So likewise you, when you shall have done all those things which are commanded you, say, We are unprofitable servants: we have done that which was our duty to do. (Luke 17)

(LUKE 17:1–10)

Lazarus Dies

¹ Now a certain *man* was sick, *named* Lazarus, of Bethany, the town of Mary and her sister Martha. ² (It was *that* Mary which anointed the Lord with ointment, and wiped his feet with her hair, whose brother Lazarus was sick.) ³ Therefore his sisters sent unto him, saying, Lord, behold, he whom you love is sick. ⁴ When Jesus heard *that,* he said, This sickness is not unto death, but for the glory of God, that the Son of God might be glorified thereby. (John 11)

⁵ <u>Now Jesus loved Martha, and her sister, and Lazarus.</u> ⁶ When he had heard therefore that he was sick, he abode two days still in the same place where he was. ⁷ Then after that said he to *his* disciples, Let us go into Judaea again. ⁸ *His* disciples said unto him, Master, the Jews of late sought to stone you; and go you thither again? ⁹ Jesus answered, Are there not twelve hours in the day? If any man walk in the day, he stumbles not, because he sees the light of this world. ¹⁰ But if a man walk in the night, he stumbles, because there is no light in him. (John 11)

¹¹ These things said he: and after that he said unto them, Our

friend Lazarus sleeps; but I go, that I may awake him out of sleep. [12] Then said his disciples, Lord, if he sleep, he shall do well. [13] Howbeit Jesus spoke of his death: but they thought that he had spoken of taking of rest in sleep. [14] Then said Jesus unto them plainly, Lazarus is dead. [15] And I am glad for your sakes that I was not there, to the intent you may believe; nevertheless let us go unto him. (John 11)

[16] Then said Thomas, which is called Didymus, unto his fellow-disciples, Let us also go, that we may die with him. (John 11)

(JOHN 11:1–16)

Jesus Raises Lazarus from the Dead

[17] THEN when Jesus came, he found that he had *lain* in the grave four days already. [18] Now Bethany was nigh unto Jerusalem, about fifteen furlongs off: [19] and many of the Jews came to Martha and Mary, to comfort them concerning their brother. [20] Then Martha, as soon as she heard that Jesus was coming, went and met him: but Mary sat *still* in the house. (John 11)

[21] Then said Martha unto Jesus, Lord, if you had been here, my brother had not died. [22] But I know, that even now, whatsoever you will ask of God, God will give *it* you. [23] Jesus said unto her, Your brother shall rise again. [24] Martha said unto him, I know that he shall rise again in the resurrection at the last day. [25] Jesus said unto her, I am the resurrection, and the life: he that believes in me, though he were dead, yet shall he live: [26] and whosoever lives and believes in me shall never die. Believe you this? [27] She said unto him, Yea, Lord: I believe that you are the Christ, the Son of God, which should come into the world. (John 11)

[28] And when she had so said, she went her way, and called Mary her sister secretly, saying, The Master is come, and calls for you. [29] As soon as she heard *that*, she arose quickly, and came unto him. [30] Now Jesus was not yet come into the town, but was in that place where Martha met him. [31] The Jews then which were with

her in the house, and comforted her, when they saw Mary, that she rose up hastily and went out, followed her, saying, She goes unto the grave to weep there. (John 11)

³² Then when Mary was come where Jesus was, and saw him, she fell down at his feet, saying unto him, Lord, if you had been here, my brother had not died. ³³ When Jesus therefore saw her weeping, and the Jews also weeping which came with her, he groaned in the spirit, and was troubled, ³⁴ and said, Where have you laid him? They said unto him, Lord, come and see. (John 11)

³⁵ Jesus wept. ³⁶ Then said the Jews, Behold how he loved him! ³⁷ And some of them said, Could not this man, which opened the eyes of the blind, have caused that even this man should not have died? ³⁸ Jesus therefore again groaning in himself came to the grave. It was a cave, and a stone lay upon it. (John 11)

³⁹ Jesus said, Take away the stone. Martha, the sister of him that was dead, said unto him, Lord, by this time he stinks: for he has been *dead* four days. ⁴⁰ Jesus said unto her, Said I not unto you, that, if you would believe, you should see the glory of God? ⁴¹ Then they took away the stone *from the place* where the dead was laid. (John 11)

⁴¹ And Jesus lifted up *his* eyes, and said, Father, I thank you that you have heard me. ⁴² And I knew that you hear me always: but because of the people which stand by I said *it*, that they may believe that you have sent me. (John 11)

⁴³ And when he thus had spoken, he cried with a loud voice, Lazarus, come forth. ⁴⁴ And he that was dead came forth, bound hand and foot with graveclothes: and his face was bound about with a napkin. Jesus said unto them, Loose him, and let him go. ⁴⁵ Then many of the Jews which came to Mary, and had seen the things which Jesus did, believed on him. (John 11)

(JOHN 11:17–45)

Chief Priests and Pharisees Counsel against Jesus

[46] BUT some of them went their ways to the Pharisees, and told them what things Jesus had done. [47] Then gathered the chief priests and the Pharisees a council, and said, What do we? For this man does many miracles. [48] If we let him thus alone, all *men* will believe on him: and the Romans shall come and take away both our place and nation. (John 11)

[49] And one of them, *named* Caiaphas, being the high priest that same year, said unto them, You know nothing at all, [50] nor consider that it is expedient for us, that one man should die for the people, and that the whole nation perish not. [51] And this spoke he not of himself: but being high priest that year, he prophesied that Jesus should die for that nation; [52] and not for that nation only, but that also he should gather together in one the children of God that were scattered abroad. (John 11)

[53] Then from that day forth they took counsel together for to put him to death. [54] Jesus therefore walked no more openly among the Jews; but went thence unto a country near to the wilderness, into a city called Ephraim, and there continued with his disciples. (John 11)

[55] And the Jews' passover was nigh at hand: and many went out of the country up to Jerusalem before the passover, to purify themselves. [56] Then sought they for Jesus, and spoke among themselves, as they stood in the temple, What think you, that he will not come to the feast? [57] Now both the chief priests and the Pharisees had given a commandment, that, if any man knew where he were, he should show *it*, that they might take him. (John 11)

(JOHN 11:46–57)

CHAPTER TWENTY-ONE

Jesus and the Ten Lepers

¹¹ AND it came to pass, as he went to Jerusalem, that he passed through the midst of Samaria and Galilee. (Luke 17)

¹² And as he entered into a certain village, there met him ten men that were lepers, which stood afar off: ¹³ and they lifted up *their* voices, and said, Jesus, Master, have mercy on us. (Luke 17)

¹⁴ And when he saw *them,* he said unto them, Go show yourselves unto the priests. And it came to pass, that, as they went, they were cleansed. (Luke 17)

¹⁵ And one of them, when he saw that he was healed, turned back, and with a loud voice glorified God, ¹⁶ and fell down on *his* face at his feet, giving him thanks: and he was a Samaritan. (Luke 17)

¹⁷ And Jesus answering said, Were there not ten cleansed? But where *are* the nine? ¹⁸ There are not found that returned to give glory to God, save this stranger. ¹⁹ And he said unto him, Arise, go your way: your faith has made you whole. (Luke 17)

(LUKE 17:11–19)

When Shall the Kingdom of God Come?

²⁰ AND when he was demanded of the Pharisees, when the kingdom of God should come, he answered them and said, The kingdom of God comes not with observation: ²¹ neither shall they say, Lo here! Or, lo there! For, behold, the kingdom of God is within you. (Luke 17)

²² And he said unto the disciples, The days will come, when you shall desire to see one of the days of the Son of man, and you shall not see *it.* ²³ And they shall say to you, See here; or, see there: go not after *them,* nor follow *them.* ²⁴ For as the lightning, that

lightens out of the one *part* under heaven, shines unto the other *part* under heaven; so shall also the Son of man be in his day. ²⁵ But first must he suffer many things, and be rejected of this generation. (Luke 17)

²⁶ And as it was in the days of Noe, so shall it be also in the days of the Son of man. ²⁷ They did eat, they drank, they married wives, they were given in marriage, until the day that Noe entered into the ark, and the flood came, and destroyed them all. (Luke 17)

²⁸ Likewise also as it was in the days of Lot; they did eat, they drank, they bought, they sold, they planted, they builded; ²⁹ but the same day that Lot went out of Sodom it rained fire and brimstone from heaven, and destroyed *them* all. ³⁰ Even thus shall it be in the day when the Son of man is revealed. ³¹ In that day, he which shall be upon the housetop, and his stuff in the house, let him not come down to take it away: and he that is in the field, let him likewise not return back. ³² Remember Lot's wife. (Luke 17)

³³ Whosoever shall seek to save his life shall lose it; and whosoever shall lose his life shall preserve it. ³⁴ I tell you, in that night there shall be two *men* in one bed; the one shall be taken, and the other shall be left. ³⁵ Two *women* shall be grinding together; the one shall be taken, and the other left. ³⁶ Two *men* shall be in the field; the one shall be taken, and the other left. ³⁷ And they answered and said unto him, Where, Lord? And he said unto them, Wheresoever the body *is,* thither will the eagles be gathered together. (Luke 17)

(LUKE 17:20–37)

Parable of the Unjust Judge

¹ AND he spoke a parable unto them *to this end,* that men ought always to pray, and not to faint; ² saying, There was in a city a judge, which feared not God, neither regarded man: ³ and there was a widow in that city; and she came unto him, saying, Avenge me of my adversary. ⁴ And he would not for a while: but afterward

he said within himself, Though I fear not God, nor regard man; ⁵ yet because this widow troubles me, I will avenge her, lest by her continual coming she weary me. (Luke 18)

⁶ And the Lord said, Hear what the unjust judge said. ⁷ And shall not God avenge his own elect, which cry day and night unto him, though he bear long with them? ⁸ I tell you that he will avenge them speedily. Nevertheless when the Son of man comes, shall he find faith on the earth? ⁹ And he spoke this parable unto certain which trusted in themselves that they were righteous, and despised others: (Luke 18)

¹⁰ Two men went up into the temple to pray; the one a Pharisee, and the other a publican. ¹¹ The Pharisee stood and prayed thus with himself, God, I thank you, that I am not as other men *are,* extortioners, unjust, adulterers, or even as this publican. ¹² I fast twice in the week, I give tithes of all that I possess. (Luke 18)

¹³ And the publican, standing afar off, would not lift up so much as *his* eyes unto heaven, but smote upon his breast, saying, God be merciful to me a sinner. ¹⁴ I tell you, this man went down to his house justified *rather* than the other: for every one that exalts himself shall be abased; and he that humbles himself shall be exalted. (Luke 18)

(LUKE 18:1–14)

Jesus Speaks on Divorce

¹ AND it came to pass, *that* when Jesus had finished these sayings, (Matthew 19) ¹ he arose from thence, (Mark 10) ¹ departed from Galilee, (Matthew 19) ¹ and came into the coasts of Judaea by the farther side of Jordan: and the people resorted unto him again; and, as he was wont, he taught them again. (Mark 10) ² And great multitudes followed him; and he healed them there. (Matthew 19) ² And (Mark 10) ³ the Pharisees also came unto him, (Matthew 19) ² and asked him, (Mark 10) ³ Is it lawful for a man to put away his wife for every cause? (Matthew 19) ² Tempting him. (Mark 10)

³ And he answered and said unto them, What did Moses command you? ⁴ And they said, Moses suffered to write a bill of divorcement, and to put *her* away. (Mark 10) ⁴ And he answered and said unto them, Have you not read, that he which made *them* at the beginning made them male and female, ⁵ and said, (Matthew 19) ⁷ For this cause shall a man leave his father and mother, (Mark 10) ⁵ and shall cleave to his wife: and they twain shall be one flesh? ⁶ Wherefore they are no more twain, but one flesh. What therefore God has joined together, let not man put asunder. (Matthew 19)

⁷ They say unto him, Why did Moses then command to give a writing of divorcement, and to put her away? (Matthew 19) ⁵ And Jesus answered and said unto them, (Mark 10) ⁸ Moses because of the hardness of your hearts, (Matthew 19) ⁵ wrote you this precept, (Mark 10) *[and]* ⁸ suffered you to put away your wives: but from the beginning it was not so. (Matthew 19)

¹⁰ And in the house his disciples asked him again of the same *matter.* ¹¹ And he said unto them, Whosoever shall put away his wife, (Mark 10) ⁹ except *it be* for fornication, and shall marry another, commits adultery (Matthew 19) ¹¹ against her: (Mark 10) ⁹ and whoso marries her which is put away does commit adultery. (Matthew 19) ¹² And if a woman shall put away her husband, and be married to another, she commits adultery. (Mark 10)

¹⁰ His disciples say unto him, If the case of the man be so with *his* wife, it is not good to marry. ¹¹ But he said unto them, All *men* cannot receive this saying, save *they* to whom it is given. ¹² For there are some eunuchs, which were so born from *their* mother's womb: and there are some eunuchs, which were made eunuchs of men: and there be eunuchs, which have made themselves eunuchs for the kingdom of heaven's sake. He that is able to receive *it*, let him receive *it.* (Matthew 19)

(MARK 10:1–12; MATTHEW 19:1–12)

Sell What You Have and Give to the Poor

¹⁵ AND they brought unto him also infants, (Luke 18) ¹³ little (Matthew 19) ¹³ young children, (Mark 10) ¹⁵ that he would touch them: (Luke 18) ¹³ that he should put *his* hands on them, and pray: (Matthew 19) ¹⁵ but when *his* disciples saw *it,* they (Luke 18) ¹³ rebuked those that brought *them.* ¹⁴ But when Jesus saw *it,* he was much displeased, (Mark 10) ¹⁶ called them *unto him,* (Luke 18) ¹⁴ and said unto them, Suffer the little children to come unto me, and forbid them not: for of such is the kingdom of God. ¹⁵ Verily I say unto you, whosoever shall not receive the kingdom of God as a little child, he (Mark 10) ¹⁷ shall in no wise enter therein. (Luke 18) ¹⁶ And he took them up in his arms, (Mark 10) ¹⁵ and he laid *his* hands on them, (Matthew 19) ¹⁶ and blessed them, (Mark 10) ¹⁵ and departed thence. (Matthew 19)

¹⁶ And, behold, (Matthew 19) ¹⁷ when he was gone forth into the way, there came (Mark 10) ¹⁸ a certain ruler, (Luke 18) ¹⁷ one running, and kneeled to him, and asked him, (Mark 10) ¹⁸ saying, Good Master, (Luke 18) ¹⁶ what good thing shall I do, (Matthew 19) ¹⁷ that I may inherit eternal life? ¹⁸ And Jesus said unto him, Why call you me good? *There is* none good but one, *that is,* (Mark 10) ¹⁷ God: but if you will enter into life, keep the commandments. ¹⁸ He said unto him, Which? Jesus said, (Matthew 19) ²⁰ You know the commandments, Do not commit adultery, Do not kill, Do not steal, Do not bear false witness, (Luke 18) ¹⁹ Defraud not, (Mark 10) ¹⁹ Honour your father and *your* mother: and, You shall love your neighbour as yourself. (Matthew 19)

²⁰ The young man (Matthew 19) ²⁰ answered and said unto him, Master, all these (Mark 10) ²⁰ things (Matthew 19) ²⁰ have I observed (Mark 10) ²⁰ from my youth up: what lack I yet? (Matthew 19) ²² Now when Jesus heard these things, (Luke 18) ²¹ Jesus beholding him loved him, and said unto him, (Mark 10) ²² Yet lack you one thing: (Luke 18) ²¹ if you will be perfect, (Matthew 19) ²¹ go your way, sell whatsoever you have, and give to the poor, and you shall have treasure in heaven: and come, take up the cross, and follow me. (Mark 10)

²² But when the young man heard that saying, (Matthew 19) ²² he was sad at that saying, and went away grieved: (Mark 10) ²³ for he was very

rich (Luke 18) *[and]* 22 had great possessions. (Mark 10) 24 And when Jesus saw that he was very sorrowful, (Luke 18) 23 Jesus looked round about, and said unto his disciples, (Mark 10) 23 Verily I say unto you, that a rich man shall hardly enter into the kingdom of heaven. (Matthew 19) 23 How hardly shall they that have riches enter into the kingdom of God! 24 And the disciples were astonished at his words. But Jesus answered again, and said unto them, Children, how hard is it for them that trust in riches to enter into the kingdom of God! (Mark 10) 24 And again I say unto you, it is easier for a camel to go through the eye of a needle, than for a rich man to enter into the kingdom of God. (Matthew 19)

25 When his disciples heard *it,* they were exceedingly amazed, (Matthew 19) 26 they were astonished out of measure, saying among themselves, Who then can be saved? 27 And Jesus looking upon them said, With men *it is* impossible, but not with God: for with God all things are possible. (Mark 10) 27 The things which are impossible with men are possible with God. (Luke 18) 27 Then answered Peter and (Matthew 19) 28 began to say unto him, (Mark 10) 27 Behold, we have forsaken all, (Matthew 19) 28 and have followed you. (Mark 10) 27 What shall we have therefore? (Matthew 19)

29 And Jesus answered and said (Mark 10) 28 unto them, Verily I say unto you, that you which have followed me, in the regeneration when the Son of man shall sit in the throne of his glory, you also shall sit upon twelve thrones, judging the twelve tribes of Israel. (Matthew 19) 29 There is no man that has left house, or brethren, or sisters, or father, or mother, or wife, or children, or lands, (Mark 10) 29 for my name's sake (Matthew 19) 29 and the gospel's; (Mark 10) 29 for the kingdom of God's sake, (Luke 18) 30 but he shall receive a hundredfold now in this (Mark 10) 30 present (Luke 18) 30 time, houses, and brethren, and sisters, and mothers, and children, and lands, with persecutions; and in the world to come (Mark 10) 29 shall inherit everlasting life. (Matthew 19) 31 But many *that are* first shall be last; (Mark 10) 30 and the last *shall be* first. (Matthew 19)

(LUKE 18:15–18, 20, 22–24, 27, 29–30;

MARK 10:13–24, 26–31; MATTHEW 19:13, 15–25, 27–30)

Kingdom of Heaven Like a Householder

¹ FOR the kingdom of heaven is like unto a man *that is* an householder, which went out early in the morning to hire labourers into his vineyard. ² And when he had agreed with the labourers for a penny a day, he sent them into his vineyard. ³ And he went out about the third hour, and saw others standing idle in the marketplace, ⁴ and said unto them; Go you also into the vineyard, and whatsoever is right I will give you. And they went their way. ⁵ Again he went out about the sixth and ninth hour, and did likewise. ⁶ And about the eleventh hour he went out, and found others standing idle, and said unto them, Why stand you here all the day idle? ⁷ They say unto him, Because no man has hired us. He said unto them, Go you also into the vineyard; and whatsoever is right, *that* shall you receive. (Matthew 20)

⁸ So when even was come, the lord of the vineyard said unto his steward, Call the labourers, and give them *their* hire, beginning from the last unto the first. ⁹ And when they came that *were hired* about the eleventh hour, they received every man a penny. ¹⁰ But when the first came, they supposed that they should have received more; and they likewise received every man a penny. ¹¹ And when they had received *it,* they murmured against the goodman of the house, ¹² saying, These last have wrought *but* one hour, and you have made them equal unto us, which have borne the burden and heat of the day. (Matthew 20)

¹³ But he answered one of them, and said, Friend, I do you no wrong: did not you agree with me for a penny? ¹⁴ Take *what* yours *is,* and go your way: I will give unto this last, even as unto you. ¹⁵ Is it not lawful for me to do what I will with my own? Is your eye evil, because I am good? ¹⁶ So the last shall be first, and the first last: for many be called, but few chosen. (Matthew 20)

(MATTHEW 20:1–16)

Jesus Tells the Disciples What Is to Come

³² AND they were in the way going up to Jerusalem; and Jesus went before them: and they were amazed; and as they followed, they were afraid. And he took (Mark 10) ³¹ *unto him* (Luke 18) ³² again the twelve (Mark 10) ¹⁷ disciples apart in the way, (Matthew 20) ³² and began to tell them what things should happen unto him, (Mark 10) ¹⁷ and said unto them, (Matthew 20) ³³ Behold, we go up to Jerusalem; (Mark 10) ³¹ and all things that are written by the prophets concerning the Son of man shall be accomplished. (Luke 18)

³² For he (Luke 18) ¹⁸ shall be betrayed (Matthew 20) *[and]* ³³ delivered unto the chief priests, and unto the scribes; and they shall condemn him to death, and shall deliver him to the Gentiles: ³⁴ and they shall mock him, and shall scourge him, and shall spit upon him, (Mark 10) *[and he shall be]* ³² spitefully entreated. (Luke 18) *[And they shall]* ¹⁹ crucify *him* (Matthew 20) ³³ and put him to death: and the third day he shall rise again. (Luke 18)

³⁴ And they understood none of these things: and this saying was hid from them, neither knew they the things which were spoken. (Luke 18)

(MARK 10:32–34; MATTHEW 20:17–19; LUKE 18:31–34)

CHAPTER TWENTY-TWO

Zebedee's Wife and Sons Approach Jesus

²⁰ THEN came to him the mother of Zebedee's children with her sons, worshipping *him,* and desiring a certain thing of him. ²¹ And he said unto her, What will you? She said unto him, Grant that these my two sons may sit, the one on your right hand, and the other on the left, in your kingdom. ^(Matthew 20)

³⁵ And James and John, the sons of Zebedee, come unto him, saying, Master, we would that you should do for us whatsoever we shall desire. ³⁶ And he said unto them, What would you that I should do for you? ³⁷ They said unto him, Grant unto us that we may sit, one on your right hand, and the other on your left hand, in your glory. ^(Mark 10)

²² But Jesus answered and said ^(Matthew 20) ³⁸ unto them, You know not what you ask: can you drink of the cup ^(Mark 10) ²² that I shall drink of, and to be baptized with the baptism that I am baptized with? ^(Matthew 20) ³⁹ And they said unto him, We can. And Jesus said unto them, You shall indeed drink of the cup that I drink of; and with the baptism that I am baptized withal shall you be baptized: ⁴⁰ but to sit on my right hand and on my left hand is not mine to give; but *it shall be given to them* for whom it is prepared ^(Mark 10) ²³ of my Father. ^(Matthew 20)

⁴¹ And when the ten heard *it,* they began to be much displeased with James and John; ^(Mark 10) ²⁴ they were moved with indignation against the two brethren. ^(Matthew 20)

⁴² But Jesus called them *to him,* and said unto them, You know that they which are accounted to rule over the Gentiles, ^(Mark 10) ²⁵ the princes of the Gentiles, ^(Matthew 20) ⁴² exercise lordship ^(Mark 10) [*and*] ²⁵ dominion ^(Matthew 20) ⁴² over them; and their great ones exercise authority upon them. ⁴³ But so shall it not be among you: but

whosoever will be great among you, (Mark 10) 26 let him be your minister. (Matthew 20) 44 And whosoever of you will be the chiefest (Mark 10)
27 among you, let him be your servant: (Matthew 20) 45 for even the Son
of man came not to be ministered unto, but to minister, and to
give his life a ransom for many. (Mark 10) *a ransom for many =*

many would come to know you a savior and lord

(MATTHEW 20:20–27; MARK 10:35–45)

Blind Bartimaeus

46 AND they came to Jericho: and as he went out of Jericho with
his disciples and a great number of people, (Mark 10) 35 a certain blind
named. man, (Luke 18) 46 Bartimaeus, the son of Timaeus, sat by the highway
side begging. (Mark 10) 36 And hearing the multitude pass by, he asked
what it meant. 37 And they told him, that Jesus of Nazareth passes
by. (Luke 18) 47 And when he heard that it was Jesus of Nazareth, he
began to cry out, and say, Jesus, *you* Son of David, have mercy on
me. (Mark 10)

39 And they which went before rebuked him, (Luke 18) 48 and many
charged him that he should hold his peace: but he cried the more
a great deal, *You* Son of David, have mercy on me. 49 And Jesus
stood still, and commanded him (Mark 10) 40 to be brought unto him.
(Luke 18) 49 And they call[ed] the blind man, saying unto him, Be of
good comfort, rise; he calls you. 50 And he, casting away his garment, rose, and came to Jesus. (Mark 10) 40 And when he was come
near, he asked him, 41 saying, What will you that I shall do unto
you? (Luke 18)

51 The blind man said unto him, Lord, that I might receive my
sight. (Mark 10) 42 And Jesus said unto him, Receive your sight: your
faith has saved you. (Luke 18) 52 Go your way; your faith has made you
whole. And immediately he received his sight, and followed Jesus
in the way, (Mark 10) 43 glorifying God: and all the people, when they
saw *it*, gave praise unto God. (Luke 18)

(MARK 10:46–52; LUKE 18:35–37, 39–43)

faith saves
faith makes whole

Zacchaeus, Chief among Publicans

named

[1] AND *Jesus* entered and passed through Jericho. [2] And, behold, *there was* a man named Zacchaeus, which was the chief among the publicans, and he was rich. [3] And he sought to see Jesus who he was; and could not for the press, because he was little of stature. [4] And he ran before, and climbed up into a sycamore tree to see him: for he was to pass that *way*. (Luke 19)

[5] And when Jesus came to the place, he looked up, and saw him, and said unto him, Zacchaeus, make haste, and come down; for to day I must abide at your house. [6] And he made haste, and came down, and received him joyfully. (Luke 19)

[7] And when they saw *it*, they all murmured, saying, that he was gone to be guest with a man that is a sinner. [8] And Zacchaeus stood, and said unto the Lord; Behold, Lord, the half of my goods I give to the poor; and if I have taken any thing from any man by false accusation, I restore *him* fourfold. [9] And Jesus said unto him, This day is salvation come to this house, forsomuch as he also is a son of Abraham. [10] For the Son of man is come to seek and to save that which was lost. (Luke 19)

(LUKE 19:1–10)

Parable of a Certain Nobleman

[11] AND as they heard these things, he added and spoke a parable, because he was nigh to Jerusalem, and because they thought that the kingdom of God should immediately appear. (Luke 19)

[12] He said therefore, A certain nobleman went into a far country to receive for himself a kingdom, and to return. [13] And he called his ten servants, and delivered them ten pounds, and said unto them, Occupy till I come. [14] But his citizens hated him, and sent a message after him, saying, We will not have this *man* to reign over us. (Luke 19)

[15] And it came to pass, that when he was returned, having received the kingdom, then he commanded these servants to be

called unto him, to whom he had given the money, that he might know how much every man had gained by trading. ¹⁶ Then came the first, saying, Lord, your pound has gained ten pounds. ¹⁷ And he said unto him, Well, you good servant: because you have been faithful in a very little, have you authority over ten cities. (Luke 19)

¹⁸ And the second came, saying, Lord, your pound has gained five pounds. ¹⁹ And he said likewise to him, Be you also over five cities. ²⁰ And another came, saying, Lord, behold, *here is* your pound, which I have kept laid up in a napkin: ²¹ for I feared you, because you are an austere man: you take up that you layed not down, and reap that you did not sow. (Luke 19)

²² And he said unto him, Out of your own mouth will I judge you, *you* wicked servant. You knew that I was an austere man, taking up that I laid not down, and reaping that I did not sow: ²³ wherefore then gave not you my money into the bank, that at my coming I might have required my own with usury? ²⁴ And he said unto them that stood by, Take from him the pound, and give *it* to him that has ten pounds. ²⁵ (And they said unto him, Lord, he has ten pounds.) (Luke 19)   those listening

²⁶ For I say unto you, that unto every one which has shall be given; and from him that has not, even that he has shall be taken away from him. ²⁷ But those my enemies, which would not that I should reign over them, bring hither, and slay them before me. LORD ²⁸ And when he had thus spoken, he went before, ascending up to Jerusalem. (Luke 19)

(LUKE 19:11–28)

Mary Anoints Jesus with Spikenard in Bethany

¹ THEN Jesus six days before the passover came to Bethany, where Lazarus was which had been dead, whom he raised from the dead. ² There they made him a supper; and Martha served: but Lazarus was one of them that sat at the table with him. ³ Then took Mary a pound of ointment of spikenard, very costly, and anointed the

feet of Jesus, and wiped his feet with her hair: and the house was filled with the odour of the ointment. (John 12)

⁴ Then said one of his disciples, Judas Iscariot, Simon's *son,* which should betray him, ⁵ Why was not this ointment sold for three hundred pence, and given to the poor? ⁶ This he said, not that he cared for the poor; but because he was a thief, and had the bag, and bore what was put therein. (John 12)

⁷ Then said Jesus, Let her alone: against the day of my burying has she kept this. ⁸ For the poor always you have with you; but me you have not always. ⁹ Much people of the Jews therefore knew that he was there: and they came not for Jesus' sake only, but that they might see Lazarus also, whom he had raised from the dead. ¹⁰ But the chief priests consulted that they might put Lazarus also to death; ¹¹ because that by reason of him many of the Jews went away, and believed on Jesus. (John 12)

(JOHN 12:1–11)

Two Disciples Sent To Loose the Colt

²⁹ AND it came to pass, (Luke 19) ¹ when they came nigh to Jerusalem, (Mark 11) ²⁹ when he was come nigh to Bethphage and Bethany, at the mount called *the mount* of Olives, (Luke 19) ¹ then sent Jesus (Matthew 21) ²⁹ two of his disciples, (Luke 19) ² and said unto them, (Mark 11) ³⁰ Go (Luke 19) ² your way into the village over against you: and as soon as you be entered into it, (Mark 11) ² you shall find an ass tied, and a colt with her, (Matthew 21) ³⁰ a colt tied, whereon yet never man sat: (Luke 19) ² loose *them,* and bring *them* unto me. ³ And if any *man* say ought unto you (Matthew 21) *[and]* ³¹ ask you, (Luke 19) ³ Why do you this? (Mark 11) ³¹ Why do you loose *him?* Thus shall you say unto him, Because (Luke 19) ³ the Lord has need of them; and straightway he will send them (Matthew 21) ³ hither. (Mark 11) ⁴ All this was done, that it might be fulfilled which was spoken by the prophet, saying, ⁵ Tell the daughter of Sion, (Matthew 21) ¹⁵ Fear not, daughter of Sion; (John 12) ⁵ behold, your King comes unto you, meek, and sitting upon an ass, and a

colt the foal of an ass.^a (Matthew 21)

³² And they that were sent, (Luke 19) ⁶ the disciples, (Matthew 21) ³² went their way, and found even as he had said unto them, (Luke 19) ⁴ and found the colt tied by the door without in a place where two ways met; and they loose[d] him, (Mark 11) ⁶ and did as Jesus commanded them. (Matthew 21) ³³ And as they were loosing the colt, the owners thereof said unto them, (Luke 19) ⁵ What do you, loosing the colt? ⁶ And they said unto them even as Jesus had commanded, (Mark 11) ³⁴ The Lord has need of him: (Luke 19) ⁶ and they let them go. ⁷ And they (Mark 11) ⁷ brought the ass, and the colt (Matthew 21) ⁷ to Jesus: (Mark 11) ⁷ and put on them their clothes, (Matthew 21) ³⁵ and they set Jesus thereon. (Luke 19) ¹⁶ These things understood not his disciples at the first: but when Jesus was glorified, then remembered they that these things were written of him, and *that* they had done these things unto him. (John 12)

(LUKE 19:29–34; MARK 11:1–7;
MATTHEW 21:1–7; JOHN 12:15–16)

---

a. O.T. prophecy in Zechariah 9:9.

CHAPTER TWENTY-THREE

Jesus Rides a Colt into Jerusalem

[12] On the next day much people that were come to the feast, when they heard that Jesus was coming to Jerusalem, [13] took branches of palm trees, and went forth to meet him. (John 12)

[8] And a very great multitude spread their garments in the way; (Matthew 21) [8] and others cut down branches off the trees, and strewed *them* in the way. (Mark 11)

[37] And when he was come nigh, even now at the descent of the mount of Olives, the whole multitude of the disciples, (Luke 19) [9] and the multitudes that went before, (Matthew 21) [9] and they that followed, (Mark 11) [37] began to rejoice and praise God with a loud voice for all the mighty works that they had seen; (Luke 19) [13] and cried, (John 12) [9] saying, (Mark 11) [9] Hosanna to the son of David! (Matthew 21) [38] Blessed *be* the King (Luke 19) [13] of Israel (John 12) [38] that comes in the name of the Lord: peace in heaven, and glory in the highest. (Luke 19) [10] Blessed be the kingdom of our father David, that comes in the name of the Lord: Hosanna in the highest.[a] (Mark 11)

[10] And when he was come into Jerusalem, all the city was moved, saying, Who is this? [11] And the multitude said, This is Jesus the prophet of Nazareth of Galilee. (Matthew 21) [17] The people therefore that was with him when he called Lazarus out of his grave, and raised him from the dead, bore record. [18] For this cause the people also met him, for that they heard that he had done this miracle. [19] The Pharisees therefore said among themselves, Perceive you how you prevail nothing? Behold, the world is gone after him. (John 12)

[39] And some of the Pharisees from among the multitude said unto him, Master, rebuke your disciples. [40] And he answered and said unto them, I tell you that, if these should hold their peace, the

---

a. O.T. prophecy in Psalm 118:26.

stones would immediately cry out. [41] And when he was come near, he beheld the city, and wept over it, [42] saying, If you had known, even you, at least in this your day, the things *which belong* unto your peace! But now they are hid from your eyes. [43] For the days shall come upon you, that your enemies shall cast a trench about you, and compass you round, and keep you in on every side, [44] and shall lay you even with the ground, and your children within you; and they shall not leave in you one stone upon another; because you knew not the time of your visitation. (Luke 19)

[11] And Jesus entered into Jerusalem, and into the temple: and when he had looked round about upon all things, and now the eventide was come, he went out unto Bethany with the twelve. (Mark 11)

[12] And on the morrow, when they were come from Bethany, (Mark 11) [18] as he returned into the city, (Matthew 21) [12] he was hungry: [13] and seeing a fig tree afar off having leaves, he came, if haply he might find anything thereon: and when he came to it, he found nothing but leaves; for the time of figs was not *yet*. [14] And Jesus answered and said unto it, (Mark 11) [19] Let no fruit grow on you henceforward for ever. (Matthew 21) [14] No man eat fruit of you hereafter for ever. [14] And his disciples heard *it*. (Mark 11) [19] And presently the fig tree withered away. (Matthew 21)

(JOHN 12:12–13, 17–19; MARK 11:8–14;
MATTHEW 21:8–11, 18–19; LUKE 19:37–44)

Jesus Throws Out the Money Changers

[15] AND they came to Jerusalem. (Mark 11) [12] And Jesus went into the temple of God, (Matthew 21) [15] and began to (Mark 11) [12] cast out all them that sold and bought in the temple, (Matthew 21) [15] and overthrew the tables of the moneychangers, and the seats of them that sold doves; [16] and would not suffer that any man should carry *any* vessel through the temple. [17] And he taught, saying unto them, Is it not written, My house shall be called of all nations the house of

prayer? But you have made it a den of thieves.ᵃ ¹⁸ And the scribes and chief priests heard *it*, and sought how they might destroy him: for they feared him, because all the people were astonished at his doctrine. (Mark 11)

¹⁴ And the blind and the lame came to him in the temple; and he healed them. ¹⁵ And when the chief priests and scribes saw the wonderful things that he did, and the children crying in the temple, and saying, Hosanna to the son of David; they were sore displeased, ¹⁶ and said unto him, Hear you what these say? And Jesus said unto them, Yea; have you never read, Out of the mouth of babes and sucklings you have perfected praise?ᵇ ¹⁷ And he left them, and went out of the city into Bethany; and he lodged there. (Matthew 21)

⁴⁷ And he taught daily in the temple. But the chief priests and the scribes and the chief of the people sought to destroy him, ⁴⁸ and could not find what they might do: for all the people were very attentive to hear him. (Luke 19) ¹⁹ And when even was come, he went out of the city. (Mark 11)

³⁷ And in the day time he was teaching in the temple; and at night he went out, and abode in the mount that is called *the mount of Olives.* ³⁸ And all the people came early in the morning to him in the temple, for to hear him. (Luke 21)

(MARK 11:15–19; MATTHEW 21:12, 14–17;
LUKE 19:47–48; 21:37–38)

Have Faith in God; Doubt Not

²⁰ AND in the morning, as they passed by, they saw the fig tree dried up from the roots. (Mark 11) ²⁰ And when the disciples saw *it,* they marvelled, saying, How soon is the fig tree withered away! (Matthew 21) ²¹ And Peter calling to remembrance said unto him, Master, behold, the fig tree which you cursed is withered away. (Mark 11)

²² And Jesus answering said unto them, Have faith in God. ²³ For

a. O.T. prophecy in Isaiah 56:7.
b. O.T. prophecy in Psalm 8:2.

verily I say unto you, (Mark 11) 21 if you have faith, and doubt not, you shall not only do this *which is done* to the fig tree, but also (Matthew 21) 23 whosoever shall say unto this mountain, Be removed, and be cast into the sea; and shall not doubt in his heart, but shall believe that those things which he said shall come to pass; (Mark 11) 21 it shall be done, (Matthew 21) *[and]* 23 he shall have whatsoever he said. (Mark 11)

24 Therefore I say unto you, what things soever you desire, when you pray, believe that you receive *them*, and you shall have *them*. (Mark 11)

25 And when you stand praying, forgive, if you have ought against any: that your Father also which is in heaven may forgive you your trespasses. 26 But if you do not forgive, neither will your Father which is in heaven forgive your trespasses. (Mark 11)

(MARK 11:20–26; MATTHEW 21:20–21)

CHAPTER TWENTY-FOUR

By Whose Authority Do You These Things?

^{1} AND it came to pass, *that* on one of those days, $^{(Luke\ 20)}$ ^{27} they come again to Jerusalem. $^{(Mark\ 11)}$ ^{23} And when he was come into the temple, $^{(Matthew\ 21)}$ ^{27} and as he was walking in the temple, $^{(Mark\ 11)}$ ^{23} the chief priests and the elders of the people $^{(Matthew\ 21)}$ ^{20} and the scribes $^{(Luke\ 20)}$ ^{23} came unto him as he was teaching $^{(Matthew\ 21)}$ ^{1} the people in the temple, and preached the gospel, ^{2} and spoke unto him, saying, Tell us, by what authority do you these things? Or who is he that gave you this authority $^{(Luke\ 20)}$ ^{28} to do these things? $^{(Mark\ 11)}$

^{29} And Jesus answered and said unto them, I will also ask of you one question, $^{(Mark\ 11)}$ ^{24} which if you tell me, I in like wise will tell you by what authority I do these things. ^{25} The baptism of John, whence was it? $^{(Matthew\ 21)}$ ^{4} Was it from heaven, or of men? $^{(Luke\ 20)}$ ^{30} Answer me. $^{(Mark\ 11)}$

^{31} And they reasoned with themselves, saying, If we shall say, From heaven; $^{(Mark\ 11)}$ ^{25} he will say unto us, $^{(Matthew\ 21)}$ ^{31} Why then did you not believe him? $^{(Mark\ 11)}$ ^{26} But if we shall say, Of men; we fear the people; $^{(Matthew\ 21)}$ ^{6} all the people will stone us: for they are persuaded that John was a prophet $^{(Luke\ 20)}$ ^{32} indeed. $^{(Mark\ 11)}$

^{33} And they answered and said unto Jesus, We cannot tell $^{(Mark\ 11)}$ ^{7} whence *it was.* $^{(Luke\ 20)}$ ^{33} And Jesus answering said unto them, Neither do I tell you by what authority I do these things. $^{(Mark\ 11)}$

(LUKE 20:1–2, 4, 6–7; MARK 11:27–33; MATTHEW 21:23–26)

Parable of a Man with Two Sons

^{28} BUT what think you? A *certain* man had two sons; and he came to the first, and said, Son, go work to day in my vineyard. ^{29} He

answered and said, I will not: but afterward he repented, and went.
³⁰ And he came to the second, and said likewise. And he answered
and said, I go, sir: and went not. ³¹ Whether of them twain did the
will of *his* father? They say unto him, The first. Jesus said unto
them, Verily I say unto you, that the publicans and the harlots go
into the kingdom of God before you. ³² For John came unto you in
the way of righteousness, and you believed him not; but the publicans and the harlots believed him: and you, when you had seen *it*,
repented not afterward, that you might believe him. ^(Matthew 21)

(MATTHEW 21:28–32)

Parable of the Husbandman

¹ AND he began to speak unto them by parables. ^(Mark 12) ⁹ Then
began he to speak to the people this parable; ^(Luke 20) ³³ Hear another parable: There was a certain householder, which planted a
vineyard, and hedged it round about, and digged a winepress in it,
^(Matthew 21) ¹ *a place for* the winevat, ^(Mark 12) ³³ and built a tower, and
let it out to husbandmen, ^(Matthew 21) ⁹ and went into a far country for
a long time. ^(Luke 20)

 ¹⁰ And at the season, ^(Luke 20) ³⁴ when the time of the fruit drew
near, ^(Matthew 21) ² he sent to the husbandmen a servant, that he might
receive from the husbandmen of the fruit of the vineyard. ³ And they
caught *him*, and beat him, and sent *him* away empty. ⁴ And again he
sent unto them another servant; ^(Mark 12) ¹¹ and they beat him also, and
entreated *him* shamefully, ^(Luke 20) ⁴ and at him they cast stones, and
wounded *him* in the head, and sent *him* away shamefully handled.
⁵ And again he sent another; ^(Mark 12) ¹² a third: and they wounded him
also, ^(Luke 20) ⁵ and him they killed, ^(Mark 12) ¹² and cast *him* out, ^(Luke 20)
⁵ and many others; beating some, and killing some. ^(Mark 12)

 ¹³ Then said the lord of the vineyard, What shall I do? I will
send my beloved son: it may be they will reverence *him* when they
see him. ^(Luke 20) ⁶ Having yet therefore one son, his wellbeloved, he
sent him also last unto them. ^(Mark 12) ³⁸ But when the husbandmen

saw the son, (Matthew 21) 14 they reasoned among themselves, saying, This is the heir: come, let us kill him, (Luke 20) 38 and let us seize on his inheritance, (Matthew 21) 7 and the inheritance shall be ours. (Mark 12) 39 And they caught him, (Matthew 21) 8 and they took him, and killed *him*, and cast *him* out of the vineyard. (Mark 12)

40 When the lord therefore of the vineyard comes, what will he do unto those husbandmen? 41 They say unto him, He will miserably destroy those wicked men, and will let out *his* vineyard unto other husbandmen, which shall render him the fruits in their seasons. (Matthew 21) 16 And when they *[others of them]* heard *it*, they said, God forbid. (Luke 20)

17 And he beheld them, and said, (Luke 20) 42 Did you never read in the scriptures (Matthew 21) *[and]* 17 what is this then that is written, (Luke 20) 42 The stone which the builders rejected, the same is become the head of the corner: this is the Lord's doing, and it is marvellous in our eyes?ᵃ 43 Therefore say I unto you, The kingdom of God shall be taken from you, and given to a nation bringing forth the fruits thereof. 44 And whosoever shall fall on this stone shall be broken: but on whomsoever it shall fall, it will grind him to powder. (Matthew 21)

45 And when the chief priests and Pharisees (Matthew 21) 19 and the scribes (Luke 20) 45 had heard his parables, they perceived that he spoke of them, (Matthew 21) 12 for they knew that he had spoken the parable against them. (Mark 12) 46 But when they sought to lay hands on him (Matthew 21) 19 the same hour, (Luke 20) 46 they feared the multitude, because they took him for a prophet. (Matthew 21) 12 And they left him, and went their way. (Mark 12)

(MARK 12:1–8, 12; MATTHEW 21:33–34, 38–46;
LUKE 20:9–14, 16–17, 19)

Parable of a King and His Son's Wedding

1 AND Jesus answered and spoke unto them again by parables, and said, 2 The kingdom of heaven is like unto a certain king,

---

a. O.T. prophecy in Psalm 118:22–23.

which made a marriage for his son, ³ and sent forth his servants to call them that were bidden to the wedding: and they would not come. ⁴ Again, he sent forth other servants, saying, Tell them which are bidden, Behold, I have prepared my dinner: my oxen and *my* fatlings *are* killed, and all things *are* ready: come unto the marriage. (Matthew 22)

⁵ But they made light of *it,* and went their ways, one to his farm, another to his merchandise: ⁶ and the remnant took his servants, and entreated *them* spitefully, and slew *them.* ⁷ But when the king heard *thereof,* he was wroth: and he sent forth his armies, and destroyed those murderers, and burned up their city. ⁸ Then said he to his servants, The wedding is ready, but they which were bidden were not worthy. (Matthew 22)

⁹ Go therefore into the highways, and as many as you shall find, bid to the marriage. ¹⁰ So those servants went out into the highways, and gathered together all as many as they found, both bad and good: and the wedding was furnished with guests. (Matthew 22)

¹¹ And when the king came in to see the guests, he saw there a man which had not on a wedding garment: ¹² and he said unto him, Friend, how came you in hither not having a wedding garment? And he was speechless. (Matthew 22)

¹³ Then said the king to the servants, Bind him hand and foot, and take him away, and cast *him* into outer darkness; there shall be weeping and gnashing of teeth. ¹⁴ For many are called, but few *are* chosen. (Matthew 22)

(MATTHEW 22:1–14)

Render unto Caesar That Which Is Caesar's

¹⁵ THEN went the Pharisees, and took counsel how they might entangle him in *his* talk. (Matthew 22) ²⁰ And they watched *him,* and sent forth spies, which should feign themselves just men, that they might take hold of his words, that so they might deliver him unto the power and authority of the governor. (Luke 20) ¹⁶ And they sent

out unto him their disciples (certain of the Pharisees, [Mark 12:13]) with the Herodians, [Matthew 22] 13 to catch him in *his* words. [Mark 12]

14 And when they were come, they say unto him, Master, we know that you are true, [Mark 12] 21 that you say and teach rightly, [Luke 20] 14 and care for no man: for you regard not the person of men, but teach the way of God in truth: [Mark 12] 17 tell us therefore, what think you? [Matthew 22] 22 Is it lawful for us to give tribute unto Caesar, or no? [Luke 20] 15 Shall we give, or shall we not give? [Mark 12]

18 But Jesus [Matthew 22] 15 knowing their hypocrisy, [Mark 12] 23 perceived their craftiness [Luke 20] *[and]* 18 their wickedness, [Matthew 22] 23 and said unto them, [Luke 20] 18 Why tempt you me, *you* hypocrites? 19 Show me the tribute money, [Matthew 22] 24 a penny, [Luke 20] 15 that I may see *it.* [Mark 12] 19 And they brought unto him a penny. [Matthew 22] 16 And he said unto them, Whose *is* this image and superscription? [Mark 12] 24 Whose image and superscription has it? [Luke 20] 16 And they [Mark 12] 24 answered and said [Luke 20] 16 unto him, Caesar's. 17 And Jesus answering said unto them, [Mark 12] 21 Render therefore unto Caesar the things which are Caesar's; and unto God the things that are God's. 22 When they had heard *these words,* [Matthew 22] 26 they could not take hold of his words before the people: and they marvelled at his answer, and held their peace [Luke 20] 22 and left him, and went their way. [Matthew 22]

(MATTHEW 22:15–19, 21–22; MARK 12:13–17; LUKE 20:20–24, 26)

The Question of Seven Brothers and One Wife

23 THE same day came to him [Matthew 22] 27 certain of the Sadducees, [Luke 20] 23 which say that there is no resurrection, [Matthew 22] 18 and they asked him, [Mark 12] 28 saying, Master, Moses wrote unto us, [Luke 20] 19 If a man's brother die, and leave *his wife behind him,* and leave no children, that his brother should [Mark 12] 24 marry [Matthew 22] 19 his wife, and raise up seed unto his brother. [Mark 12]

25 Now there were with us seven brethren: [Matthew 22] 29 and the first took a wife, [Luke 20] 20 and dying left no seed, [Mark 12] 29 and died

without children (deceased, and, having no issue, left his wife unto his brother, (Matthew 22:25)). 30 And the second took her to wife, and he died childless, (Luke 20) 21 neither left he any seed. (Mark 12) 31 And the third took her; and in like manner the seven also: and they left no children, and died. (Luke 20) [So] 22 the seven had her, and left no seed: (Mark 12) 27 and last of all the woman died also. (Matthew 22) 23 In the resurrection therefore, when they shall rise, whose wife shall she be (Mark 12) 28 of the seven? For they all had her (Matthew 22) 23 to wife. (Mark 12)

24 And Jesus answering said unto them, Do you not therefore err, because you know not the scriptures, neither the power of God? (Mark 12) 34 The children of this world marry, and are given in marriage: 35 But they which shall be accounted worthy to obtain that world, and the resurrection from the dead, (Luke 20) 25 when they shall rise from the dead, they (Mark 12) 35 neither marry, nor are given in marriage: 36 neither can they die any more: for they are equal unto the angels (Luke 20) 25 which are in heaven; (Mark 12) 36 and are the children of God, being the children of the resurrection. (Luke 20)

26 And as touching the dead, that they rise: have you not read in the book of Moses, how in the bush God spoke unto him, saying, I am the God of Abraham, and the God of Isaac, and the God of Jacob? (Mark 12) 38 For (Luke 20) 32 God is not the God of the dead, (Matthew 22) 27 but the God of the living: you therefore do greatly err: (Mark 12) 38 for all live unto him. (Luke 20)

33 And when the multitude heard this, they were astonished at his doctrine. (Matthew 22) 39 Then certain of the scribes answering said, Master, you have well said. 40 And after that they dare not ask him any question at all. (Luke 20)

(MATTHEW 22:23–25, 27–28, 32–33; MARK 12:18–27;
LUKE 20:27–31, 34–36, 38–40)

The First and Great Commandment

34 BUT when the Pharisees had heard that he had put the Sadducees

to silence, they were gathered together. (Matthew 22) 28 And one of the scribes came, (Mark 12) 35 *which was* a lawyer, (Matthew 22) 28 and having heard them reasoning together, and perceiving that he had answered them well, asked him (Mark 12) 35 *a question,* tempting him, and saying, 36 Master, which *is* the great commandment in the law? (Matthew 22) 28 Which is the first commandment of all? (Mark 12)

29 And Jesus answered him, (Mark 12) *[and]* 37 said unto him, (Matthew 22) 29 The first of all the commandments *is,* Hear, O Israel; The Lord our God is one Lord: 30 and you shall love the Lord your God with all your heart, and with all your soul, and with all your mind, and with all your strength; (Mark 12) 38 this is the first and great commandment. 39 And the second *is* like unto it, (Matthew 22) 31 *namely* this, You shall love your neighbour as yourself. There is none other commandment greater than these. (Mark 12) 40 On these two commandments hang all the law and the prophets. (Matthew 22)

32 And the scribe said unto him, Well, Master, you have said the truth: for there is one God; and there is none other but he: 33 and to love him with all the heart, and with all the understanding, and with all the soul, and with all the strength, and to love *his* neighbour as himself, is more than all whole burnt offerings and sacrifices. 34 And when Jesus saw that he answered discreetly, he said unto him, You are not far from the kingdom of God. And no man after that dare ask him *any question.* (Mark 12)

(MATTHEW 22:34–40; MARK 12:28–34)

What Think You of Christ?

41 WHILE the Pharisees were gathered together, Jesus asked them, 42 saying, What think you of Christ? Whose son is he? They say unto him, *The son* of David. (Matthew 22) 35 And Jesus answered and said (Mark 12) 41 unto them, (Luke 20) 35 while he taught in the temple, How say the scribes that Christ is the son of David? 36 For David himself said by the Holy Ghost, (Mark 12) 42 in the book of Psalms, The Lord said unto my Lord, Sit on my right hand, 43 till I make your enemies

your footstool.^a (Luke 20) 37 David therefore himself calls him Lord; and whence is he *then* his son? (Mark 12) 46 And no man was able to answer him a word, neither dare any *man* from that day forth ask him any more *questions*. (Matthew 22) 37 And the common people heard him gladly. (Mark 12)

(MATTHEW 22:41–42, 46; MARK 12:35–37; LUKE 20:41–43)

Woe unto You Scribes and Pharisees

1 THEN spoke Jesus to the multitude, and to his disciples, (Matthew 23) 38 in his doctrine, (Mark 12) 2 saying, The scribes and the Pharisees sit in Moses' seat: 3 all therefore whatsoever they bid you observe, *that* observe and do; but do not you after their works: for they say, and do not. 4 For they bind heavy burdens and grievous to be borne, and lay *them* on men's shoulders; but they *themselves* will not move them with one of their fingers. 5 But all their works they do for to be seen of men: they make broad their phylacteries, and enlarge the borders of their garments, (Matthew 23) 46 which desire to walk in long robes, (Luke 20) 6 and love the uppermost rooms at feasts, and the chief seats in the synagogues, (Matthew 23) 38 and *love* salutations in the marketplaces, (Mark 12) 7 and to be called of men, Rabbi, Rabbi; (Matthew 23) 47 which devour widows' houses, and for a show make long prayers: the same shall receive greater damnation. (Luke 20)

8 But be not you called Rabbi: for one is your Master, *even* Christ; and all you are brethren. 9 And call no *man* your father upon the earth: for one is your Father, which is in heaven. 10 Neither be you called masters: for one is your Master, *even* Christ. 11 But he that is greatest among you shall be your servant. 12 And whosoever shall exalt himself shall be abased; and he that shall humble himself shall be exalted. (Matthew 23)

13 But woe unto you, scribes and Pharisees, hypocrites! For you shut up the kingdom of heaven against men: for you neither go in *yourselves,* neither suffer you them that are entering to go in. (Matthew 23)

---

a. O.T. prophecy in Psalm 110:1.

¹⁴ Woe unto you, scribes and Pharisees, hypocrites! For you devour widows' houses, and for a pretence make long prayer: therefore you shall receive the greater damnation. (Matthew 23)

¹⁵ Woe unto you, scribes and Pharisees, hypocrites! For you compass sea and land to make one proselyte, and when he is made, you make him twofold more the child of hell than yourselves. (Matthew 23)

¹⁶ Woe unto you, *you* blind guides, which say, Whosoever shall swear by the temple, it is nothing; but whosoever shall swear by the gold of the temple, he is a debtor! ¹⁷ *You* fools and blind: for whether is greater, the gold, or the temple that sanctifies the gold? ¹⁸ And, Whosoever shall swear by the altar, it is nothing; but whosoever swears by the gift that is upon it, he is guilty. ¹⁹ *You* fools and blind: for whether *is* greater, the gift, or the altar that sanctifies the gift? ²⁰ Whoso therefore shall swear by the altar, swears by it, and by all things thereon. ²¹ And whoso shall swear by the temple, swears by it, and by him that dwells therein. ²² And he that shall swear by heaven, swears by the throne of God, and by him that sits thereon. (Matthew 23)

²³ Woe unto you, scribes and Pharisees, hypocrites! For you pay tithe of mint and anise and cummin, and have omitted the weightier *matters* of the law, judgment, mercy, and faith: these ought you to have done, and not to leave the other undone. ²⁴ *You* blind guides, which strain at a gnat, and swallow a camel. (Matthew 23)

²⁵ Woe unto you, scribes and Pharisees, hypocrites! For you make clean the outside of the cup and of the platter, but within they are full of extortion and excess. ²⁶ *You* blind Pharisee, cleanse first that *which is* within the cup and platter, that the outside of them may be clean also. (Matthew 23)

²⁷ Woe unto you, scribes and Pharisees, hypocrites! For you are like unto whited sepulchres, which indeed appear beautiful outward, but are within full of dead *men's* bones, and of all uncleanness. ²⁸ Even so you also outwardly appear righteous unto men, but within you are full of hypocrisy and iniquity. (Matthew 23)

²⁹ Woe unto you, scribes and Pharisees, hypocrites! Because you build the tombs of the prophets, and garnish the sepulchres of the

righteous, ³⁰ and say, If we had been in the days of our fathers, we would not have been partakers with them in the blood of the prophets. ³¹ Wherefore you be witnesses unto yourselves, that you are the children of them which killed the prophets. ³² Fill you up then the measure of your fathers. ³³ *You* serpents, *you* generation of vipers, how can you escape the damnation of hell? (Matthew 23)

³⁴ Wherefore, behold, I send unto you prophets, and wise men, and scribes: and *some* of them you shall kill and crucify; and *some* of them shall you scourge in your synagogues, and persecute *them* from city to city: ³⁵ that upon you may come all the righteous blood shed upon the earth, from the blood of righteous Abel unto the blood of Zacharias son of Barachias, whom you slew between the temple and the altar. ³⁶ Verily I say unto you, all these things shall come upon this generation. (Matthew 23)

³⁷ O Jerusalem, Jerusalem, *you* that kill the prophets, and stone them which are sent unto you, how often would I have gathered your children together, even as a hen gathers her chickens under *her* wings, and you would not! ³⁸ Behold, your house is left unto you desolate. ³⁹ For I say unto you, you shall not see me henceforth, till you shall say, Blessed *is* he that comes in the name of the Lord. (Matthew 23)

(MATTHEW 23:1–39; LUKE 20:46–47; MARK 12:38)

CHAPTER TWENTY-FIVE

The Widow's Two Mites

⁴¹ AND Jesus sat over against the treasury, ^(Mark 12) ¹ and he looked up, ^(Luke 21) ⁴¹ and beheld how the people cast money into the treasury: and many that were rich cast in much, ^(Mark 12) ¹ their gifts. ^(Luke 21) ⁴² And there came a certain poor widow, and she threw in two mites, which make a farthing. ⁴³ And he called *unto him* his disciples, and said unto them, Verily I say unto you, that this poor widow has cast more in, than all they which have cast into the treasury: ^(Mark 12) ⁴ for all these have of their abundance cast in unto the offerings of God: but she of her penury (want, ^{Mark 12:44}) has cast in all the living that she had. ^(Luke 21) *ALL*

(MARK 12:41–44; LUKE 21:1, 4)

A Voice Comes from Heaven

²⁰ AND there were certain Greeks among them that came up to worship at the feast: ²¹ the same came therefore to Philip, which was of Bethsaida of Galilee, and desired him, saying, Sir, we would see Jesus. ²² Philip comes and tells Andrew: and again Andrew and Philip tell Jesus. ^(John 12)

²³ And Jesus answered them, saying, The hour is come, that the Son of man should be glorified. ²⁴ Verily, verily, I say unto you, except a corn of wheat fall into the ground and die, it abides alone: but if it die, it brings forth much fruit. ²⁵ He that loves his life shall lose it; and he that hates his life in this world shall keep it unto life eternal. ²⁶ If any man serve me, let him follow me; and where I am, there shall also my servant be: if any man serve me, him will *my* Father honour. ^(John 12)

[27] Now is my soul troubled; and what shall I say? Father, save me from this hour: but for this cause came I unto this hour. [28] Father, glorify your name. Then came there a voice from heaven, *saying*, I have both glorified *it,* and will glorify *it* again. [29] The people therefore, that stood by, and heard *it,* said that it thundered: others said, An angel spoke to him. (John 12)

[30] Jesus answered and said, This voice came not because of me, but for your sakes. [31] Now is the judgment of this world: now shall the prince of this world be cast out. [32] And I, if I be lifted up from the earth, will draw all *men* unto me. [33] This he said, signifying what death he should die. [34] The people answered him, We have heard out of the law that Christ abides for ever: and how say you, The Son of man must be lifted up? Who is this Son of man? [35] Then Jesus said unto them, Yet a little while is the light with you. Walk while you have the light, lest darkness come upon you: for he that walks in darkness knows not whither he goes. [36] While you have light, believe in the light, that you may be the children of light. These things spoke Jesus, and departed, and did hide himself from them. (John 12)

[37] But though he had done so many miracles before them, yet they believed not on him: [38] that the saying of Esaias the prophet might be fulfilled, which he spoke, Lord, who has believed our report? And to whom has the arm of the Lord been revealed?[a] [39] Therefore they could not believe, because that Esaias said again, [40] He has blinded their eyes, and hardened their heart; that they should not see with *their* eyes, nor understand with *their* heart, and be converted, and I should heal them.[b] [41] These things said Esaias, when he saw his glory, and spoke of him. [42] Nevertheless among the chief rulers also many believed on him; but because of the Pharisees they did not confess *him,* lest they should be put out of the synagogue: [43] for they loved the praise of men more than the praise of God. (John 12)

[44] Jesus cried and said, He that believes on me, believes not

---

a. O.T. prophecy in Isaiah 53:1.
b. O.T. prophecy in Isaiah 6:9–10.

on me, but on him that sent me. ^{45} And he that sees me sees him that sent me. ^{46} I am come a light into the world, that whosoever believes on me should not abide in darkness. ^{47} And if any man hears my words, and believes not, I judge him not: for I came not to judge the world, but to save the world. ^{48} He that rejects me, and receives not my words, has one that judges him: the word that I have spoken, the same shall judge him in the last day. ^{49} For I have not spoken of myself; but the Father which sent me, he gave me a commandment, what I should say, and what I should speak. ^{50} And I know that his commandment is life everlasting: whatsoever I speak therefore, even as the Father said unto me, so I speak. (John 12)

(JOHN 12:20–50)

End of Days; Beginning of Sorrows

^{1} AND Jesus went out, and departed from the temple. (Matthew 24) ^{1} And as he went out of the temple, (Mark 13) ^{1} his disciples came to *him* for to show him the buildings of the temple. (Matthew 24) ^{5} And as some spoke of the temple, how it was adorned with goodly stones and gifts, (Luke 21) ^{1} one of his disciples said unto him, Master, see what manner of stones and what buildings *are here!* (Mark 13)

^{2} And Jesus answering said unto him, See you these great buildings? (Mark 13) ^{2} See you not all these things? Verily I say unto you, (Matthew 24) ^{6} *as for* these things which you behold, the days will come, in the which there shall not be (Luke 21) ^{2} left here one stone upon another, that shall not be thrown down. (Matthew 24) ^{3} And as he sat upon the mount of Olives over against the temple, (Mark 13) ^{3} the disciples (Matthew 24) ^{3} Peter and James and John and Andrew (Mark 13) ^{3} came unto him privately, (Matthew 24) ^{7} and they asked him, saying, Master, (Luke 21) ^{4} tell us, (Mark 13) ^{7} when shall these things be? And what sign *will there be* when (Luke 21) ^{4} all these things shall be fulfilled? (Mark 13) ^{3} And what *shall be* the sign of your coming, and of the end of the world? (Matthew 24)

⁵ And Jesus answering them began to say, Take heed lest any *man* deceive you: ⁶ for many shall come in my name, saying, I am *Christ;* (Mark 13) ⁸ and the time draws near; (Luke 21) ⁵ and shall deceive many. (Matthew 24) ⁸ Go you not therefore after them. (Luke 21) ⁷ And when you shall hear of wars and rumours of wars (Mark 12) ⁹ and commotions, be not terrified: (Luke 21) ⁶ see that you be not troubled: (Matthew 24) ⁷ for *such things* must needs be; but the end *shall* not *be* yet. (Mark 13) ⁶ For all *these things* (Matthew 24) ⁹ must first come to pass; but the end *is* not by and by. ¹⁰ Then said he unto them, (Luke 21) ⁸ For nation shall rise against nation, and kingdom against kingdom: and there shall be (Mark 13) ¹¹ great earthquakes (Luke 21) ⁸ in divers places, and there shall be famines and troubles (Mark 13) ⁷ and pestilences (Matthew 24) ¹¹ and fearful sights and great signs shall there be from heaven. (Luke 21)

⁸ All these *are* the beginning of sorrows. (Matthew 24) ⁹ But take heed to yourselves: for (Mark 13) ¹² before all these, they shall lay their hands on you, and persecute *you,* delivering *you* up to the synagogues, (Luke 21) ⁹ and in the synagogues you shall be beaten: (Mark 13) ¹² and into prisons. (Luke 21) ⁹ Then shall they deliver you up (Matthew 24) ⁹ to councils, (Mark 13) ⁹ to be afflicted, and shall kill you: (Matthew 24) ⁹ and you shall be brought before rulers and kings (Mark 13) ¹² for my name's sake. ¹³ And it shall turn to you for a testimony, (Luke 21) ⁹ for a testimony against them. (Mark 13) ¹⁴ And this gospel of the kingdom (Matthew 24) ¹⁰ must first be published (Mark 13) ¹⁴ in all the world for a witness unto all nations; and then shall the end come. (Matthew 24)

¹¹ But when they shall lead *you,* and deliver you up, take no thought beforehand what you shall speak, neither do you premeditate: but whatsoever shall be given you in that hour, that speak you: for it is not you that speak, but the Holy Ghost. (Mark 13) ¹⁴ Settle *it* therefore in your hearts, not to meditate before what you shall answer: ¹⁵ for I will give you a mouth and wisdom, which all your adversaries shall not be able to gainsay nor resist. (Luke 21)

¹⁰ And then shall many be offended, and shall betray one another, and shall hate one another. (Matthew 24) ¹² Now the brother shall betray the brother to death, and the father the son; and children

shall rise up against *their* parents, and shall cause them to be put to death. (Mark 13) ¹⁶ And you shall be betrayed both by parents, and brethren, and kinsfolks, and friends; and *some* of you shall they cause to be put to death. (Luke 21)

¹¹ And many false prophets shall rise, and shall deceive many. ¹² And because iniquity shall abound, the love of many shall wax cold. (Matthew 24) ¹³ And you shall be hated of all nations for my name's sake. (Mark 13) ¹³ But he that shall endure unto the end, the same shall be saved. (Matthew 24) ¹⁸ But there shall not an hair of your head perish. ¹⁹ In your patience possess you your souls. (Luke 21)

(MATTHEW 24:1–3, 5–14; MARK 13:1–13; LUKE 21:5–16, 18–19)

Abomination of Desolation

²⁰ AND when you shall see Jerusalem compassed with armies, then know that the desolation thereof is nigh. ²¹ Then let them which are in Judaea flee to the mountains; and let them which are in the midst of it depart out; and let not them that are in the countries enter thereinto. ²² For these be the days of vengeance, that all things which are written may be fulfilled. ²³ But woe unto them that are with child, and to them that give suck, in those days! For there shall be great distress in the land, and wrath upon this people. ²⁴ And they shall fall by the edge of the sword, and shall be led away captive into all nations: and Jerusalem shall be trodden down of the Gentiles, until the times of the Gentiles be fulfilled. (Luke 21)

¹⁵ When you therefore shall see the abomination of desolation, spoken of by Daniel the prophet, stand in the holy place, (Matthew 24) ¹⁴ where it ought not, (Mark 13) ¹⁵ (whoso reads, let him understand:) (Matthew 24) ¹⁴ then let them that be in Judaea flee to the mountains: ¹⁵ and let him that is on the housetop not go down into the house, neither enter *therein,* to take any thing out of his house: ¹⁶ and let him that is in the field not turn back again for to take up his garment. (Mark 13)

[17] But woe to them that are with child, and to them that give suck in those days! (Mark 13) [20] But pray that your flight be not in the winter, neither on the sabbath day: [21] For then shall be great tribulation, such as was not since the beginning of the world to this time, no, nor ever shall be. (Matthew 24) [19] For *in* those days shall be affliction, such as was not from the beginning of the creation which God created unto this time, neither shall be. (Mark 13)

[20] And except that the Lord had shortened those days, (Mark 13) [22] there should no flesh be saved: (Matthew 24) [20] but for the elect's sake, whom he has chosen, he has shortened the days; (Mark 13) [22] those days shall be shortened. (Matthew 24) [21] And then if any man shall say to you, Lo, here *is* Christ; or, lo, *he is* there; believe *him* not: [22] for false Christs and false prophets shall rise, (Mark 13) [24] and shall show great signs and wonders; insomuch that, if *it were* possible, they shall deceive (Matthew 24) [22] even (Mark 13) [24] the very elect. (Matthew 24) [23] But take you heed: behold, I have foretold you all things. (Mark 13)

[26] Wherefore if they shall say unto you, Behold, he is in the desert; go not forth: behold, *he is* in the secret chambers; believe *it* not. [27] For as the lightning comes out of the east, and shines even unto the west; so shall also the coming of the Son of man be. [28] For wheresoever the carcase is, there will the eagles be gathered together. (Matthew 24)

[24] But in those days, (Mark 13) [29] immediately after (Matthew 24) [24] that tribulation, (Mark 13) [25] there shall be signs in the sun, and in the moon, and in the stars; and upon the earth distress of nations, with perplexity; the sea and the waves roaring; [26] men's hearts failing them for fear, and for looking after those things which are coming on the earth: (Luke 21) [24] the sun shall be darkened, and the moon shall not give her light, [25] and the stars of heaven shall fall, and the powers that are in heaven shall be shaken. (Mark 13)

[30] And then shall appear the sign of the Son of man in heaven: and then shall all the tribes of the earth mourn. (Matthew 24) [27] And then shall they see the Son of man (Luke 21) [30] coming in the clouds of heaven (Matthew 24) [26] with great power (Mark 13) [30] and great glory. (Matthew 24) [27] And then shall he send his angels, (Mark 13) [31] with a great

sound of a trumpet, and they shall gather together his elect from the four winds, from one end of heaven to the other, (Matthew 24) ²⁷ from the uttermost part of the earth to the uttermost part of heaven. (Mark 13) ²⁸ And when these things begin to come to pass, then look up, and lift up your heads; for your redemption draws nigh. (Luke 21)

(LUKE 21:20–28; MARK 13:14–17, 19–27; MATTHEW 24:15, 20–22, 24, 26–31)

The Coming of the Son of Man

²⁸ Now learn a parable of the fig tree; When her branch is yet tender, and puts forth leaves, you know that summer is near. (Mark 13) ²⁹ And he spoke to them a parable; Behold the fig tree, and all the trees; ³⁰ when they now shoot forth, you see and know of your own selves that summer is now nigh at hand. (Luke 21) ²⁹ So you in like manner, when you shall see (Mark 13) ³³ all these things (Matthew 24) ²⁹ come to pass, (Mark 13) ³¹ know that the kingdom of God is nigh at hand, (Luke 21) ³³ it is near, *even* at the doors. (Matthew 24)

³² Verily I say unto you, (Luke 21) ³⁰ that (Mark 13) ³² this generation shall not pass away, (Luke 21) ³⁴ till all these things be fulfilled. (Matthew 24) ³³ Heaven and earth shall pass away: but my words shall not pass away. (Luke 21) ³² But of that day and *that* hour knows no man, no, not the angels which are in heaven, neither the Son, (Mark 13) ³⁶ but my Father only. (Matthew 24) ³⁴ And take heed to yourselves, lest at any time your hearts be overcharged with surfeiting, and drunkenness, and cares of this life, and *so* that day come upon you unawares. (Luke 21) ³³ Take heed, watch and pray: for you know not when the time is. (Mark 13)

³⁵ For as a snare shall it come on all them that dwell on the face of the whole earth. ³⁶ Watch therefore, and pray always, that you may be accounted worthy to escape all these things that shall come to pass, and to stand before the Son of man. (Luke 21)

³⁷ But as the days of Noe *were,* so shall also the coming of the

Son of man be. [38] For as in the days that were before the flood they were eating and drinking, marrying and giving in marriage, until the day that Noe entered into the ark, [39] and knew not until the flood came, and took them all away; so shall also the coming of the Son of man be. [40] Then shall two be in the field; the one shall be taken, and the other left. [41] Two *women shall be* grinding at the mill; the one shall be taken, and the other left. (Matthew 24)

[36] And you yourselves *[be]* like unto men that wait for their lord, when he will return from the wedding; that when he comes and knocks, they may open unto him immediately. [37] Blessed *are* those servants, whom the lord when he comes shall find watching: verily I say unto you, that he shall gird himself, and make them to sit down to meat, and will come forth and serve them. [38] And if he shall come in the second watch, or come in the third watch, and find *them* so, blessed are those servants. (Luke 12)

[34] *For the Son of man is* as a man taking a far journey, who left his house, and gave authority to his servants, and to every man his work, and commanded the porter to watch. [35] Watch therefore: for you know not when the master of the house comes, at even, or at midnight, or at the cockcrowing, or in the morning: [36] lest coming suddenly he find you sleeping. [37] And what I say unto you I say unto all, (Mark 13) [42] watch therefore: for you know not what hour your Lord does come. (Matthew 24)

[43] But know this, that if the goodman of the house had known in what watch the thief would come, he would have watched, and would not have suffered his house to be broken up. [44] Therefore be you also ready: for in such an hour as you think not the Son of man will come. (Matthew 24)

(MARK 13:28–30, 32–37; MATTHEW 24:33–34, 36–44;
LUKE 12:36–38; 21:29–36)

Who Is the Faithful and Wise Steward?

[41] THEN Peter said unto him, Lord, speak you this parable unto us,

or even to all? ⁴²And the Lord said, ⁽Luke 12⁾ ⁴⁵Who then is a faithful and wise steward, whom his lord has made ruler over his household, to give them ⁽Matthew 24⁾ ⁴²*their* portion of meat in due season? ⁽Luke 12⁾ ⁴⁶Blessed *is* that servant, whom his lord when he comes shall find so doing. ⁽Matthew 24⁾ ⁴⁴Of a truth I say unto you, that he will make him ruler over all that he has, ⁽Luke 12⁾ ⁴⁷over all his goods. ⁽Matthew 24⁾

⁴⁸But and if that evil servant shall say in his heart, My lord delays his coming; ⁽Matthew 24⁾ ⁴⁵and shall begin to beat the menservants and maidens, ⁽Luke 12⁾ ⁴⁹*his* fellowservants, ⁽Matthew 24⁾ ⁴⁵and to eat and drink, and to be drunken; ⁴⁶the lord of that servant will come in a day when he looks not for *him*, ⁽Luke 12⁾ ⁵⁰and in an hour that he is not aware of, ⁽Matthew 24⁾ ⁴⁶and will cut him in sunder, and will appoint him his portion with the unbelievers ⁽Luke 12⁾ *[and]* ⁵¹the hypocrites: there shall be weeping and gnashing of teeth. ⁽Matthew 24⁾

⁴⁷And that servant, which knew his lord's will, and prepared not *himself,* neither did according to his will, shall be beaten with many *stripes.* ⁴⁸But he that knew not, and did commit things worthy of stripes, shall be beaten with few *stripes.* For unto whomsoever much is given, of him shall be much required: and to whom men have committed much, of him they will ask the more. ⁽Luke 12⁾

(LUKE 12:41–42, 44–48; MATTHEW 24:45–51)

Kingdom of Heaven Is Like Ten Virgins

¹THEN shall the kingdom of heaven be likened unto ten virgins, which took their lamps, and went forth to meet the bridegroom. ²And five of them were wise, and five *were* foolish. ³They that *were* foolish took their lamps, and took no oil with them: ⁴but the wise took oil in their vessels with their lamps. ⁵While the bridegroom tarried, they all slumbered and slept. ⁽Matthew 25⁾

⁶And at midnight there was a cry made, Behold, the bridegroom comes; go out to meet him. ⁷Then all those virgins arose, and trimmed their lamps. ⁸And the foolish said unto the wise, Give us

of your oil; for our lamps are gone out. [9] But the wise answered, saying, *Not so;* lest there be not enough for us and you: but go rather to them that sell, and buy for yourselves. [10] And while they went to buy, the bridegroom came; and they that were ready went in with him to the marriage: and the door was shut. (Matthew 25)

[11] Afterward came also the other virgins, saying, Lord, Lord, open to us. [12] But he answered and said, Verily I say unto you, I know you not. [13] Watch therefore, for you know neither the day nor the hour wherein the Son of man comes. (Matthew 25)

(MATTHEW 25:1–13)

Kingdom of Heaven Like a Traveling Man

[14] FOR *the kingdom of heaven is* as a man travelling into a far country, *who* called his own servants, and delivered unto them his goods. [15] And unto one he gave five talents, to another two, and to another one; to every man according to his several ability; and straightway took his journey. [16] Then he that had received the five talents went and traded with the same, and made *them* other five talents. [17] And likewise he that *had received* two, he also gained other two. [18] But he that had received one went and digged in the earth, and hid his lord's money. (Matthew 25)

[19] After a long time the lord of those servants comes, and reckons with them. [20] And so he that had received five talents came and brought other five talents, saying, Lord, you delivered unto me five talents: behold, I have gained beside them five talents more. [21] His lord said unto him, Well done, *you* good and faithful servant: you have been faithful over a few things, I will make you ruler over many things: enter into the joy of your lord. [22] He also that had received two talents came and said, Lord, you delivered unto me two talents: behold, I have gained two other talents beside them. [23] His lord said unto him, Well done, good and faithful servant; you have been faithful over a few things, I will make you ruler over many things: enter into the joy of your lord. (Matthew 25)

²⁴ Then he which had received the one talent came and said, Lord, I knew you that you are an hard man, reaping where you have not sown, and gathering where you have not strewed: ²⁵ and I was afraid, and went and hid your talent in the earth: lo, *there* you have *that is* yours. (Matthew 25)

²⁶ His lord answered and said unto him, *You* wicked and slothful servant, you knew that I reap where I sowed not, and gather where I have not strewed: ²⁷ you ought therefore to have put my money to the exchangers, and *then* at my coming I should have received my own with usury. ²⁸ Take therefore the talent from him, and give *it* unto him which has ten talents. ²⁹ For unto every one that has shall be given, and he shall have abundance: but from him that has not shall be taken away even that which he has. ³⁰ And cast the unprofitable servant into outer darkness: there shall be weeping and gnashing of teeth. (Matthew 25)

(MATTHEW 25:14–30)

When the Son of Man Comes

³¹ WHEN the Son of man shall come in his glory, and all the holy angels with him, then shall he sit upon the throne of his glory: ³² and before him shall be gathered all nations: and he shall separate them one from another, as a shepherd divides *his* sheep from the goats: ³³ and he shall set the sheep on his right hand, but the goats on the left. ³⁴ Then shall the King say unto them on his right hand, Come, you blessed of my Father, inherit the kingdom prepared for you from the foundation of the world: ³⁵ for I was an hungred, and you gave me meat: I was thirsty, and you gave me drink: I was a stranger, and you took me in: ³⁶ naked, and you clothed me: I was sick, and you visited me: I was in prison, and you came unto me. (Matthew 25)

³⁷ Then shall the righteous answer him, saying, Lord, when saw we you an hungred, and fed *you*? Or thirsty, and gave *you* drink? ³⁸ When saw we you a stranger, and took *you* in? Or naked, and

clothed *you?* [39] Or when saw we you sick, or in prison, and came unto you? (Matthew 25)

[40] And the King shall answer and say unto them, Verily I say unto you, inasmuch as you have done *it* unto one of the least of these my brethren, you have done *it* unto me. [41] Then shall he say also unto them on the left hand, Depart from me, you cursed, into everlasting fire, prepared for the devil and his angels: [42] for I was an hungred, and you gave me no meat: I was thirsty, and you gave me no drink: [43] I was a stranger, and you took me not in: naked, and you clothed me not: sick, and in prison, and you visited me not. (Matthew 25)

[44] Then shall they also answer him, saying, Lord, when saw we you an hungred, or athirst, or a stranger, or naked, or sick, or in prison, and did not minister unto you? (Matthew 25)

[45] Then shall he answer them, saying, Verily I say unto you, inasmuch as you did *it* not to one of the least of these, you did *it* not to me. [46] And these shall go away into everlasting punishment: but the righteous into life eternal. (Matthew 25)

[1] And it came to pass, when Jesus had finished all these sayings, he said unto his disciples, [2] You know that after two days is *the feast of* the passover, and the Son of man is betrayed to be crucified. (Matthew 26)

[1] Now the feast of unleavened bread drew nigh, which is called the Passover. (Luke 22) [3] Then assembled together the chief priests, and the scribes, and the elders of the people, unto the palace of the high priest, who was called Caiaphas, [4] and consulted that (sought how, Mark 14:1) they might take Jesus by subtlety, and kill *him.* [5] But they said, Not on the feast *day,* lest there be an uproar among the people. (Matthew 26) [2] For they feared the people. (Luke 22)

(MATTHEW 25:31–46; 26:1–5; LUKE 22:1–2)

CHAPTER TWENTY-SIX

The Alabaster Box of Oil

⁶ Now when Jesus was in Bethany, (Matthew 26) ³ in the house of Simon the leper, as he sat at meat, there came (Mark 14) ⁷ unto him (Matthew 26) ³ a woman having an alabaster box of ointment of spikenard very precious; and she broke the box, and poured *it* on his head. (Mark 14) ⁸ But when his disciples saw *it,* they had indignation, saying, To what purpose *is* this waste? ⁹ For this ointment (Matthew 26) ⁵ might have been sold for more than three hundred pence, and have been given to the poor. And they murmured against her. (Mark 14)

¹⁰ When Jesus understood *it,* he said unto them, (Matthew 26) ⁶ Let her alone; (Mark 14) ¹⁰ why trouble you the woman? For she has wrought a good work upon me. (Matthew 26) ⁷ For you have the poor with you always, and whensoever you will you may do them good: but me you have not always. ⁸ She has done what she could: she is come aforehand to anoint my body to the burying. (Mark 14) ¹² For in that she has poured this ointment on my body, she did *it* for my burial. (Matthew 26) ⁹ Verily I say unto you, wheresoever this gospel shall be preached throughout the whole world, *this* also that she has done shall be spoken of for a memorial of her. (Mark 14)

³ Then entered Satan into Judas surnamed Iscariot, being of the number of the twelve. ⁴ And he went his way, and communed with the chief priests and captains, how he might betray him unto them. (Luke 22) ¹⁵ And said *unto them,* What will you give me, and I will deliver him unto you? (Matthew 26)

¹¹ And when they heard *it,* they were glad, and (Mark 14) ¹⁵ covenanted with him (Matthew 26) ⁵ to give him (Luke 22) ¹⁵ thirty pieces of silver. (Matthew 26) ⁶ And he promised, (Luke 22) ¹⁶ and from that time he sought opportunity (Matthew 26) ¹¹ how he might conveniently betray

him (Mark 14) 6 unto them in the absence of the multitude. (Luke 22)

(MATTHEW 26:6–10, 12, 15–16; LUKE 22:3–6; MARK 14:3, 5–9, 11)

Passover Week: The First Day of Unleavened Bread

7 THEN came (Luke 22) 17 the first *day* of the *feast of* unleavened bread,
(Matthew 26) 7 when the passsover must be killed. 8 And he *[Jesus]* sent
Peter and John, saying, Go and prepare us the passover, that we
may eat. 9 And they said unto him, (Luke 22) 12 Where will you that
we go and prepare that you may eat the passover? (Mark 14) 10 And
he said unto them, (Luke 22) 13 Go into the city, and (Mark 14) 10 behold,
when you are entered into the city, (Luke 22) 13 there shall meet you a
man bearing a pitcher of water: follow him. 14 And wheresoever he
shall go in, say to the goodman of the house, (Mark 14) 11 The Master
says unto you, (Luke 22) 18 My time is at hand; (Matthew 26) 14 where is the
guestchamber, where I shall eat the passover with my disciples?
(Mark 14) 18 I will keep the passover at your house with my disciples.
(Matthew 26) 15 And he will show you a large upper room furnished
and prepared: there make ready for us. 16 And his disciples went
forth, and came into the city, and found as he had said unto them:
(Mark 14) 19 and the disciples did as Jesus had appointed them; and
they made ready the passover. (Matthew 26)

20 Now when the even was come, (Matthew 26) 17 he came (Mark 14)
[and] 14 he sat down, and the twelve apostles with him. (Luke 22)
24 And there was also a strife among them, which of them should
be accounted the greatest. 25 And he said unto them, The kings of
the Gentiles exercise lordship over them; and they that exercise
authority upon them are called benefactors. 26 But you *shall* not *be*
so: but he that is greatest among you, let him be as the younger;
and he that is chief, as he that does serve. 27 For whether *is* greater,
he that sits at meat, or he that serves? *Is* not he that sits at meat?
But I am among you as he that serves. 28 You are they which have
continued with me in my temptations. 29 And I appoint unto you a
kingdom, as my Father has appointed unto me; 30 that you may eat

and drink at my table in my kingdom, and sit on thrones judging the twelve tribes of Israel. (Luke 22)

(LUKE 22:7–11, 14, 24–30; MATTHEW 26:17–20; MARK 14:12–17)

Jesus Washes the Feet of His Disciples

¹ Now before the feast of the passover, when Jesus knew that his hour was come that he should depart out of this world unto the Father, having loved his own which were in the world, he loved them unto the end. ² And supper being ended, the devil having now put into the heart of Judas Iscariot, Simon's *son,* to betray him; ³ Jesus knowing that the Father had given all things into his hands, and that he was come from God, and went to God; ⁴ he rose from supper, and laid aside his garments; and took a towel, and girded himself. (John 13)

⁵ After that he poured water into a bason, and began to wash the disciples' feet, and to wipe *them* with the towel wherewith he was girded. ⁶ Then came he to Simon Peter: and Peter said unto him, Lord, do you wash my feet? ⁷ Jesus answered and said unto him, What I do you know not now; but you shall know hereafter. ⁸ Peter said unto him, You shall never wash my feet. Jesus answered him, If I wash you not, you have no part with me. ⁹ Simon Peter said unto him, Lord, not my feet only, but also *my* hands and *my* head. ¹⁰ Jesus said to him, He that is washed needs not save to wash *his* feet, but is clean every whit: and you are clean, but not all. ¹¹ For he knew who should betray him; therefore said he, You are not all clean. (John 13)

¹² So after he had washed their feet, and had taken his garments, and was set down again, he said unto them, Know you what I have done to you? ¹³ You call me Master and Lord: and you say well; for *so* I am. ¹⁴ If I then, *your* Lord and Master, have washed your feet; you also ought to wash one another's feet. ¹⁵ For I have given you an example, that you should do as I have done to you. (John 13)

¹⁶ Verily, verily, I say unto you, the servant is not greater than his lord; neither he that is sent greater than he that sent him. ¹⁷ If you know these things, happy are you if you do them. ¹⁸ I speak not of you all: I know whom I have chosen: but that the scripture may be fulfilled, He that eats bread with me has lifted up his heel against me.^a ¹⁹ Now I tell you before it come, that, when it is come to pass, you may believe that I am *he*. ²⁰ Verily, verily, I say unto you, he that receives whomsoever I send receives me; and he that receives me receives him that sent me. ^(John 13)

(JOHN 13:1–20)

The Lord's Supper

²¹ WHEN Jesus had thus said, ^(John 13) ¹⁸ as they sat and did eat, ^(Mark 14) ²¹ he was troubled in spirit, and testified, and said, Verily, verily, I say unto you, that one of you ^(John 13) ¹⁸ which eats with me shall betray me. ^(Mark 14) ²¹ But, behold, the hand of him that betrays me *is* with me on the table. ²² And truly the Son of man goes as it was determined ^(Luke 22) *[and]* ²¹ written of him: ^(Mark 14) ²² but woe unto that man by whom ^(Luke 22) ²¹ the Son of man is betrayed! Good were it for that man if he had never been born. ^(Mark 14)

²² Then the disciples ^(John 13) ²² were exceeding sorrowful, ^(Matthew 26) ²² looked one on another, doubting of whom he spoke. ^(John 13) ²³ And they began to inquire among themselves, which of them it was that should do this thing. ^(Luke 22) ²² And began every one of them to say ^(Matthew 26) ¹⁹ unto him one by one, ^(Mark 14) ²² Lord, is it I? ^(Matthew 26) ¹⁹ And another *said, Is* it I? ²⁰ And he answered and said unto them, ^(Mark 14) ²³ He that dips *his* hand with me in the dish, the same shall betray me. ^(Matthew 26) ²⁰ *It is* one of the twelve, that dips with me in the dish. ^(Mark 14)

²³ Now there was leaning on Jesus' bosom one of his disciples, whom Jesus loved. ²⁴ Simon Peter therefore beckoned to him, that he should ask who it should be of whom he spoke. ²⁵ He then lying

a. O.T. prophecy in Psalm 41:9.

on Jesus' breast said unto him, Lord, who is it? ²⁶ Jesus answered, He it is, to whom I shall give a sop, when I have dipped *it*. ^(John 13)

²⁶ And when he had dipped the sop, he gave *it* to Judas Iscariot, *the son* of Simon. ²⁷ And after the sop Satan entered into him. ^(John 13) ²⁵ Then Judas, which betrayed him, answered and said, Master, is it I? He said unto him, You have said. ^(Matthew 26) ²⁷ Then said Jesus unto him, That you do, do quickly. ²⁸ Now no man at the table knew for what intent he spoke this unto him. ²⁹ For some *of them* thought, because Judas had the bag, that Jesus had said unto him, Buy *those things* that we have need of against the feast; or, that he should give something to the poor. ³⁰ He then having received the sop went immediately out: and it was night. ^(John 13)

³¹ Therefore, when he was gone out, Jesus said, Now is the Son of man glorified, and God is glorified in him. ³² If God be glorified in him, God shall also glorify him in himself, and shall straightway glorify him. ³³ Little children, yet a little while I am with you. You shall seek me: and as I said unto the Jews, Whither I go, you cannot come; so now I say to you. ³⁴ A new commandment I give unto you, That you love one another; as I have loved you, that you also love one another. ³⁵ By this shall all *men* know that you are my disciples, if you have love one to another. ^(John 13)

²⁷ And Jesus said unto them, All you shall be offended because of me this night: for it is written, I will smite the shepherd, ^(Mark 14) ³¹ and the sheep of the flock shall be scattered abroad.^a ^(Matthew 26) ²⁸ But after that I am risen ^(Mark 14) ³² again, ^(Matthew 26) ²⁸ I will go before you into Galilee. ²⁹ But Peter ^(Mark 14) ³³ answered and said unto him, ^(Matthew 26) ²⁹ Although all ^(Mark 14) ³³ *men* shall be offended because of you, *yet* will I never be offended. ^(Matthew 26) ³¹ And the Lord said, Simon, Simon, behold, Satan has desired *to have* you, that he may sift *you* as wheat: ³² but I have prayed for you, that your faith fails not: and when you are converted, strengthen your brethren. ^(Luke 22)

³⁶ Simon Peter said unto him, Lord, whither go you? Jesus answered him, Whither I go, you can not follow me now; but you

---

a. O.T. prophecy in Zechariah 13:7.

shall follow me afterwards. [37] Peter said unto him, Lord, why cannot I follow you now? I will lay down my life for your sake. (John 13) [33] Lord, I am ready to go with you, both into prison, and to death. (Luke 22)

[38] Jesus answered him, Will you lay down your life for my sake? Verily, verily, I say unto you, (John 13) [34] Peter, (Luke 22) [30] that this day, *even* in this night, before the cock crow twice, (Mark 14) [34] you shall thrice deny that you know me. (Luke 22) [31] But (Mark 14) [35] Peter (Matthew 26) [31] spoke the more vehemently, If I should die with you, I will not deny you in any wise. (Mark 14) [35] Likewise also said all the disciples. (Matthew 26)

[35] And he said unto them, When I sent you without purse, and scrip, and shoes, lacked you any thing? And they said, Nothing. [36] Then said he unto them, But now, he that has a purse, let him take *it*, and likewise *his* scrip: and he that has no sword, let him sell his garment, and buy one. [37] For I say unto you, that this that is written must yet be accomplished in me, And he was reckoned among the transgressors:[a] for the things concerning me have an end. [38] And they said, Lord, behold, here *are* two swords. And he said unto them, It is enough. (Luke 22)

[26] And as they were eating, Jesus (Matthew 26) [15] said unto them, With desire I have desired to eat this passover with you before I suffer: [16] for I say unto you, I will not any more eat thereof, until it be fulfilled in the kingdom of God. [17] And he took the cup, and gave thanks, and said, Take this, and divide *it* among yourselves: [18] for I say unto you, I will not drink of the fruit of the vine, until the kingdom of God shall come. (Luke 22) [22] And as they did eat, Jesus took bread, (Mark 14) [26] and blessed *it*, and broke *it*, and gave *it* to the disciples, and said, (Matthew 26) [22] Take, eat: (Mark 14) [19] this is my body which is given for you: this do in remembrance of me. (Luke 22)

[23] And he took the cup (Mark 14) [20] after supper, (Luke 22) [23] and when he had given thanks, he gave *it* to them: (Mark 14) [27] saying, Drink you all of it; (Matthew 26) [23] and they all drank of it. [24] And he said unto them, (Mark 14) [28] This is my blood of the new testament, which

---

a. O.T. prophecy in Isaiah 53:12.

is shed for many for the remission of sins. ^(Matthew 26) 25 Verily I say unto you, I will drink no more of the fruit of the vine, until that day that I drink it new ^(Mark 14) 29 with you in my Father's kingdom.

(Matthew 26)

(JOHN 13:21–38; MATTHEW 26:22–23, 25–29, 31–33, 35;
MARK 14:18–25, 27–29; LUKE 22:15–23, 31–38)

many for the remission of sins

CHAPTER TWENTY-SEVEN

Let Not Your Heart Be Troubled

¹ LET not your heart be troubled: you believe in God, believe also in me. ² In my Father's house are many mansions: if *it were* not *so*, I would have told you. I go to prepare a place for you. ³ And if I go and prepare a place for you, I will come again, and receive you unto myself; that where I am, *there* you may be also. ⁴ And whither I go you know, and the way you know. (John 14)

⁵ Thomas said unto him, Lord, we know not whither you go; and how can we know the way? ⁶ Jesus said unto him, I am the way, the truth, and the life: no man comes unto the Father, but by me. ⁷ If you had known me, you should have known my Father also: and from henceforth you know him, and have seen him. ⁸ Philip said unto him, Lord, show us the Father, and it suffices us. (John 14)

⁹ Jesus said unto him, Have I been so long time with you, and yet have you not known me, Philip? He that has seen me has seen the Father; and how say you *then*, Show us the Father? ¹⁰ Believe you not that I *am* in the Father, and the Father in me? The words that I speak unto you I speak not of myself: but the Father that dwells in me, he does the works. (John 14)

¹¹ Believe me that I am in the Father, and the Father in me: or else believe me for the very works' sake. ¹² Verily, verily, I say unto you, he that believes on me, the works that I do shall he do also; and greater *works* than these shall he do; because I go unto my Father. ¹³ And whatsoever you shall ask in my name, that will I do, that the Father may be glorified in the Son. ¹⁴ If you shall ask any thing in my name, I will do *it*. ¹⁵ If you love me, keep my commandments. ¹⁶ And I will pray the Father, and he shall give you another Comforter, that he may abide with you for ever; ¹⁷ *even*

the Spirit of truth; whom the world cannot receive, because it sees him not, neither knows him: but you know him; for he dwells with you, and shall be in you. ¹⁸ I will not leave you comfortless: I will come to you. (John 14)

¹⁹ Yet a little while, and the world sees me no more; but you see me: because I live, you shall live also. ²⁰ At that day you shall know that I *am* in my Father, and you in me, and I in you. ²¹ He that has my commandments, and keeps them, he it is that loves me: and he that loves me shall be loved of my Father, and I will love him, and will manifest myself to him. (John 14)

OBEY

²² Judas said unto him, not Iscariot, Lord, how is it that you will manifest yourself unto us, and not unto the world? ²³ Jesus answered and said unto him, If a man love me, he will keep my words: and my Father will love him, and we will come unto him, and make our abode with him. ²⁴ He that loves me not keeps not my sayings: and the word which you hear is not mine, but the Father's which sent me. ²⁵ These things have I spoken unto you, being *yet* present with you. (John 14)

²⁶ But the Comforter, *which* is the Holy Ghost, whom the Father will send in my name, he shall teach you all things, and bring all things to your remembrance, whatsoever I have said unto you. ²⁷ Peace I leave with you, my peace I give unto you: not as the world gives, give I unto you. Let not your heart be troubled, neither let it be afraid. ²⁸ You have heard how I said unto you, I go away, and come *again* unto you. If you loved me, you would rejoice, because I said, I go unto the Father: for my Father is greater than I. ²⁹ And now I have told you before it come to pass, that, when it is come to pass, you might believe. (John 14)

not to worry not to be afraid

(JOHN 14:1-29)

I Am the Vine and You Are the Branches

³⁰ HEREAFTER I will not talk much with you: for the prince of this world comes, and has nothing in me. ³¹ But that the world may

Jesus loves the Father
Jesus obeyed the Father

know that I love the Father; and as the Father gave me commandment, even so I do. Arise, let us go hence. (John 14)

[1] I am the true vine, and my Father is the husbandman. [2] Every branch in me that bears not fruit he takes away: and every *branch* that bears fruit, he purges it, that it may bring forth more fruit. [3] Now you are clean through the word which I have spoken unto you. [4] Abide in me, and I in you. As the branch cannot bear fruit of itself, except it abide in the vine; no more can you, except you abide in me. [5] I am the vine, you *are* the branches: he that abides in me, and I in him, the same brings forth much fruit: for without me you can do nothing. (John 15) *w/out Jesus can do nothing*

[6] If a man abide not in me, he is cast forth as a branch, and is withered; and men gather them, and cast *them* into the fire, and they are burned. [7] If you abide in me, and my words abide in you, you shall ask what you will, and it shall be done unto you. *ASK* [8] Herein is my Father glorified, that you bear much fruit; so shall you be my disciples. [9] As the Father has loved me, so have I loved you: continue in my love. [10] If you keep my commandments, you *OBEY* shall abide in my love; even as I have kept my Father's commandments, and abide in his love. (John 15)

[11] These things have I spoken unto you, that my joy might *JOY* remain in you, and *that* your joy might be full. [12] This is my commandment, that you love one another, as I have loved you. *LOVE* [13] Greater love has no man than this, that a man lay down his life for his friends. [14] You are my friends, if you do whatsoever I command you. [15] Henceforth I call you not servants; for the servant knows not what his lord does: but I have called you friends; for all things that I have heard of my Father I have made known unto you. (John 15)

[16] You have not chosen me, but I have chosen you, and ordained you, that you should go and bring forth fruit, and *that* your fruit should remain: that whatsoever you shall ask of the Father in my name, he may give it you. (John 15)

[17] These things I command you, that you love one another. [18] If the world hate you, you know that it hated me before *it hated* you.

abide obey bear fruit   Love one another

¹⁹ If you were of the world, the world would love his own: but because you are not of the world, but I have chosen you out of the world, therefore the world hates you. (John 15)

²⁰ Remember the word that I said unto you, The servant is not greater than his lord. If they have persecuted me, they will also persecute you; if they have kept my saying, they will keep yours also. ²¹ But all these things will they do unto you for my name's sake, because they know not him that sent me. ²² If I had not come and spoken unto them, they had not had sin: but now they have no cloak for their sin. ²³ He that hates me hates my Father also. ²⁴ If I had not done among them the works which none other man did, they had not had sin: but now have they both seen and hated both me and my Father. ²⁵ But *this comes to pass*, that the word might be fulfilled that is written in their law, They hated me without a cause.ᵃ (John 15)

(JOHN 14:30–31; 15:1–25)

When the Comforter, the Spirit of Truth Is Come

²⁶ BUT when the Comforter is come, whom I will send unto you from the Father, *even* the Spirit of truth, which proceeds from the Father, he shall testify of me: ²⁷ and you also shall bear witness, because you have been with me from the beginning. (John 15) 1 These things have I spoken unto you, that you should not be offended. (John 16)

² They shall put you out of the synagogues: yea, the time comes, that whosoever kills you will think that he does God service. ³ And these things will they do unto you, because they have not known the Father, nor me. ⁴ But these things have I told you, that when the time shall come, you may remember that I told you of them. And these things I said not unto you at the beginning, because I was with you. ⁵ But now I go my way to him that sent me; and none of you asks me, Whither go you? ⁶ But because I have said these things unto you, sorrow has filled your heart. (John 16)

a. O.T. prophecy in Psalm 35:19; 109:3; 119:161.

⁷ Nevertheless I tell you the truth; It is expedient for you that I go away: for if I go not away, the Comforter will not come unto you; but if I depart, I will send him unto you. ⁸ And when he is come, he will reprove the world of sin, and of righteousness, and of judgment: ⁹ of sin, because they believe not on me; ¹⁰ of righteousness, because I go to my Father, and you see me no more; ¹¹ of judgment, because the prince of this world is judged. ^(John 16)

¹² I have yet many things to say unto you, but you cannot bear them now. ¹³ Howbeit when he, the Spirit of truth, is come, he will guide you into all truth: for he shall not speak of himself; but whatsoever he shall hear, *that* shall he speak: and he will show you things to come. ¹⁴ He shall glorify me: for he shall receive of mine, and shall show *it* unto you. ¹⁵ All things that the Father has are mine: therefore said I, that he shall take of mine, and shall show *it* unto you. ¹⁶ A little while, and you shall not see me: and again, a little while, and you shall see me, because I go to the Father. ^(John 16)

(JOHN 15:26–27; 16:1–16)

I Have Overcome the World

¹⁷ THEN said *some* of his disciples among themselves, What is this that he says unto us, A little while, and you shall not see me: and again, a little while, and you shall see me: and, Because I go to the Father? ¹⁸ They said therefore, What is this that he says, A little while? We cannot tell what he says. ^(John 16)

¹⁹ Now Jesus knew that they were desirous to ask him, and said unto them, Do you enquire among yourselves of that I said, A little while, and you shall not see me: and again, a little while, and you shall see me? ²⁰ Verily, verily, I say unto you, that you shall weep and lament, but the world shall rejoice: and you shall be sorrowful, but your sorrow shall be turned into joy. ²¹ A woman when she is in travail has sorrow, because her hour is come: but as soon as she is delivered of the child, she remembers no more the anguish, for joy that a man is born into the world. ²² And you now therefore

have sorrow: but I will see you again, and your heart shall rejoice, and your joy no man takes from you. (John 16)

²³ And in that day you shall ask me nothing. Verily, verily, I say unto you, whatsoever you shall ask the Father in my name, he will give it you. ²⁴ Hitherto have you asked nothing in my name: ask, and you shall receive, that your joy may be full. ²⁵ These things have I spoken unto you in proverbs: but the time comes, when I shall no more speak unto you in proverbs, but I shall show you plainly of the Father. ²⁶ At that day you shall ask in my name: and I say not unto you, that I will pray the Father for you: ²⁷ for the Father himself loves you, because you have loved me, and have believed that I came out from God. ²⁸ I came forth from the Father, and am come into the world: again, I leave the world, and go to the Father. (John 16)

²⁹ His disciples said unto him, Lo, now speak you plainly, and speak no proverb. ³⁰ Now are we sure that you know all things, and need not that any man should ask you: by this we believe that you came forth from God. ³¹ Jesus answered them, Do you now believe? ³² Behold, the hour comes, yea, is now come, that you shall be scattered, every man to his own, and shall leave me alone: and yet I am not alone, because the Father is with me. ³³ These things I have spoken unto you, that in me you might have peace. In the world you shall have tribulation: but be of good cheer; I have overcome the world. (John 16)

(JOHN 16:17–33)

Father, Glorify Your Son

¹ THESE words spoke Jesus, and lifted up his eyes to heaven, and said, Father, the hour is come; glorify your Son, that your Son also may glorify you: ² as you have given him power over all flesh, that he should give eternal life to as many as you have given him. ³ And this is life eternal, that they might know you the only true God, and Jesus Christ, whom you have sent. ⁴ I have glorified you on

the earth: I have finished the work which you gave me to do. [5] And now, O Father, glorify you me with your own self with the glory which I had with you before the world was. (John 17)

[6] I have manifested your name unto the men which you gave me out of the world: yours they were, and you gave them me; and they have kept your word. [7] Now they have known that all things whatsoever you have given me are of you. [8] For I have given unto them the words which you gave me; and they have received *them*, and have known surely that I came out from you, and they have believed that you did send me. [9] I pray for them: I pray not for the world, but for them which you have given me; for they are yours. [10] And all mine are yours, and yours are mine; and I am glorified in them. (John 17)

[11] And now I am no more in the world, but these are in the world, and I come to you. Holy Father, keep through your own name those whom you have given me, that they may be one, as we *are.* [12] While I was with them in the world, I kept them in your name: those that you gave me I have kept, and none of them is lost, but the son of perdition; that the scripture might be fulfilled. [13] And now come I to you; and these things I speak in the world, that they might have my joy fulfilled in themselves. [14] I have given them your word; and the world has hated them, because they are not of the world, even as I am not of the world. (John 17)

[15] I pray not that you should take them out of the world, but that you should keep them from the evil. [16] They are not of the world, even as I am not of the world. [17] Sanctify them through your truth: your word is truth. [18] As you have sent me into the world, even so have I also sent them into the world. [19] And for their sakes I sanctify myself, that they also might be sanctified through the truth. [20] Neither pray I for these alone, but for them also which shall believe on me through their word; [21] that they all may be one; as you, Father, *are* in me, and I in you, that they also may be one in us: that the world may believe that you have sent me. (John 17)

[22] And the glory which you gave me I have given them; that they may be one, even as we are one: [23] I in them, and you in me, that

they may be made perfect in one; and that the world may know that you have sent me, and have loved them, as you have loved me. [24] Father, I will that they also, whom you have given me, be with me where I am; that they may behold my glory, which you have given me: for you loved me before the foundation of the world. [25] O righteous Father, the world has not known you: but I have known you, and these have known that you have sent me. [26] And I have declared unto them your name, and will declare *it:* that the love wherewith you have loved me may be in them, and I in them. (John 17)

[1] When Jesus had spoken these words, (John 18) [26] and when they had sung an hymn, they went out into the mount of Olives. (Mark 14) [1] He went forth with his disciples over the brook Cedron, where was a garden, into the which he entered, and his disciples. (John 18)

(JOHN 17:1–26; 18:1; MARK 14:26)

CHAPTER TWENTY-EIGHT

Jesus at the Mount of Olives To Pray; Gethsemane

[39] AND he came out, and went, as he was wont, to the mount of Olives; and his disciples also followed him. (Luke 22) [32] And they came to a place which was named Gethsemane: and he said to his disciples, (Mark 14) [36] Sit here, while I go and pray yonder. [37] And he took with him Peter and the two sons of Zebedee, (Matthew 26) [33] James and John, and began to be sore amazed, and (Mark 14) [37] to be sorrowful and (Matthew 26) [33] very heavy. (Mark 14) [38] Then said he unto them, My soul is exceeding sorrowful, even unto death: tarry here, and watch with me. (Matthew 26) [40] Pray that you enter not into temptation. (Luke 22)

[35] And he went forward a little, (Mark 14) [41] from them about a stone's cast, and kneeled down, (Luke 22) [39] and fell on his face, (Matthew 26) [35] on the ground, and prayed that, if it were possible, the hour might pass from him. [36] And he said, Abba, Father, all things *are* possible unto you; (Mark 14) [42] if you be willing, (Luke 22) [36] take away this cup from me: nevertheless not what I will, but what you will; (Mark 14) [42] not my will, but yours, be done. [43] And there appeared an angel unto him from heaven, strengthening him. [44] And being in an agony he prayed more earnestly: and his sweat was as it were great drops of blood falling down to the ground. (Luke 22)

[45] And when he rose up from prayer, and was come to his disciples, he found them sleeping for sorrow, (Luke 22) [37] and said unto Peter, (Mark 14) [40] What, (Matthew 26) [37] Simon, sleep you? Could not you (Mark 14) [40] watch with me one hour? (Matthew 26) [46] Why sleep you? Rise, (Luke 22) [38] watch and pray, lest you enter into temptation. The spirit truly *is* ready, but the flesh *is* weak. (Mark 14) [41] The spirit indeed *is* willing, but the flesh *is* weak. (Matthew 26)

[39] And again he went away, (Mark 14) [42] the second time, (Matthew 26)

³⁹ and prayed, and spoke the same words, (Mark 14) ⁴² saying, O my Father, if this cup may not pass away from me, except I drink it, your will be done. (Matthew 26)

⁴⁰ And when he returned, he found them asleep again, (for their eyes were heavy,) neither knew they what to answer him. (Mark 14) ⁴⁴ And he left them, and went away again, and prayed the third time, saying the same words. (Matthew 26) ⁴¹ And he came the third time (Mark 14) ⁴⁵ to his disciples, (Matthew 26) ⁴¹ and said unto them, Sleep on now, and take *your* rest: it is enough, the hour is come; behold, the Son of man is betrayed into the hands of sinners. ⁴² Rise up, let us go; lo, he that betrays me is at hand. (Mark 14)

(LUKE 22:39–46; MARK 14:32–33, 35–42;
MATTHEW 26:36–42, 44–45)

Judas Iscariot Betrays Jesus

⁴³ AND immediately, while he yet spoke, came (Mark 14) ⁴⁷ he that was called Judas, one of the twelve. (Luke 22) ² And Judas also, which betrayed him, knew the place: for Jesus oftentimes resorted thither with his disciples. ³ Judas then, having received a band *of men* and officers from the chief priests and Pharisees (John 18) ⁴³ and the scribes and the elders (Mark 14) ⁴⁷ of the people, (Matthew 26) ³ came thither, (John 18) ⁴³ and with him a great multitude, (Mark 14) ³ with lanterns and torches and weapons, (John 18) ⁴³ swords and staves. (Mark 14)

⁴ Jesus therefore, knowing all things that should come upon him, went forth, and said unto them, Whom seek you? ⁵ They answered him, Jesus of Nazareth. Jesus said unto them, I am *he*. And Judas also, which betrayed him, stood with them. ⁶ As soon then as he had said unto them, I am *he,* they went backward, and fell to the ground. ⁷ Then asked he them again, Whom seek you? And they said, Jesus of Nazareth. ⁸ Jesus answered, I have told you that I am *he:* if therefore you seek me, let these go their way: ⁹ that the saying might be fulfilled, which he spoke, Of them which you gave me have I lost none. (John 18)

⁴⁴ And he that betrayed him had given them a token, ^(Mark 14) ⁴⁸ a sign, ^(Matthew 26) ⁴⁴ saying, Whomsoever I shall kiss, that same is he; take him, ^(Mark 14) ⁴⁸ hold him fast, ^(Matthew 26) ⁴⁴ and lead *him* away safely. ⁴⁵ And as soon as he was come, he went straightway ^(Mark 14) ⁴⁷ before them, and drew near unto Jesus to kiss him, ^(Luke 22) ⁴⁵ and said, ^(Mark 14) ⁴⁹ Hail, ^(Matthew 26) ⁴⁵ Master, master; and kissed him. ^(Mark 14) ⁵⁰ And Jesus said unto him, ^(Matthew 26) ⁴⁸ Judas, ^(Luke 22) ⁵⁰ friend, wherefore are you come? ^(Matthew 26) ⁴⁸ Betray you the Son of man with a kiss? ^(Luke 22) ⁵⁰ Then came they, and laid hands on Jesus, and took him. ^(Matthew 26) ⁴⁹ When they which were about him saw what would follow, they said unto him, Lord, shall we smite with the sword? ^(Luke 22) ⁵¹ And, behold, one of them which were with Jesus ^(Matthew 26) ⁴⁷ that stood by, ^(Mark 14) ¹⁰ Simon Peter having a sword, ^(John 18) ⁵¹ stretched out *his* hand, and drew his sword, ^(Matthew 26) ¹⁰ and smote the high priest's servant, and cut off his right ear. The servant's name was Malchus. ^(John 18)

¹¹ Then said Jesus unto Peter, Put up ^(John 18) ⁵² again ^(Matthew 26) ¹¹ your sword into the sheath: the cup which my Father has given me, shall I not drink it? ^(John 18) ⁵² For all they that take the sword shall perish with the sword. ⁵³ Think you that I cannot now pray to my Father, and he shall presently give me more than twelve legions of angels? ⁵⁴ But how then shall the scriptures be fulfilled, that thus it must be? ^(Matthew 26) ⁵¹ And Jesus answered and said, Suffer you thus far. And he touched his ear, and healed him. ^(Luke 22)

⁵⁵ In that same hour ^(Matthew 26) ⁵² Jesus said unto the chief priests, and captains of the temple, and the elders, ^(Luke 22) ⁵⁵ *[and]* ⁵⁵ to the multitudes ^(Matthew 26) ⁵² which were come to him, ^(Luke 22) ⁵⁵ Are you come out, as against a thief, with swords and staves for to take me? ^(Matthew 26) ⁴⁹ I was daily with you in the temple teaching, and you took me not: ^(Mark 14) ⁵³ you stretched forth no hands against me: ^(Luke 22) ⁵⁵ you laid no hold on me. ^(Matthew 26) ⁵³ But this is your hour, and the power of darkness. ^(Luke 22) ⁵⁶ But all this was done, that the scriptures of the prophets might be fulfilled. Then all the disciples forsook him, and fled. ^(Matthew 26) ⁵¹ And there followed him a certain young man, having a linen cloth cast about *his* naked

body; and the young men laid hold on him: ⁵² and he left the linen cloth, and fled from them naked. (Mark 14)

¹² Then the band and the captain and officers of the Jews took Jesus, and bound him, ¹³ and led him away to Annas first; for he was father in law to Caiaphas, which was the high priest that same year. ¹⁴ Now Caiaphas was he, which gave counsel to the Jews, that it was expedient that one man should die for the people. (John 18)

⁵⁷ And they that had laid hold on Jesus (Matthew 26) ⁵⁴ took him, and led *him* (Luke 22) ⁵⁷ away to Caiaphas the high priest, (Matthew 26) ⁵⁴ and brought him unto the high priest's house, (Luke 22) ⁵⁷ where (Matthew 26) ⁵³ all the chief priests and (Mark 14) ⁵⁷ the scribes and the elders were assembled. (Matthew 26)

(MARK 14:43–45, 47, 49, 51–53; MATTHEW 26:47–57;
LUKE 22:47–49, 51–54; JOHN 18:2–14)

Peter Denies Knowing Jesus

¹⁵ AND Simon Peter followed Jesus, (John 18) ⁵⁴ afar off, (Mark 14) ⁵⁸ to see the end, (Matthew 26) ¹⁵ and *so did* another disciple: that disciple was known unto the high priest, and went in with Jesus into the palace of the high priest. ¹⁶ But Peter stood at the door without. Then went out that other disciple, which was known unto the high priest, and spoke unto her that kept the door, and brought in Peter. (John 18) ⁵⁵ And when they had kindled a fire in the midst of the hall, and were sat down together, Peter sat down among them. (Luke 22) ¹⁸ And the servants and officers stood there, who had made a fire of coals; for it was cold: and they warmed themselves: and Peter stood with them (John 18) ⁵⁴ and warmed himself at the fire. (Mark 14)

⁶⁶ And as Peter was beneath in the palace, there came one of the maids of the high priest, (Mark 14) ¹⁷ the damsel that kept the door. (John 18) ⁶⁷ And when she saw Peter warming himself, (Mark 14) ⁵⁶ as he sat by the fire, (Luke 22) ⁶⁷ she (Mark 14) ⁵⁶ earnestly looked upon him, and said, (Luke 22) ¹⁷ Are not you also *one* of this man's disciples? (John 18) ⁶⁷ And you also were with Jesus of Nazareth (Mark 14) ⁶⁹ of

Galilee. (Matthew 26) *[And she said to the others,]* ⁵⁶ This man was also with him. (Luke 22) ⁷⁰ But he denied (Matthew 26) ⁵⁷ him (Luke 22) ⁷⁰ before *them* all, saying, (Matthew 26) ⁶⁸ I know not, neither understand I what you say. (Mark 14) ⁵⁷ Woman, I know him not. (Luke 22) ⁶⁸ And he went out into the porch; and the cock crew. (Mark 14)

⁷¹ And when he was gone out into the porch, another *maid* saw him (Matthew 26) ⁶⁹ again, and began to say to them that stood by, This is *one* of them. (Mark 14) ⁷¹ This *fellow* was also with Jesus of Nazareth. (Matthew 26) ⁵⁸ And after a little while another saw him, and said, You are also of them. (Luke 22) ²⁵ And Simon Peter stood and warmed himself. They said therefore unto him, Are not you also *one* of his disciples? (John 18) ⁵⁸ And Peter (Luke 22) ⁷⁰ denied it again (Mark 14) ⁷² with an oath, (Matthew 26) ⁵⁸ Man, I am not. (Luke 22) ⁷² I do not know the man. (Matthew 26)

⁵⁹ And about the space of one hour after another confidently affirmed, saying, Of a truth this *fellow* also was with him: for he is a Galilaean. (Luke 22) ²⁶ One of the servants of the high priest, being *his* kinsman whose ear Peter cut off, said, Did not I see you in the garden with him? (John 18) ⁷⁰ They that stood by said again to Peter, Surely you are *one* of them: for you are a Galilaean, and your speech agrees *thereto;* (Mark 14) ⁷³ for your speech betrays you. (Matthew 26)

⁶⁰ And Peter said, Man, I know not what you say. (Luke 22) ²⁷ Peter then (John 18) ⁷¹ began to curse and to swear, *saying,* I know not this man of whom you speak. (Mark 14) ⁶⁰ And immediately, while he yet spoke, (Luke 22) ⁷² the second time the cock crew. (Mark 14) ⁶¹ And the Lord turned, and looked upon Peter. And Peter remembered the word of the Lord (Luke 22) ⁷⁵ Jesus, (Matthew 26) ⁶¹ how he had said unto him, (Luke 22) ⁷² Before the cock crow twice, (Mark 14) ⁶¹ you shall deny me thrice. (Luke 22) ⁷² And when he thought thereon, (Mark 14) ⁶² Peter went out, and wept bitterly. (Luke 22)

¹⁹ The high priest then asked Jesus of his disciples, and of his doctrine. ²⁰ Jesus answered him, I spoke openly to the world; I ever taught in the synagogue, and in the temple, whither the Jews always resort; and in secret have I said nothing. ²¹ Why ask you me?

Ask them which heard me, what I have said unto them: behold, they know what I said. ²² And when he had thus spoken, one of the officers which stood by struck Jesus with the palm of his hand, saying, Answer you the high priest so? ²³ Jesus answered him, If I have spoken evil, bear witness of the evil: but if well, why smite you me? ²⁴ Now Annas had sent him bound unto Caiaphas the high priest. (John 18)

(JOHN 18:15–27; MATTHEW 26:58, 69–73, 75; MARK 14:54, 66–72; LUKE 22:55–62)

Jesus in the Council of Elders, Scribes, and Chief Priests

⁶⁶ AND as soon as it was day, the elders of the people and the chief priests and the scribes came together, and led him into their council. (Luke 22) ⁵⁹ Now the chief priests, and elders, and all the council, sought (Matthew 26) ⁵⁵ for (Mark 14) ⁵⁹ false witness against Jesus, to put him to death; ⁶⁰ but found none. (Matthew 26) ⁵⁶ For many bore false witness against him, but their witness agreed not together. (Mark 14) ⁶⁰ Yea, though many false witnesses came, yet found they none. (Matthew 26) ⁵⁷ And (Mark 14) ⁶⁰ at the last (Matthew 26) ⁵⁷ there arose (Mark 14) ⁶⁰ two false witnesses, (Matthew 26) ⁵⁷ and bore false witness against him, saying, ⁵⁸ We heard (Mark 14) ⁶¹ this *fellow* (Matthew 26) ⁵⁸ say, I will destroy this temple (Mark 14) ⁶¹ of God, (Matthew 26) ⁵⁸ that is made with hands, and within three days I will build another made without hands. (Mark 14)

⁵⁹ But neither so did their witness agree together. ⁶⁰ And the high priest (Mark 14) ⁶² arose, (Matthew 26) ⁶⁰ stood up in the midst, and asked Jesus, saying, Answer you nothing? What *is it which* these witness against you? (Mark 14) ⁶³ But Jesus held his peace, (Matthew 26) ⁶¹ and answered nothing. Again the high priest asked him, and said unto him, Are you the Christ, the Son of the Blessed? (Mark 14) ⁶⁷ Tell us. And he said unto them, If I tell you, you will not believe: ⁶⁸ and if I also ask *you*, you will not answer me, nor let *me* go. (Luke 22) ⁶³ And the high priest answered and said unto him, I adjure you by the living God, that you tell us whether you be the Christ,

the Son of God. (Matthew 26) 70 Then said they all, Are you then the Son of God? And he said unto them, You say that I am. (Luke 22) 62 And Jesus said, I am. (Mark 14) 64 You have said: nevertheless I say unto you, (Matthew 26) 69 hereafter shall (Luke 22) 64 you see (Matthew 26) 69 the Son of man sit on the right hand of the power of God, (Luke 22) 64 and coming in the clouds of heaven. (Matthew 26)

63 Then the high priest rent his clothes, and said, (Mark 14) 65 He has spoken blasphemy; what further need have we of (Matthew 26) 71 any further (Luke 22) 65 witnesses? Behold, now you have heard his blasphemy. (Matthew 26) 71 For we ourselves have heard of his own mouth. (Luke 22) 64 What think you? And they all condemned him to be guilty of death. 65 And some (Mark 14) *[of]* 63 the men that held Jesus (Luke 22) 65 began to spit (Mark 14) 67 in his face, (Matthew 26) 65 and to cover his face, and to buffet him. (Mark 14) *[They]* 63 mocked him, and smote *him.* 64 And when they had blindfolded him, they struck him on the face, and asked him, saying, (Luke 22) 68 Prophesy unto us, you Christ, (Matthew 26) 64 who is it that smote you? (Luke 22) 65 And the servants did strike him with the palms of their hands. (Mark 14) 65 And many other things blasphemously spoke they against him. (Luke 22)

(LUKE 22:63–71; MATTHEW 26:59–65, 67–68;
MARK 14:55–65)

CHAPTER TWENTY-NINE

Jesus Taken to Pontius Pilate

¹ AND straightway in the morning ⁽Mark 15⁾ ¹ all the chief priests ⁽Matthew 27⁾ ¹ held a consultation with the elders ⁽Mark 15⁾ ¹ of the people ⁽Matthew 27⁾ ¹ and scribes and the whole council, ⁽Mark 15⁾ ¹ against Jesus to put him to death. ⁽Matthew 27⁾

¹ And the whole multitude of them arose, ⁽Luke 23⁾ ¹ bound Jesus, and carried *him* away, ⁽Mark 15⁾ ¹ and led him ⁽Luke 23⁾ ²⁸ from Caiaphas unto the hall of judgment, ⁽John 18⁾ ² and delivered him to Pontius Pilate the governor. ⁽Matthew 27⁾ ²⁸ And it was early; and they themselves went not into the judgment hall, lest they should be defiled; but that they might eat the passover. ⁽John 18⁾

²⁹ Pilate then went out unto them, and said, What accusation bring you against this man? ³⁰ They answered and said unto him, If he were not a malefactor, we would not have delivered him up unto you. ⁽John 18⁾ ² And they began to accuse him, saying, We found this *fellow* perverting the nation, and forbidding to give tribute to Caesar, saying that he himself is Christ a King. ⁽Luke 23⁾ ³¹ Then said Pilate unto them, Take him, and judge him according to your law. ⁽John 18⁾

³¹ The Jews therefore said unto him, It is not lawful for us to put any man to death: ³² that the saying of Jesus might be fulfilled, which he spoke, signifying what death he should die. ³³ Then Pilate entered into the judgment hall again, and called Jesus. ⁽John 18⁾

¹¹ And Jesus stood before the governor: and the governor asked him, saying, Are you the King of the Jews? ⁽Matthew 27⁾ ³ And he answered him and said, You say *it*. ⁽Luke 23⁾ ³⁴ Say you this thing of yourself, or did others tell it you of me? ³⁵ Pilate answered, Am I a Jew? Your own nation and the chief priests have delivered you unto me: what have you done? ⁽John 18⁾

³⁶ Jesus answered, My kingdom is not of this world: if my kingdom were of this world, then would my servants fight, that I should not be delivered to the Jews: but now is my kingdom not from hence. ³⁷ Pilate therefore said unto him, Are you a king then? Jesus answered, You say that I am a king. To this end was I born, and for this cause came I into the world, that I should bear witness unto the truth. Every one that is of the truth hears my voice. ³⁸ Pilate said unto him, What is truth? ^(John 18)

³⁸ And when he had said this, he went out again unto the Jews, and said unto ^(John 18) ⁴ the chief priests and *to* the people, I find no fault ^(Luke 23) ³⁸ *at all* ^(John 18) ⁴ in this man. ⁵ And they were the more fierce, saying, He stirs up the people, teaching throughout all Jewry, beginning from Galilee to this place. ^(Luke 23)

¹² And when he was accused of the chief priests and elders, ^(Matthew 27) ³ of many things, ^(Mark 15) ¹² he answered nothing. ^(Matthew 27) ⁴ And Pilate asked him again, saying, Answer you nothing? ^(Mark 15) ¹³ Hear you not ^(Matthew 27) ⁴ how many things they witness against you. ⁵ But Jesus yet answered nothing, ^(Mark 15) ¹⁴ insomuch that the governor ^(Matthew 27) ⁵ Pilate ^(Mark 15) ¹⁴ marvelled greatly. ^(Matthew 27)

(MARK 15:1, 3–5; MATTHEW 27:1–2, 11–14;
JOHN 18:28–38; LUKE 23:1–5)

Pilate Sends Jesus to Herod

⁶ WHEN Pilate heard of Galilee, he asked whether the man were a Galilaean. ⁷ And as soon as he knew that he belonged unto Herod's jurisdiction, he sent him to Herod, who himself also was at Jerusalem at that time. ⁸ And when Herod saw Jesus, he was exceeding glad: for he was desirous to see him of a long *season,* because he had heard many things of him; and he hoped to have seen some miracle done by him. ⁹ Then he questioned with him in many words; but he answered him nothing. ^(Luke 23)

¹⁰ And the chief priests and scribes stood and vehemently accused him. ¹¹ And Herod with his men of war set him at nought,

and mocked *him,* and arrayed him in a gorgeous robe, and sent him again to Pilate. ¹² And the same day Pilate and Herod were made friends together: for before they were at enmity between themselves. (Luke 23)

¹³ And Pilate, when he had called together the chief priests and the rulers and the people, ¹⁴ said unto them, You have brought this man unto me, as one that perverts the people: and, behold, I, having examined *him* before you, have found no fault in this man touching those things whereof you accuse him: ¹⁵ no, nor yet Herod: for I sent you to him; and, lo, nothing worthy of death is done unto him. ¹⁶ I will therefore chastise him, and release *him.* (Luke 23)

(LUKE 23:6–16)

"Crucify Him! Crucify Him!"

¹⁵ Now at *that* feast the governor was wont to release unto the people a prisoner, (Matthew 27) ⁶ whomsoever they desired. (Mark 15) ¹⁷ (For of necessity he must release one unto them at the feast.) (Luke 23) ⁷ And there was *one* (Mark 15) ¹⁶ notable prisoner (Matthew 27) ⁷ named Barabbas, (Mark 15) ⁴⁰ a robber, (John 18) ⁷ *which lay* bound with them that had made insurrection (Mark 15) ¹⁹ in the city (Luke 23) ⁷ with him, who had committed murder in the insurrection. ⁸ And the multitude crying aloud began to desire *him to do* as he had ever done unto them. (Mark 15) ¹⁷ Therefore when they were gathered together, Pilate said unto them, (Matthew 27) ³⁹ You have a custom, that I should release unto you one at the passover. (John 18) ¹⁷ Whom will you that I release unto you? Barabbas, or Jesus which is called Christ? (Matthew 27) ⁹ Will you (Mark 15) ³⁹ therefore (John 18) ⁹ that I release unto you the King of the Jews? ¹⁰ For he knew that the chief priests had delivered him for envy. (Mark 15)

¹⁸ And they cried out all at once, saying, Away with this *man,* and release unto us Barabbas: ¹⁹ (Who for a certain sedition made in the city, and for murder, was cast into prison.) ²⁰ Pilate therefore,

willing to release Jesus, spoke again to them. ²¹ But they cried, saying, Crucify *him*, crucify him. ²² And he said unto them the third
time, Why, what evil has he done? I have found no cause of death
in him: I will therefore chastise him, and let *him* go. (Luke 23)

¹ Then Pilate therefore took Jesus, and scourged *him*. (John 19)
²⁷ Then the soldiers of the governor took Jesus into the common
hall, (Matthew 27) ¹⁶ called Praetorium, (Mark 15) ²⁷ and gathered unto
him the whole band *of soldiers.* ²⁸ And they stripped him, and
put on him a scarlet robe. ²⁹ And when they had platted a crown
of thorns, they put *it* upon his head, and a reed in his right hand;
and they bowed the knee before him, (Matthew 27) ¹⁹ worshipped him
(Mark 15) ²⁹ and mocked him, (Matthew 27) ¹⁸ and began to salute him,
(Mark 15) ²⁹ saying, Hail, King of the Jews! ³⁰ And they spit upon him,
and took the reed, and smote him on the head, (Matthew 27) ³ and they
smote him with their hands. ⁴ Pilate therefore went forth again,
and said unto them, Behold, I bring him forth to you, that you
may know that I find no fault in him. ⁵ Then came Jesus forth,
wearing the crown of thorns, and the purple robe. (John 18)

⁵ And *Pilate* said unto them, Behold the man! ⁶ When the chief
priests therefore and officers saw him, they cried out, saying, Crucify *him,* crucify *him.* Pilate said unto them, Take him, and crucify
him: for I find no fault in him. ⁷ The Jews answered him, We have
a law, and by our law he ought to die, because he made himself the
Son of God. ⁸ When Pilate therefore heard that saying, he was the
more afraid; ⁹ and went again into the judgment hall, and said unto
Jesus, Whence are you? But Jesus gave him no answer. ¹⁰ Then said
Pilate unto him, Speak you not unto me? Know you not that I have
power to crucify you, and have power to release you? (John 19)

¹¹ Jesus answered, You could have no power *at all* against me,
except it were given you from above: therefore he that delivered me
unto you has the greater sin. ¹² And from thenceforth Pilate sought
to release him: but the Jews cried out, saying, If you let this man
go, you are not Caesar's friend: whosoever makes himself a king
speaks against Caesar. (John 19)

¹³ When Pilate therefore heard that saying, he brought Jesus

forth, and sat down in the judgment seat in a place that is called the Pavement, but in the Hebrew, Gabbatha. (John 19) 19 When he was set down on the judgment seat, his wife sent unto him, saying, Have you nothing to do with that just man: for I have suffered many things this day in a dream because of him. (Matthew 27) 14 And it was the preparation of the passover, and about the sixth hour: and he said unto the Jews, Behold your King! (John 19)

(MATTHEW 27:15–17, 19, 27–30; MARK 15:6–10, 16, 18–19;
LUKE 23:17–22; JOHN 18:39–40; 19:1–14)

Barabbas Released Instead of Jesus

20 BUT the chief priests and elders persuaded the multitude that they should ask (Matthew 27) 11 that he should rather release Barabbas unto them, (Mark 15) 20 and destroy Jesus. 21 The governor answered and said unto them, Whether of the twain will you that I release unto you? They said, Barabbas. (Matthew 27) 12 And Pilate answered and said again unto them, What will you then that I shall do *unto him* whom you call the King of the Jews, (Mark 15) 22 Jesus which is called Christ? *They* all say unto him, (Matthew 27) 15 Away with *him,* away with *him,* crucify him. (John 19) 14 Then (Mark 15) 23 the governor (Matthew 27) 14 Pilate said unto them, Why, what evil has he done? (Mark 15) 15 Shall I crucify your King? The chief priests answered, We have no king but Caesar. (John 19) 14 And they cried out the more exceedingly, Crucify him. (Mark 15) 23 And they were instant with loud voices, requiring that he might be crucified. (Luke 23)

24 When Pilate saw that he could prevail nothing, but *that* rather a tumult was made, he took water, and washed *his* hands before the multitude, saying, I am innocent of the blood of this just person: see you *to it.* 25 Then answered all the people, and said, His blood *be* on us, and on our children. (Matthew 27) 23 And the voices of them and of the chief priests prevailed. (Luke 23) 15 And *so* Pilate, willing to content the people, (Mark 15) 24 gave sentence that it should be as they required. 25 And he released unto them him that for sedition

and murder was cast into prison, (Luke 23) 15 Barabbas (Mark 15) 25 whom they had desired, (Luke 23) 26 and when he had scourged Jesus, he delivered *him* (Matthew 27) 25 to their will, (Luke 23) 15 to be crucified. (Mark 15)

31 And after that they had mocked him, they took (Matthew 27) 20 the purple (Mark 15) 31 robe off from him, and put his own raiment on him, and led him away to crucify *him*. (Matthew 27)

(MATTHEW 27:20–26, 31; MARK 15:11–12, 14–15, 20;
LUKE 23:23–25; JOHN 19:15)

Judas Returns the Thirty Pieces of Silver

3 THEN Judas, which had betrayed him, when he saw that he was condemned, repented himself, and brought again the thirty pieces of silver to the chief priests and elders, 4 saying, I have sinned in that I have betrayed the innocent blood. (Matthew 27)

4 And they said, What *is that* to us? See you *to that*. 5 And he cast down the pieces of silver in the temple, and departed, and went and hanged himself. (Matthew 27)

6 And the chief priests took the silver pieces, and said, It is not lawful for to put them into the treasury, because it is the price of blood. 7 And they took counsel, and bought with them the potter's field, to bury strangers in. 8 Wherefore that field was called, The field of blood, unto this day. 9 Then was fulfilled that which was spoken by Jeremy the prophet, saying, And they took the thirty pieces of silver, the price of him that was valued, whom they of the children of Israel did value; 10 and gave them for the potter's field, as the Lord appointed me.ᵃ (Matthew 27)

(MATTHEW 27:3–10)

---

a. O.T. prophecy in Zechariah 11:12–13.

CHAPTER THIRTY

Jesus Goes to Calvary (Golgotha)

32 AND as they came out, (Matthew 27) 26 and as they led him away, (Luke 23) 17 and he bearing his cross, (John 19) 32 they found a man of Cyrene, Simon by name: (Matthew 27) 21 who passed by, coming out of the country, the father of Alexander and Rufus, (Mark 15) 26 and on him they laid the cross, (Luke 23) *[and]* 32 him they compelled (Matthew 27) 26 that he might bear *it* after Jesus. 27 And there followed him a great company of people, and of women, which also bewailed and lamented him. (Luke 23)

28 But Jesus turning unto them said, Daughters of Jerusalem, weep not for me, but weep for yourselves, and for your children. 29 For, behold, the days are coming, in the which they shall say, Blessed *are* the barren, and the wombs that never bore, and the paps which never gave suck. 30 Then shall they begin to say to the mountains, Fall on us; and to the hills, Cover us. 31 For if they do these things in a green tree, what shall be done in the dry? (Luke 23)

32 And there were also two other, malefactors, led with him to be put to death. (Luke 23) 22 And they bring him unto the place (Mark 15) 33 which is called Calvary, (Luke 23) 17 *the place* of a skull, which is called in the Hebrew Golgotha. (John 19) 34 They gave him vinegar to drink mingled with gall[a]: and when he had tasted *thereof,* he would not drink. (Matthew 27)

23 And they gave him to drink wine mingled with myrrh: but he received *it* not. (Mark 15)

(MATTHEW 27:32, 34; LUKE 23:26–33;
MARK 15:21–23; JOHN 19:17)

---

a. O.T. prophecy in Psalm 69:21.

Jesus of Nazareth Is Crucified

35 AND they crucified him. (Matthew 27) 27 And with him they crucified two thieves; the one on his right hand, and the other on his left, (Mark 15) 18 and Jesus in the midst. (John 19) 28 And the scripture was fulfilled, which says, And he was numbered with the transgressors.a (Mark 15) 25 And it was the third hour, and they crucified him. (Mark 15) 34 Then said Jesus, Father, forgive them; for they know not what they do. (Luke 23)

23 Then the soldiers, when they had crucified Jesus, took his garments, and made four parts, to every soldier a part; and also *his* coat: now the coat was without seam, woven from the top throughout. 24 They said therefore among themselves, Let us not rend it, but cast lots for it, whose it shall be (John 19) *[and]* 24 what every man should take, (Mark 15) 24 that the scripture (John 19) 35 which was spoken by the prophet (Matthew 27) 24 might be fulfilled, which says, They parted my raiment among them, and for my vesture they did cast lots.b These things therefore the soldiers did. (John 19) 36 And sitting down they watched him there. (Matthew 27)

19 And Pilate wrote a title, (John 19) 26 the superscription of his accusation, (Mark 15) 19 and put *it* on the cross (John 19) 37 over his head. (Matthew 27) 19 And the writing was, (John 19) 37 THIS IS (Matthew 27) 19 JESUS OF NAZARETH THE KING OF THE JEWS. 20 This title then read many of the Jews: for the place where Jesus was crucified was nigh to the city: and it was written in Hebrew, *and* Greek, *and* Latin. 21 Then said the chief priests of the Jews to Pilate, Write not, The King of the Jews; but that he said, I am King of the Jews. 22 Pilate answered, What I have written I have written. (John 19)

29 And they that passed by railed on him, (Mark 15) 39 reviled him, (Matthew 27) 29 wagging their heads, and saying, Ah, you that destroy the temple, and build *it* in three days, 30 save yourself. (Mark 15) 40 If you be the Son of God, come down from the cross. (Matthew 27)

35 And the people stood beholding. And the rulers also with

---

a. O.T. prophecy in Isaiah 53:12.
b. O.T. prophecy in Psalm 22:18.

them derided *him*. (Luke 23) 31 Likewise also the chief priests mock-ing said among themselves with the scribes (Mark 15) 41 and elders, (Matthew 27) 31 He saved others; himself he cannot save. 32 Let Christ the King of Israel descend now from the cross, (Mark 15) 42 if he be the King of Israel. (Matthew 27) 35 Let him save himself, if he be Christ, the chosen of God, (Luke 23) 32 that we may see (Mark 15) 42 and we will believe him. 43 He trusted in God; let him deliver him now, if he will have him: for he said, I am the Son of God.a (Matthew 27) 36 And the soldiers also mocked him, coming to him, and offering him vinegar, 37 and saying, If you be the king of the Jews, save yourself. (Luke 23)

44 The thieves also, which were crucified with him, cast the same in his teeth. (Matthew 27) 39 And one of the malefactors which were hanged railed on him, saying, If you be Christ, save yourself and us. 40 But the other answering rebuked him, saying, Do not you fear God, seeing you are in the same condemnation? 41 And we indeed justly; for we receive the due reward of our deeds: but this man has done nothing amiss. 42 And he said unto Jesus, Lord, remember me when you come into your kingdom. 43 And Jesus said unto him, Verily I say unto you, Today shall you be with me in paradise. (Luke 23)

(MATTHEW 27:35–37, 39–44; MARK 15:24–32;
LUKE 23:34–37, 39–43; JOHN 19:18–24)

Mary Beholds Her Son Crucified

25 Now there stood by the cross of Jesus his mother, and his mother's sister, Mary the *wife* of Cleophas, and Mary Magdalene. 26 When Jesus therefore saw his mother, and the disciple standing by, whom he loved, he said unto his mother, Woman, behold your son! 27 Then said he to the disciple, Behold your mother! And from that hour that disciple took her unto his own *home*. (John 19) 33 And when the sixth hour was come, there was darkness over the

---

a. O.T. prophecy in Psalm 22:8.

whole land until the ninth hour. [34] And at the ninth hour Jesus cried with a loud voice, saying, Eloi, Eloi, lama sabachthani? Which is, being interpreted, My God, my God, why have you forsaken me?[a] [35] And some of them that stood by, when they heard *it*, said, Behold, (Mark 15) [47] this *man* calls for Elias. (Matthew 27) *Knowing = GOD*

[28] After this, Jesus knowing that all things were now accomplished, that the scripture might be fulfilled, said, I thirst.[b] [29] Now there was set a vessel full of vinegar: (John 19) [48] and straightway one of them ran, and took a sponge, and filled *it* with vinegar, and put *it* on a reed, (Matthew 27) [29] hyssop, and put *it* to his mouth (John 19) [48] and gave him to drink. [49] The rest said, Let be, let us see whether Elias will come to save him (Matthew 27) *[and]* [36] take him down. (Mark 15) [30] When Jesus therefore had received the vinegar, he said, It is finished. (John 19) [46] And when Jesus had cried with a loud voice, he said, Father, into your hands I commend my spirit: and having said thus, (Luke 23) [30] he bowed his head, and gave up the ghost. (John 19) *thirst = man*

[45] And the sun was darkened, (Luke 23) [51] and, behold, the veil of the temple was rent in twain (Matthew 27) [45] in the midst, (Luke 23) [51] from the top to the bottom; and the earth did quake, and the rocks rent; [52] and the graves were opened; and many bodies of the saints which slept arose, [53] and came out of the graves after his resurrection, and went into the holy city, and appeared unto many. (Matthew 27)

[54] Now when the centurion, (Matthew 27) [39] which stood over against him, saw that he so cried out, and gave up the ghost, (Mark 15) [47] he glorified God, saying, Certainly this was a righteous man. (Luke 23) [39] Truly this man was the Son of God. (Mark 15) [54] And they that were with him, watching Jesus, saw the earthquake, and those things that were done, *[and]* they feared greatly, saying, Truly this was the Son of God. (Matthew 27) [48] And all the people that came together to that sight, beholding the things which were done, smote their breasts, and returned. (Luke 23)

[40] There were also (Mark 15) [55] many (Matthew 27) [40] women (Mark 15) [49] and

---

a. O.T. prophecy in Psalm 22:1.
b. O.T. prophecy in Psalm 69:21.

all his acquaintance, (Luke 23) 40 looking on afar off, (Mark 15) 49 beholding these things: (Luke 23) 40 among whom was Mary Magdalene, and Mary the mother of James the less and of Joses, and Salome (the mother of Zebedee's children, Matthew 27:56); (Mark 15) 41 (Who also, when he was in Galilee, followed him, and ministered unto him;) and many other women which came up with him unto Jerusalem. (Mark 15)

31 The Jews therefore, because it was the preparation, that the bodies should not remain upon the cross on the sabbath day, (for that sabbath day was an high day,) besought Pilate that their legs might be broken, and *that* they might be taken away. 32 Then came the soldiers, and broke the legs of the first, and of the other which was crucified with him. (John 19)

33 But when they came to Jesus, and saw that he was dead already, they broke not his legs: 34 but one of the soldiers with a spear pierced his side, and forthwith came there out blood and water. 35 And he that saw *it* bore record, and his record is true: and he knows that he says true, that you might believe. 36 For these things were done, that the scripture should be fulfilled, A bone of him shall not be broken.a 37 And again another scripture says, They shall look on him whom they pierced.b (John 19)

(JOHN 19:25–37; MATTHEW 27:47–49, 51–56;
MARK 15:33–36, 39–41; LUKE 23:45–49)

Joseph of Arimathaea and Nicodemus
Prepare Jesus' Body for Burial

42 AND now when the even was come, because it was the preparation, that is, the day before the Sabbath, (Mark 15) 57 there came a rich man of Arimathaea, named Joseph, (Matthew 27) 43 an honorable counselor, (Mark 15) 50 *and he was* a good man, and a just: 51 (The same had not consented to the counsel and deed of them;) *he was* of Arimathaea, a city of the Jews: who also himself waited for the

---

a. O.T. prophecy in Psalm 34:20.
b. O.T. prophecy in Zechariah 12:10.

kingdom of God, (Luke 23) 38 being a disciple of Jesus, but secretly for fear of the Jews. (John 19) 52 This *man* (Luke 23) 43 came, and went in boldly unto Pilate, and (Mark 15) 38 besought Pilate that he might take away the body of Jesus. (John 19)

44 And Pilate marvelled if he were already dead: and calling *unto him* the centurion, he asked him whether he had been any while dead. 45 And when he knew *it* of the centurion, (Mark 15) 58 Pilate commanded the body to be delivered (Matthew 27) 45 to Joseph. (Mark 15) 38 He came therefore, and took the body of Jesus. (John 19)

39 And there came also Nicodemus, which at the first came to Jesus by night, and brought a mixture of myrrh and aloes, about an hundred pound *weight,* (John 19) *[and Joseph]* 46 bought fine linen. (Mark 15) 40 Then took they the body of Jesus, and wound it in (John 19) 59 clean (Matthew 27) 40 linen clothes with the spices, as the manner of the Jews is to bury. (John 19)

41 Now in the place where he was crucified there was a garden; and in the garden 42 laid they Jesus therefore, (John 19) *[in Joseph's]* 60 own new tomb, which he had hewn out in the rock: (Matthew 27) 53 wherein never man before was laid, (Luke 23) 42 because of the Jews' preparation *day;* for the sepulchre was nigh at hand, (John 19) 54 and the sabbath drew on. 55 And the women also, which came with him from Galilee, (Luke 23) 47 Mary Magdalene and Mary *the mother* of Joses, (Mark 15) 55 followed after, and beheld the sepulchre, (Luke 23) 61 sitting over against the sepulchre, (Matthew 27) *[and]* 47 beheld where he was laid, (Mark 15) 55 and how his body was laid. 56 And they returned, and prepared spices and ointments; and rested the sabbath day according to the commandment. (Luke 23) 60 And he *[Joseph]* rolled a great stone to the door of the sepulchre, and departed. (Matthew 27)

(MARK 15:42–47; MATTHEW 27:57–61; JOHN 19:38–42; LUKE 23:50–56)

A Watch Is Set at Jesus' Tomb

⁶² Now the next day, that followed the day of the preparation, the chief priests and Pharisees came together unto Pilate, ⁶³ saying, Sir, we remember that that deceiver said, while he was yet alive, After three days I will rise again. ⁶⁴ Command therefore that the sepulchre be made sure until the third day, lest his disciples come by night, and steal him away, and say unto the people, He is risen from the dead: so the last error shall be worse than the first. (Matthew 27)

⁶⁵ Pilate said unto them, You have a watch: go your way, make *it* as sure as you can. ⁶⁶ So they went, and made the sepulchre sure, sealing the stone, and setting a watch. (Matthew 27)

(MATTHEW 27:62–66)

CHAPTER THIRTY-ONE

Resurrection Day

¹ IN the end of the sabbath, as it began to dawn toward the first *day* of the week, ² behold, there was a great earthquake: for the angel of the Lord descended from heaven, and came and rolled back the stone from the door, and sat upon it. ³ His countenance was like lightning, and his raiment white as snow: ⁴ and for fear of him the keepers did shake, and became as dead *men*. (Matthew 28)

¹ And when the sabbath was past, Mary Magdalene, and Mary the *mother* of James, and Salome, had bought sweet spices, that they might come and anoint him. ² And very early in the morning the first *day* of the week, (Mark 16) ¹ when it was yet dark, (John 20) ² they (Mark 16) ¹ and certain *others* with them, (Luke 24) ² came unto the sepulchre at the rising of the sun. (Mark 16)

³ And they said among themselves, Who shall roll us away the stone from the door of the sepulchre? ⁴ And when they looked, they saw that the stone was rolled away (Mark 16) ² from the sepulchre: (Luke 24) ⁴ for it was very great. (Mark 16) ³ And they entered in, and found not the body of the Lord Jesus. (Luke 24)

² Then she *[Mary Magdalene]* ran, and came to Simon Peter, and to the other disciple, whom Jesus loved, and said unto them, They have taken away the Lord out of the sepulchre, and we know not where they have laid him. ³ Peter therefore went forth, and that other disciple, and came to the sepulchre. ⁴ So they ran both together: and the other disciple did outrun Peter, and came first to the sepulchre. ⁵ And he stooping down, *and looking in*, saw the linen clothes lying; yet went he not in. (John 20)

⁶ Then came Simon Peter following him, and went into the sepulchre, and saw the linen clothes lie, ⁷ and the napkin, that was about his head, not lying with the linen clothes, but wrapped together in a

place by itself. ⁸ Then went in also that other disciple, which came first to the sepulchre, and he saw, and believed. ⁹ For as yet they knew not the scripture, that he must rise again from the dead. ¹⁰ Then the disciples went away again unto their own home, ⁽John 20⁾ *[Peter]* ¹² wondering in himself at that which was come to pass. ⁽Luke 24⁾

¹¹ But Mary stood without at the sepulchre weeping: and as she wept, she stooped down, *and looked* into the sepulchre, ¹² and saw two angels in white sitting, the one at the head, and the other at the feet, where the body of Jesus had lain. ¹³ And they say unto her, Woman, why weep you? She said unto them, Because they have taken away my Lord, and I know not where they have laid him. ¹⁴ And when she had thus said, she turned herself back, and saw Jesus standing, and knew not that it was Jesus. ⁽John 20⁾

¹⁵ Jesus said unto her, Woman, why weep you? Whom seek you? She, supposing him to be the gardener, said unto him, Sir, if you have borne him hence, tell me where you have laid him, and I will take him away. ¹⁶ Jesus said unto her, Mary. She turned herself, and said unto him, Rabboni; which is to say, Master. ¹⁷ Jesus said unto her, Touch me not; for I am not yet ascended to my Father: but go to my brethren, and say unto them, I ascend unto my Father, and your Father; and *to* my God, and your God. ¹⁸ Mary Magdalene came and told the disciples that she had seen the Lord, and that he had spoken these things unto her. ⁽John 20⁾

(MATTHEW 28:1–4; MARK 16:1–4;
JOHN 20:1–18; LUKE 24:1–3, 12)

The Other Women at the Sepulchre

[During the time that Mary went to tell Peter and John, the other women stayed at the sepulchre.] ⁴ And it came to pass ⁽Luke 24⁾ *[upon their]* ⁵ entering into the sepulchre, ⁽Mark 16⁾ ⁴ as they were much perplexed thereabout, behold, two men stood by them in shining garments. ⁽Luke 24⁾ *[One of them was]* ⁵ a young man sitting on the right side, clothed in a long white garment; and they were

affrighted, (Mark 16) 5 and bowed down *their* faces to the earth. (Luke 24)

5 And the angel answered and said unto the women, Fear not: for I know that you seek Jesus (Matthew 28) 6 of Nazareth, (Mark 16) 5 which was crucified. (Matthew 28) 5 Why seek you the living among the dead? 6 He is not here, (Luke 24) 6 for he is risen, as he said. (Matthew 28) 6 Remember how he spoke unto you when he was yet in Galilee, 7 saying, The Son of man must be delivered into the hands of sinful men, and be crucified, and the third day rise again. (Luke 24)

6 Come, see the place where the Lord lay. (Matthew 28) 7 But go your way (Mark 16) 7 quickly, and (Matthew 28) 7 tell his disciples and Peter that (Mark 16) 7 he is risen from the dead; and, behold, he goes before you into Galilee; there shall you see him: (Matthew 28) 7 as he said unto you. (Mark 16) 7 Lo, I have told you. (Matthew 28) 8 And they remembered his words, (Luke 24) 8 and they went out quickly, and fled from the sepulchre; for they trembled and were amazed (Mark 16) 8 with fear and great joy; (Matthew 28) 8 neither said they any thing to any *man*; for they were afraid, (Mark 16) 8 and did run to bring his disciples word. (Matthew 28)

9 And as they went to tell his disciples, behold, Jesus met them, saying, All hail. And they came and held him by the feet, and worshipped him. 10 Then said Jesus unto them, Be not afraid: go tell my brethren that they go into Galilee, and there shall they see me. (Matthew 28)

11 Now when they were going, behold, some of the watch came into the city, and showed unto the chief priests all the things that were done. 12 And when they were assembled with the elders, and had taken counsel, they gave large money unto the soldiers, 13 saying, Say, His disciples came by night, and stole him *away* while we slept. 14 And if this come to the governor's ears, we will persuade him, and secure you. 15 So they took the money, and did as they were taught: and this saying is commonly reported among the Jews until this day. (Matthew 28)

9 And *[they]* returned from the sepulchre, and told all these things unto the eleven, and to all the rest. 10 It was Mary Magdalene, and Joanna, and Mary *the mother* of James, and other

women that were with them, which told these things unto the apostles. [11] And their words seemed to them as idle tales, and they believed them not. (Luke 24)

(LUKE 24:4–11; MATTHEW 28:5–15; MARK 16:5–8)

Jesus Meets Two Disciples on the Road to Emmaus

[13] AND, behold, two of them went that same day to a village called Emmaus, which was from Jerusalem *about* threescore furlongs. [14] And they talked together of all these things which had happened. [15] And it came to pass, that, while they communed *together* and reasoned, Jesus himself drew near, and went with them. [16] But their eyes were kept that they should not know him. (Luke 24)

[17] And he said unto them, What manner of communications *are* these that you have one to another, as you walk, and are sad? [18] And the one of them, whose name was Cleopas, answering said unto him, Are you only a stranger in Jerusalem, and have not known the things which are come to pass there in these days? [19] And he said unto them, What things? And they said unto him, Concerning Jesus of Nazareth, which was a prophet mighty in deed and word before God and all the people: [20] and how the chief priests and our rulers delivered him to be condemned to death, and have crucified him. (Luke 24)

[21] But we trusted that it had been he which should have redeemed Israel: and beside all this, to day is the third day since these things were done. [22] Yea, and certain women also of our company made us astonished, which were early at the sepulchre; [23] and when they found not his body, they came, saying, that they had also seen a vision of angels, which said that he was alive. [24] And certain of them which were with us went to the sepulchre, and found *it* even so as the women had said: but him they saw not. (Luke 24)

[25] Then he said unto them, O fools, and slow of heart to believe all that the prophets have spoken: [26] ought not Christ to have

suffered these things, and to enter into his glory? ²⁷ And beginning at Moses and all the prophets, he expounded unto them in all the scriptures the things concerning himself. (Luke 24)

²⁸ And they drew nigh unto the village, whither they went: and he made as though he would have gone further. ²⁹ But they constrained him, saying, Abide with us: for it is toward evening, and the day is far spent. And he went in to tarry with them. (Luke 24)

³⁰ And it came to pass, as he sat at meat with them, he took bread, and blessed *it,* and broke, and gave to them. ³¹ And their eyes were opened, and they knew him; and he vanished out of their sight. ³² And they said one to another, Did not our heart burn within us, while he talked with us by the way, and while he opened to us the scriptures? (Luke 24)

³³ And they rose up the same hour, and returned to Jerusalem, and found the eleven gathered together, and them that were with them, ³⁴ saying, The Lord is risen indeed, and has appeared to Simon. ³⁵ And they told what things *were done* in the way, and how he was known of them in breaking of bread. (Luke 24)

(LUKE 24:13–35)

Jesus Appears in the Midst of the Disciples

³⁶ AND as they thus spoke, (Luke 24) ¹⁹ the same day at evening, being the first *day* of the week, when the doors were shut where the disciples were assembled for fear of the Jews, (John 20) ³⁶ Jesus himself stood in the midst of them, and said unto them, Peace *be* unto you. ³⁷ But they were terrified and affrighted, and supposed that they had seen a spirit. (Luke 24)

³⁸ And he said unto them, Why are you troubled? And why do thoughts arise in your hearts? ³⁹ Behold my hands and my feet, that it is I myself: handle me, and see; for a spirit has not flesh and bones, as you see me have. ⁴⁰ And when he had thus spoken, he showed them *his* hands and *his* feet (Luke 24) ²⁰ and his side. Then were the disciples glad, when they saw the Lord. (John 20) ⁴¹ And

while they yet believed not for joy, and wondered, he said unto them, Have you here any meat? (Luke 24)

42 And they gave him a piece of a broiled fish, and of an honeycomb. 43 And he took *it,* and did eat before them. 44 And he said unto them, These *are* the words which I spoke unto you, while I was yet with you, that all things must be fulfilled, which were written in the law of Moses, and *in* the prophets, and *in* the psalms, concerning me. (Luke 24)

45 Then opened he their understanding, that they might understand the scriptures, 46 and said unto them, Thus it is written, and thus it behooved Christ to suffer, and to rise from the dead the third day: 47 and that repentance and remission of sins should be preached in his name among all nations, beginning at Jerusalem. 48 And you are witnesses of these things. (Luke 24)

49 And, behold, I send the promise of my Father upon you: but tarry you in the city of Jerusalem, until you be endued with power from on high. (Luke 24)

21 Then said Jesus to them again, Peace *be* unto you: as *my* Father has sent me, even so send I you. 22 And when he had said this, he breathed on *them,* and said unto them, Receive the Holy Ghost: 23 whose soever sins you remit, they are remitted unto them; *and* whose soever *sins* you retain, they are retained. (John 20)

24 But Thomas, one of the twelve, called Didymus, was not with them when Jesus came. 25 The other disciples therefore said unto him, We have seen the Lord. But he said unto them, Except I shall see in his hands the print of the nails, and put my finger into the print of the nails, and thrust my hand into his side, I will not believe. (John 20)

(LUKE 24:36–49; JOHN 20:19–25)

Jesus Appears to Thomas and at the Sea of Tiberias

26 AND after eight days again his disciples were within, and Thomas with them: *then* came Jesus, the doors being shut, and stood in

the midst, and said, Peace *be* unto you. [27] Then said he to Thomas, Reach hither your finger, and behold my hands; and reach hither your hand, and thrust *it* into my side: and be not faithless, but believing. [28] And Thomas answered and said unto him, My Lord and my God. [29] Jesus said unto him, Thomas, because you have seen me, you have believed: blessed *are* they that have not seen, and *yet* have believed. (John 20)

[1] After these things Jesus showed himself again to the disciples at the sea of Tiberias; and on this wise showed he *himself*. [2] There were together Simon Peter, and Thomas called Didymus, and Nathanael of Cana in Galilee, and the *sons* of Zebedee, and two other of his disciples. [3] Simon Peter said unto them, I go a-fishing. They say unto him, We also go with you. They went forth, and entered into a ship immediately; and that night they caught nothing. (John 21)

[4] But when the morning was now come, Jesus stood on the shore: but the disciples knew not that it was Jesus. [5] Then Jesus said unto them, Children, have you any meat? They answered him, No. [6] And he said unto them, Cast the net on the right side of the ship, and you shall find. They cast therefore, and now they were not able to draw it for the multitude of fishes. [7] Therefore that disciple whom Jesus loved said unto Peter, It is the Lord. Now when Simon Peter heard that it was the Lord, he girt *his* fisher's coat *unto him*, (for he was naked,) and did cast himself into the sea. (John 21)

[8] And the other disciples came in a little ship; (for they were not far from land, but as it were two hundred cubits,) dragging the net with fishes. [9] As soon then as they were come to land, they saw a fire of coals there, and fish laid thereon, and bread. [10] Jesus said unto them, Bring of the fish which you have now caught. [11] Simon Peter went up, and drew the net to land full of great fishes, an hundred and fifty and three: and for all there were so many, yet was not the net broken. (John 21)

[12] Jesus said unto them, Come *and* dine. And none of the disciples dared ask him, Who are you? Knowing that it was the Lord.

¹³ Jesus then came, and took bread, and gave them, and fish likewise. ¹⁴ This is now the third time that Jesus showed himself to his disciples, after that he was risen from the dead. ¹⁵ So when they had dined, Jesus said to Simon Peter, Simon, *son* of Jonas, love you me more than these? He said unto him, Yea, Lord; you know that I love you. He said unto him, Feed my lambs. ^(John 21)

¹⁶ He said to him again the second time, Simon, *son* of Jonas, love you me? He said unto him, Yea, Lord; you know that I love you. He said unto him, Feed my sheep. ¹⁷ He said unto him the third time, Simon, *son* of Jonas, love you me? Peter was grieved because he said unto him the third time, Love you me? And he said unto him, Lord, you know all things; you know that I love you. Jesus said unto him, Feed my sheep. ^(John 21)

¹⁸ Verily, verily, I say unto you, when you were young, you girded yourself, and walked whither you would: but when you shall be old, you shall stretch forth your hands, and another shall gird you, and carry *you* whither you would not. ¹⁹ This spoke he, signifying by what death he should glorify God. And when he had spoken this, he said unto him, Follow me. ²⁰ Then Peter, turning about, saw the disciple whom Jesus loved following; which also leaned on his breast at supper, and said, Lord, which is he that betrays you? ^(John 21)

²¹ Peter seeing him said to Jesus, Lord, and what *shall* this man *do*? ²² Jesus said unto him, If I will that he tarry till I come, what *is that* to you? Follow me. ²³ Then went this saying abroad among the brethren, that that disciple should not die: yet Jesus said not unto him, He shall not die; but, If I will that he tarry till I come, what *is that* to you? ²⁴ This is the disciple which testified of these things, and wrote these things: and we know that his testimony is true. ^(John 21)

(JOHN 20:26–29; 21:1–24)

Go Therefore and Teach All Nations

¹⁶ THEN the eleven disciples went away into Galilee, into a mountain where Jesus had appointed them. ¹⁷ And when they saw him, they worshipped him: but some doubted. ¹⁸ And Jesus came and spoke unto them, saying, All power is given unto me in heaven and in earth. ¹⁹ Go therefore, and teach all nations, baptizing them in the name of the Father, and of the Son, and of the Holy Ghost: ²⁰ teaching them to observe all things whatsoever I have commanded you: and, lo, I am with you always, *even* unto the end of the world. Amen. (Matthew 28)

(MATTHEW 28:16–20)

Jesus Ascends

⁹ Now when *Jesus* was risen early the first *day* of the week, he appeared first to Mary Magdalene, out of whom he had cast seven devils. ¹⁰ *And* she went and told them that had been with him, as they mourned and wept. ¹¹ And they, when they had heard that he was alive, and had been seen of her, believed not. (Mark 16)

¹² After that he appeared in another form unto two of them, as they walked, and went into the country. ¹³ And they went and told *it* unto the residue: neither believed they them. ¹⁴ Afterward he appeared unto the eleven as they sat at meat, and upbraided them with their unbelief and hardness of heart, because they believed not them which had seen him after he was risen. (Mark 16)

¹⁵ And he said unto them, Go into all the world, and preach the gospel to every creature. ¹⁶ He that believes and is baptized shall be saved; but he that believes not shall be damned. ¹⁷ And these signs shall follow them that believe; in my name shall they cast out devils; they shall speak with new tongues; ¹⁸ they shall take up serpents; and if they drink any deadly thing, it shall not hurt them; they shall lay hands on the sick, and they shall recover. (Mark 16)

⁵⁰ And he led them out as far as to Bethany, and he lifted up his

hands, and blessed them. [51] And it came to pass, while he blessed them, he was parted from them, and carried up into heaven. [52] And they worshipped him, and returned to Jerusalem with great joy: [53] and were continually in the temple, praising and blessing God. Amen. (Luke 24)

[19] So then after the Lord had spoken unto them, he was received up into heaven, and sat on the right hand of God. [20] And they went forth, and preached every where, the Lord working with *them,* and confirming the word with signs following. Amen. (Mark 16)

[30] And many other signs truly did Jesus in the presence of his disciples. (John 20) [25] And there are also many other things which Jesus did, (John 21) [30] which are not written in this book. (John 20) [25] If they should be written every one, I suppose that even the world itself could not contain the books that should be written. (John 21) [31] But these are written, that you might believe that Jesus is the Christ, the Son of God; and that believing you might have life through his name. (John 20) [25] Amen. (John 21)

(MARK 16:9–20; LUKE 24:50–53; JOHN 20:30–31; 21:25)

Epilogue

[1] THE former treatise have I made, O Theophilus *[you who love God]*, of all that Jesus began both to do and teach, [2] until the day in which he was taken up, after that he through the Holy Ghost had given commandments unto the apostles whom he had chosen: [3] to whom also he showed himself alive after his passion by many infallible proofs, being seen of them forty days, and speaking of the things pertaining to the kingdom of God. (Acts 1)

[4] And, being assembled together with *them,* commanded them that they should not depart from Jerusalem, but wait for the promise of the Father, which, *said he,* you have heard of me. [5] For John truly baptized with water; but you shall be baptized with the Holy Ghost not many days hence. (Acts 1)

[6] When they therefore were come together, they asked of him,

saying, Lord, will you at this time restore again the kingdom to Israel? ⁷ And he said unto them, It is not for you to know the times or the seasons, which the Father has put in his own power. ⁸ But you shall receive power, after that the Holy Ghost is come upon you: and you shall be witnesses unto me both in Jerusalem, and in all Judaea, and in Samaria, and unto the uttermost part of the earth. ^(Acts 1)

⁹ And when he had spoken these things, while they beheld, he was taken up; and a cloud received him out of their sight. ¹⁰ And while they looked stedfastly toward heaven as he went up, behold, two men stood by them in white apparel; ¹¹ which also said, You men of Galilee, why stand you gazing up into heaven? This same Jesus, which is taken up from you into heaven, shall so come in like manner as you have seen him go into heaven. ^(Acts 1)

(ACTS 1:1–11)

TO YOU WHO DO NOT KNOW THE LORD

Salvation from sin is the greatest gift a person can receive from the Lord!

"For God so loved the world, that he gave his only begotten Son, that whosoever believes in him should not perish, but have everlasting life." (John 3:16)

Jesus Christ is a Person. He is God. He died for you. He shed His blood for your sins. He created you and He came to give meaning to your life.

No matter how hard a person tries to achieve something in life, the life of a person as a whole can never fulfill its appointed purpose without knowledge of the Creator. He is the one that gave us our lives.

Every person is born in sin. Sin is not only an action that is contrary to given moral standards. Sin is first and foremost a condition in which a person does not know the Creator, and thus is not functioning in the purpose for which he or she was created. The Lord has a plan for each person's life and everybody that strays from that plan, and walks in his or her own ways instead, is missing the purpose for which he or she has been created. This is sin: to miss God's will and purpose for your life and walk in your own ways, ignoring your Maker.

Jesus Christ is not a religion! He is not about belonging to a church; He is not a doctrine, creed or tradition! **He is a Person!** He loves you and wants to communicate with you. He longs for your communication.

Surrender your life to Him! There is no other name given to us under Heaven, through which a person can find eternal salvation, satisfaction and purpose in life. The heart of every person longs for Him, whether they realize it or not. There is no substitute that can fill that void—no glory, no power, no riches, no achievements or successes—only the Person of Jesus Christ, Who gave His life, so you can have life. The rightful and deserving punishment for our sins is eternal death, but Jesus came to give eternal life to all who will choose to believe in Him.

All you have to do is to invite Him to come in your life and He will do it. This will be the greatest and most important decision you will ever have to make in life. Jesus will come and enter in your heart. That is why, with your own words from your heart, please pray a prayer similar to the following:

> "Lord, please come into my heart. I repent for my sins and ask You to forgive me, that I have not sought You up until now. I want to live for You. I want to accomplish Your will and purpose in my life. I want to serve You. Please come, Lord Jesus! I believe with my heart that You came to this earth, died on the cross for my sins, and were raised from the dead on the third day. Thank You for Your love towards me. Amen!"

If this prayer has come from your heart with faith, you have just become a member of God's family, consisting of millions of believers all over the world. Please contact us to let us know of your decision, so we can further help you in your walk with God through advice or counsel, through prayer, through literature, and all else we can do to help. Please feel free to contact Nikola at nikolahelen@gmail.com. Thank you in advance!

APPENDIX I

*Family Lineage of Jesus Christ According to
the Gospels of Matthew and Luke*

The generations of Jesus Christ are given both in Matthew and in Luke. Both lines come through King David, but through two different sons. The generations given in Matthew are through David's son Solomon up to Jacob, the father of Joseph, who became the husband of the Virgin Mary, who supernaturally conceived. The generations given in Luke are through David's son Nathan (2 Samuel 5:14) up to Heli, the father of the Virgin Mary. Please note that Luke 3:23 identifies Joseph as "the son" of Heli. Mary is indeed the daughter of Heli, but since women are not typically mentioned in Hebrew genealogies, Joseph is in the genealogy as his son.

Generations of Jesus Christ According to Matthew

¹ THE book of the generation of Jesus Christ, the son of David, the son of Abraham. ² Abraham begat Isaac; and Isaac begat Jacob; and Jacob begat Judas and his brethren; ³ And Judas begat Phares and Zara of Thamar; and Phares begat Esrom; and Esrom begat Aram; ⁴ And Aram begat Aminanab; and Aminadab begat Naasson; and Naasson begat Salmon. ⁽Matthew 1⁾

⁵ And Salmon begat Booz of Rachab; and Booz begat Obed of Ruth; and Obed begat Jesse; ⁶ And Jesse begat David the king; and David the king begat Solomon of her *that had been the wife* of Urias; ⁷ And Solomon begat Roboam; and Roboam begat Abia; and Abia begat Asa; ⁸ And Asa begat Josaphat; and Josaphat begat Joram; and Joram begat Ozias; ⁹ And Ozias begat Joatham; and Joatham begat Achaz; and Achaz begat Ezekias. ⁽Matthew 1⁾

¹⁰ And Ezekias begat Manasses; and Manasses begat Amon; and Amon begat Josias; ¹¹ And Josias begat Jechonias and his brethren,

about the time they were carried away to Babylon: [12] And after they were brought to Babylon, Jechonias begat Salathiel; and Salathiel begat Zorobabel; [13] And Zorobabel begat Abiud; and Abiud begat Eliakim; and Eliakim begat Azor; [14] And Azor begat Sadoc; and Sadoc begat Achim; and Achim begat Eliud; [15] And Eliud begat Eleazar; and Eleazar begat Matthan; and Matthan begat Jacob. (Matthew 1)

[16] And Jacob begat Joseph the husband of Mary, of whom was born Jesus, who is called Christ. [17] So all the generations from Abraham to David *are* fourteen generations; and from David until the carrying away into Babylon *are* fourteen generations; and from the carrying away into Babylon unto Christ *are* fourteen generations. (Matthew 1)

(MATTHEW 1:1–17)

Generations of Jesus Christ according to Luke

[23] AND Jesus himself began to be about thirty years of age, being (as was supposed) the son of Joseph, which was *the son* of Heli, [24] Which was *the son* of Matthat, which was *the son* of Levi, which was *the son* of Melchi, which was *the son* of Janna, which was *the son* of Joseph, [25] Which was *the son* of Mattathias, which was *the son* of Amos, which was *the son* of Naum, which was *the son* of Esli, which was *the son* of Nagge, [26] Which was *the son* of Maath, which was *the son* of Mattathias, which was *the son* of Semei, which was *the son* of Joseph, which was *the son* of Juda, (Luke 3)

[27] Which was *the son* of Joanna, which was *the son* of Rhesa, which was *the son* of Zorobabel, which was *the son* of Salathiel, which was *the son* of Neri, [28] Which was *the son* of Melchi, which was *the son* of Addi, which was *the son* of Cosam, which was *the son* of Elmodam, which was *the son* of Er, [29] Which was *the son* of Jose, which was *the son* of Eliezer, which was *the son* of Jorim, which was *the son* of Matthat, which was *the son* of Levi, (Luke 3)

³⁰ Which was *the son* of Simeon, which was *the son* of Juda, which was *the son* of Joseph, which was *the son* of Jonan, which was *the son* of Eliakim, ³¹ Which was *the son* of Melea, which was *the son* of Menan, which was *the son* of Mattatha, which was *the son* of Nathan, which was *the son* of David, (Luke 3)

³² Which was *the son* of Jesse, which was *the son* of Obed, which was *the son* of Booz, which was *the son* of Salmon, which was *the son* of Naasson, ³³ Which was *the son* of Aminadab, which was *the son* of Aram, which was *the son* of Esrom, which was *the son* of Phares, which was *the son* of Juda, (Luke 3)

³⁴ Which was *the son* of Jacob, which was *the son* of Isaac, which was *the son* of Abraham, which was *the son* of Thara, which was *the son* of Nachor, ³⁵ Which was *the son* of Saruch, which was *the son* of Ragau, which was *the son* of Phalec, which was *the son* of Heber, which was *the son* of Sala, ³⁶ Which was *the son* of Cainan, which was *the son* of Arphaxad, which was *the son* of Sem, which was *the son* of Noe, which was *the son* of Lamech, (Luke 3)

³⁷ Which was *the son* of Mathusala, which was *the son* of Enoch, which was *the son* of Jared, which was *the son* of Maleleel, which was *the son* of Cainan, ³⁸ Which was *the son* of Enos, which was *the son* of Seth, which was *the son* of Adam, which was *the son* of God. (Luke 3)

(LUKE 3:23–38)

APPENDIX II

General Explanations

The Chronology. I have done my best to place all events in proper chronological order, checking numerous sources for Biblical chronology, such as theological works, debates, chronological tables, and other works that have attempted a similar study. Those include Matthew Henry's Tabular Harmony of the Gospels, the International Standard Bible Encyclopedia, The Interlinear Bible, Strong's Concordance, Dake's Annotated Reference Bible, e-Sword Bible software, Charles Templeton's New Testament in Modern Speech, Aaron Bible University Chronological Bible, The Bulgarian Orthodox Bible's Chronological Charts, and several other available sources. As previously mentioned, please note that this is not intended to be a substitute for the four Gospels, nor is it a theological work, but rather it is meant to be an accessible key to understanding the four Biblical perspectives of Matthew, Mark, Luke, and John.

The Methodology. An understanding of the methodology used to compile this work will assist the reader in recognizing and receiving the full potential of this material.

The Gospel of Mark has been used as the base Gospel because of its systematic structure and chronological order. In general, the Gospel of Mark is in chronological order; however, there are some exceptions. For example, in order for the context of a story not to be broken, it is finished, then an out-of-order verse may follow, saying something that has happened before that story. Conversely, there may be a collective or summary verse saying that a story or event has happened, and then there may be a whole chapter or more explaining in detail how exactly the story or event happened. Thus we see that the Gospel of Mark is not wholly chronological.

One example in Mark of placing the collective or summary verse after the story is Mark 15:25. Mark 15:25 surely must have happened BEFORE Mark 15:24, and not after it. This is because Mark 15:24 says that, **when they had crucified him,** the soldiers parted Jesus' garments, casting lots upon them. Mark 15:25 says that it was the third hour and **they crucified him.** Logically, deductive reasoning suggests that the events of Mark 15:25 happened before Mark 15:24:

> **Mark 15:25** And it was the third hour, and they crucified him.
>
> **Mark 15:24** And when they had crucified him, they parted his garments, casting lots upon them, what every man should take.

An example of placing the collective or summary verse first, in *The Four in One Gospel of Jesus,* and then explaining it in detail is Luke 4:14. Here we see Jesus, after the temptation in the wilderness, come to Galilee and start His preaching, teaching, healing, and deliverance ministry. Yet, events that transpired between His coming out of the wilderness and the beginning of His ministry are explained in detail in John 1:9 through John 3:36. So, Luke 4:14 is a collective or summary verse, describing in one sentence what is being explained in almost three chapters: Jesus' coming to Galilee to start His ministry:

> **Luke 4:14** And Jesus returned in the power of the Spirit into Galilee: and there went out a fame of him through all the region round about.
>
> **John 1:9–John 3:36** (Not presented here due to its length.)

There are many other examples of collective or summary verses, especially in Matthew. Instead of giving complete details concerning an event or a story, Matthew compiled historical Biblical events through deductive reasoning with little regard for chronology.

In some places, a Gospel is repetitive. This is no mistake. One such example is Matthew 12:22–24 and Matthew 9:32–34:

> **Matthew 12:22–24** Then was brought unto him one pos-

sessed with a devil, blind, and dumb: and he healed him, insomuch that the blind and dumb both spoke and saw. And all the people were amazed, and said, Is not this the son of David? But when the Pharisees heard *it,* they said, This *fellow* does not cast out devils, but by Beelzebub the prince of the devils.

Matthew 9:32–34 As they went out, behold, they brought to him a dumb man possessed with a devil. And when the devil was cast out, the dumb spoke: and the multitudes marvelled, saying, It was never so seen in Israel. But the Pharisees said, He casts out devils through the prince of the devils.

The same story may appear repeatedly even in the same Gospel. Although it may appear to be the same story and the Pharisees speak similar words, there may in fact be more than one story with the Pharisees speaking nearly identical words. This is no mistake. Jesus did so many things and healed so many people, many of whom with comparable if not identical problems, that repetition is not only common, but inevitable. Matthew 16:19 and Matthew 18:18 provide another example of the use of similar words:

Matthew 16:19 And I will give unto you the keys of the kingdom of heaven: and whatsoever you shall bind on earth shall be bound in heaven: and whatsoever you shall loose on earth shall be loosed in heaven.

Matthew 18:18 Verily I say unto you, Whatsoever you shall bind on earth shall be bound in heaven: and whatsoever you shall loose on earth shall be loosed in heaven.

There are also cases where a story is told in two, three, or even four of the Gospels. The story may seem identical, but we cannot be sure if it is, or if there are several similar stories. For example, Jesus shares two stories of a person who invites guests who decline the invitation for various reasons. The stories are told in Luke 14:16–24 and Matthew 22:1–8:

Luke 14:16–24 Then said he unto him, A certain man made a great supper, and bade many: And sent his servant at supper time to say to them that were bidden, Come; for all things are now ready. And they all with one *consent* began to make excuse. The first said unto him, I have bought a piece of ground, and I must needs go and see it: I pray you have me excused. And another said, I have bought five yoke of oxen, and I go to prove them: I pray you have me excused. And another said, I have married a wife, and therefore I cannot come. So that servant came, and showed his lord these things. Then the master of the house being angry said to his servant, Go out quickly into the streets and lanes of the city, and bring in hither the poor, and the maimed, and the halt, and the blind. And the servant said, Lord, it is done as you have commanded, and yet there is room. And the lord said unto the servant, Go out into the highways and hedges, and compel *them* to come in, that my house may be filled. For I say unto you, That none of those men which were bidden shall taste of my supper.

Matthew 22:1–8 And Jesus answered and spoke unto them again by parables, and said, The kingdom of heaven is like unto a certain king, which made a marriage for his son, And sent forth his servants to call them that were bidden to the wedding: and they would not come. Again, he sent forth other servants, saying, Tell them which are bidden, Behold, I have prepared my dinner: my oxen and *my* fatlings *are* killed, and all things *are* ready: come unto the marriage. But they made light of *it,* and went their ways, one to his farm, another to his merchandise: And the remnant took his servants, and entreated *them* spitefully, and slew *them.* But when the king heard *thereof,* he was wroth: and he sent forth his armies, and destroyed those murderers, and burned up their city. Then said he to his servants, The wedding is ready, but they which were bidden were not worthy.

The stories seem identical at first glance, but they are not. They are told in different settings and in different times. A similar example is Matthew 25:14–30 and Luke 19:11–28, two conceptually related but different stories.

The story of when the women see the angels and Jesus after the Resurrection differs in the different sources. I have chosen to go with Matthew Henry's Tabular Harmony and the Orthodox Bible on this, as follows:

1. Early in the morning Mary Magdalene visits the tomb with some other women. They enter in and see that the body of Jesus is not there.

2. Mary Magdalene runs to tell Peter and John, while the other women remain at the tomb and experience the two angels, who tell them Jesus has risen, so they are to go and tell the disciples. The women leave the tomb and on their way to the disciples they see Jesus. Mary Magdalene couldn't have been with them, because when she goes to Peter and John, she tells them somebody has taken the Lord and she has no idea where they put Him. Moreover, when she sees Jesus, before recognizing Him, she thinks He is the gardener. So, at that point, she couldn't have seen the angels the other women saw, or she would know Jesus had risen. *[handwritten: two women see]*

3. When the other women leave the tomb, Mary Magdalene arrives with Peter and John. They both see the tomb empty and return home, while Mary stays and sees Jesus. She then goes to the disciples too and along with the other women, they tell the disciples. *[handwritten: Mary M. sees.]*

The Translation. We have seriously weighed making changes to the venerated King James text. We hope those who love and admire the original will understand our evangelical intent to reach a new crowd of modern readers. We especially desire to reach young people who may have no previous relationship with the Bible or the church. *[handwritten: but not disciples (they see an angel]*

We have simplified archaic Early Modern English word forms to contemporary usage for easier readability. These changes include verbs with "est" and "eth" endings, and "thee" and "thou" pronouns, for example. In this, The changes we have made do not include any innovation to the King James original Greek or English, usage or syntax, other than to modernize certain Early Modern English words, now long out of ordinary use.

APPENDIX III

Identical Scriptures

What follows is a list of the identical, similar, or contextually close
Bible verses, by chapter:

Chapter Three

> Matthew 3:6 and part of Mark 1:5
> Matthew 3:8 and Luke 3:8
> Mark 1:8 and Matthew 3:11
> Luke 3:9 and Matthew 3:10
> Luke 3:17 and Matthew 3:12
> Mark 1:10 and Matthew 3:16
> Matthew 3:17, with parts of Mark 1:11 and Luke 3:22
> Matthew 4:10 and Luke 4:8

Chapter Five

> Mark 1:16 and Matthew 4:18
> Mark 1:24 and Luke 4:34
> Mark 1:25 and Luke 4:35
> Matthew 8:14, with parts of Mark 1:29, 30 and Luke 4:38
> Mark 1:34, Luke 4:41, and Matthew 8:16
> Luke 4:44, with parts of Matthew 4:23 and Mark 1:39
> Luke 5:13 and Mark 1:41–42
> Matthew 9:7, with parts of Mark 2:12 and Luke 5:25
> Matthew 8:3 and Mark 1:41–42
> Matthew 4:20 and Mark 1:18
> Luke 4:37 and Mark 1:28
> Luke 5:14 and Mark 1:43–44
> Luke 5:20 and Matthew 9:2
> Luke 5:23 and Mark 2:9
> Luke 4:44 and Matthew 4:23

Chapter Six

Mark 2:17 and Matthew 9:12–13
Luke 5:35 and Mark 2:20
Luke 5:38, with parts of Matthew 9:17 and Mark 2:22
Matthew 12:16 and Mark 3:12
Matthew 9:14 and Mark 2:18
Matthew 12:3 and Mark 2:25
Luke 6:5 and Mark 2:27–28
Mark 3:3 and Luke 6:8

Chapter Seven

Mark 3:18 and Matthew 10:2–4
Luke 6:28 and Matthew 5:44

An interesting chronology issue appears in this chapter. The events from Luke 6:17–19 seem to be the same as Matthew 12:15 and Mark 3:7–8 from chapter 6:

Luke 6:17–19 And he came down with them, and stood in the plain, and the company of his disciples, and a great multitude of people out of all Judaea and Jerusalem, and from the sea coast of Tyre and Sidon, which came to hear him, and to be healed of their diseases; And they that were vexed with unclean spirits: and they were healed. And the whole multitude sought to touch him: for there went virtue out of him, and healed *them* all.

Matthew 12:15 But when Jesus knew *it,* he withdrew himself from thence: and great multitudes followed him, and he healed them all;

Mark 3:7–8 But Jesus withdrew himself with his disciples to the sea: and a great multitude from Galilee followed him, and from Judaea, And from Jerusalem, and from Idumaea, and *from* beyond Jordan; and they about Tyre and Sidon, a great multitude, when they had heard what great things he did, came unto him.

We must be very careful though, because there are several words that seem to show us the right order of events. It goes like this: Jesus withdraws to **the sea** (Mark 3:7), and great multitudes gather while He is there. Then, He **goes up** into a mountain to pray (Luke 6:12 and Mark 3:13) and the result is that He chooses twelve apostles to whom He gives power and authority.

> **Luke 6:12** And it came to pass in those days, that he went out into a mountain to pray, and continued all night in prayer to God.
> **Mark 3:13** And he went up into a mountain, and called *unto him* whom he would: and they came unto him.

Then He **comes down** with them and abides **in the plain** for a time (Luke 6:17). And seeing the multitudes, He **goes up** into a mountain again (Matthew 5:1) and then He delivers His Sermon on the Mount (Matthew 5 through 7).

> **Matthew 5:1** And seeing the multitudes, he went up into a mountain: and when he was set, his disciples came unto him:

Chapter Eight

Matthew 11:9 and Luke 7:26
Luke 7:27 and Matthew 11:10
Matthew 7:4–5 and Luke 6:42
Luke 6:31 and Matthew 7:12
Matthew 8:5 and Luke 7:1, 3
Matthew 8:9 and Luke 7:8
Matthew 11:4–6 and Luke 7:22–23
Matthew 11:17–19 and Luke 7:32–35

Chapter Nine

Mark 3:33 and Matthew 12:48
Matthew 12:41 and Luke 11:32
Luke 11:15 and Mark 3:22

Matthew 12:29 and Mark 3:27
Matthew 12:43 and Luke 11:24
Luke 11:25 and Matthew 12:44
Luke 11:26 and Matthew 12:45

Chapter Ten

Matthew 13:4 and Mark 4:4
Matthew 13:6 and Mark 4:6
Matthew 19:9, Mark 4:9, and Luke 8:8
Luke 8:10, and Matthew 13:11, 13
Mark 4:16 and Matthew 13:20
Mark 4:18 and Matthew 13:22
Mark 4:22 and Luke 8:17
Luke 13:21 and Matthew 13:33

Chapter Eleven

Matthew 13:58 and Mark 6:5–6
Matthew 13:57 and Mark 6:3–4
Matthew 13:54 and Mark 6:1–2
Luke 8:49 and Mark 5:35
Luke 8:54 and Mark 5:40–41
Matthew 9:25 and Mark 5:40–42
Matthew 13:53 and the context of Mark 6:1

Chapter Twelve

Luke 9:4 and Mark 6:10
Mark 6:15 and Luke 9:8
Matthew 14:4 and Mark 6:18
Matthew 14:11 and Mark 6:28
Matthew 14:13, with parts of Luke 9:10 and Mark 6:32–33
Matthew 14:14, Mark 6:34, and Luke 9:11
Matthew 14:17 and Luke 9:13
Matthew 14:19 and Mark 6:39–41

Matthew 14:20 and Mark 6:39–41
Matthew 14:20, Mark 6:42–43, and John 6:13

Chapter Thirteen

Mark 6:46 and Matthew 14:23
John 6:20 and Mark 6:50
Matthew 14:34 and Mark 6:53
Matthew 15:7 and Mark 7:6
Mark 7:7 and Matthew 15:9
Matthew 15:5 and Mark 7:11

Chapter Fourteen

Mark 8:16 and Matthew 16:7
Matthew 16:15 and Mark 8:29
Mark 8:8 and Matthew 15:37
Matthew 16:9–10 and Mark 8:17–20
Luke 9:22 and Mark 8:31
Matthew 16:24 and Luke 9:23
Luke 9:24 and Mark 8:35
Matthew 16:26 and Mark 8:36–37

Chapter Fifteen

Mark 9:7 and Luke 9:34–35
Mark 9:11 and Matthew 17:10
Matthew 17:19 and Mark 9:28
Mark 9:29 and Matthew 17:21
Mark 9:32 and Luke 9:45
Matthew 10:1, Luke 9:46, and the context of Mark 9:33–34
Mark 9:45–46 and the context of Matthew 18:8

Chapter Seventeen

Luke 10:14–15 and Matthew 11:22–23
Matthew 11:25–27, with part of Luke 10:21–22

Chapter Twenty-One

Mark 10:25 and Luke 18:25, with part of Matthew 19:24
Mark 10:9 and Matthew 19:6
Mark 10:6 and Matthew 19:4
Mark 10:8 and Matthew 19:5–6
Matthew 19:14 and Mark 10:14
Luke 18:19 and Mark 10:18
Luke 18:21 and Matthew 19:20
Luke 18:28 and Mark 10:28
Matthew 19:26 and Mark 10:27
Luke 18:26 and Matthew 19:25

Chapter Twenty-Two

Matthew 20:28 and Mark 10:45
Luke 18:38 and Mark 10:47
John 12:14, Luke 19:35, and the context of Matthew 21:7 and
    Mark 11:7

Chapter 22 contains the story of blind Bartimaeus (Mark 10:46–52; Luke 18:35–43). Both Mark and Luke say that there was only one blind man, named Bartimaeus. Matthew 20:29–34 shares the story of two blind men. The story is almost identical in that it happens in the same location, near Jericho, but since Matthew does not specifically mention that one of these blind men was Bartimaeus, we reference this story as a separate one:

Matthew 20:29–34 And as they departed from Jericho, a great multitude followed him. And, behold, two blind men sitting by the way side, when they heard that Jesus passed by, cried out, saying, Have mercy on us, O Lord, *you* son of David. And the multitude rebuked them, because they should hold their peace: but they cried the more, saying, Have mercy on us, O Lord, *you* son of David. And Jesus stood still, and called them, and said, What will you that I shall do unto you? They say unto him, Lord, that our eyes may be opened.

So Jesus had compassion *on them,* and touched their eyes: and immediately their eyes received sight, and they followed him.

Chapter Twenty-Three

Luke 19:36, Matthew 21:8, and Mark 11:8
Luke 19:45 and Matthew 21:12
Matthew 21:13, Luke 19:46, and Mark 11:17
Matthew 21:22 and Mark 11:24

Chapter Twenty-Four

Luke 20:32 and Matthew 22:27
Matthew 22:20 and Mark 12:16
Luke 20:3 and Mark 11:29
Luke 20:5 and Mark 11:31
Matthew 21:27, Luke 20:8, and Mark 11:33
Matthew 21:35–36, Mark 12:2–5, and Luke 20:10–12
Matthew 21:37 and Mark 12:6
Luke 20:15 and Mark 12:8
Luke 20:18 and Matthew 21:44
Matthew 22:30–31 and Mark 12:25–26
Luke 20:33 and Mark 12:23
Matthew 22:29 and Mark 12:24
Luke 20:37 and Mark 12:26
Matthew 22:43–45, Luke 20:42–43, and Mark 12:37
Mark 12:9–11 and Matthew 21:40–42
Luke 20:25 and Matthew 22:21
Matthew 22:26 and Luke 20:31
Luke 20:44 and Mark 12:37
Luke 20:45 and Matthew 23:1
Mark 12:39 and Matthew 23:6
Mark 12:40 and Luke 20:47

Chapter Twenty-Five

Matthew 24:35, Mark 13:31, and Luke 21:33
Luke 21:2–3 and Mark 12:42–43
Matthew 24:4 and Mark 13:5
Luke 21:17 and Matthew 24:9
Mark 13:13 and Matthew 24:9, 13
Mark 13:18 and Matthew 24:20
Matthew 24:16–19 and Mark 13:14–17
Matthew 24:23 and Mark 13:21
Matthew 24:25 and Mark 13:23
Matthew 24:32 and Mark 13:28
Mark 14:1–2, Luke 22:1, and Matthew 26:3–5
Luke 12:39 and Matthew 24:43
Luke 12:40 and Matthew 24:44
Luke 12:43 and Matthew 24:46

Chapter Twenty-Six

Mark 14:4 and Matthew 26:8
Matthew 26:11 and Mark 14:7
Matthew 26:13 and Mark 14:9
Matthew 26:14, Mark 14:10, and Luke 22:3–4
Luke 22:12–13 and Mark 14:15–16
Matthew 26:21, Mark 14:18, and John 13:21
Matthew 26:24 and Mark 14:21
Matthew 26:34, Luke 22:34, and Mark 14:30

Chapter Twenty-Seven

Matthew 26:30 and Mark 14:26

Chapter Twenty-Eight

Mark 14:34 and Matthew 26:38
Matthew 26:43 and Mark 14:40
Matthew 26:46 and Mark 14:42

Mark 14:46 and Matthew 26:50
Luke 22:50, Matthew 26:51, and John 18:10
Mark 14:48 and Matthew 26:55
Mark 14:50 and Matthew 26:56
Matthew 26:74, Mark 14:71, and Luke 22:60
Matthew 26:66 and Mark 14:64

Chapter Twenty-Nine

Mark 15:2 and Matthew 27:11
Matthew 27:18 and Mark 15:10
Mark 15:13 and Matthew 27:22
Mark 15:17 and Matthew 27:28–29
John 19:2 and Matthew 27:28–29
John 19:16, Matthew 27:26, and Luke 23:25

Chapter Thirty

Matthew 27:33 and Mark 15:22
Luke 23:38, John 19:19–20, and Mark 15:26
Matthew 27:38 and Mark 15:27
Matthew 27:45, Luke 23:44, and Mark 15:33
Matthew 27:46 and Mark 15:34
Mark 15:37, Matthew 27:50, Luke 23:46, and John 19:30
Mark 15:38 and Matthew 27:51

APPENDIX IV

Old Testament Prophecies
Fulfilled in the New Testament, by Chapter

Chapter 2

Isaiah 7:14 fulfilled in Matthew 1:23
Micah 5:2 fulfilled in Matthew 2:6
Hosea 11:1 fulfilled in Matthew 2:15
Jeremiah 31:15 fulfilled in Matthew 2:18

Chapter 3

Isaiah 40:3–5 and Malachi 3:1 fulfilled in Mark 1:2–3 and
　　Luke 3:4–6
Isaiah 40:3 fulfilled in John 1:23

Chapter 4

Psalm 69:9 fulfilled in John 2:17

Chapter 5

Isaiah 9:1–2 fulfilled in Matthew 4:15–16
Isaiah 53:4 fulfilled in Matthew 8:17
Isaiah 61:1–2 fulfilled in Luke 4:18–19

Chapter 6

Isaiah 42:1–4 fulfilled in Matthew 12:18 and Mark 4:12

Chapter 10

Isaiah 6:9–10 fulfilled in Matthew 13:14–15
Psalm 78:2 fulfilled in Matthew 13:35

Chapter 13

    Isaiah 54:13 fulfilled in John 6:45

    Isaiah 29:13 fulfilled in Matthew 15:8–9

Chapter 16

    Isaiah 11:1 and 10, Jeremiah 23:5, and Micah 5:1–2 fulfilled in John 7:42

Chapter 22

    Zechariah 9:9 fulfilled in Matthew 21:5 and John 12:15

Chapter 23

    Psalm 118:26 fulfilled in Matthew 21:9, Mark 11:9, Luke 19:38, and John 12:13

    Isaiah 56:7 fulfilled in Mark 11:17

    Psalm 8:2 fulfilled in Matthew 21:16

Chapter 24

    Psalm 118:22–23 fulfilled in Matthew 21:42 and Luke 20:17

    Psalm 110:1 fulfilled in Luke 20:42–43

Chapter 25

    Isaiah 53:1 fulfilled in John 12:38

    Isaiah 6:9–10 fulfilled in John 12:40

Chapter 26

    Psalm 41:9 fulfilled in John 13:18

    Zechariah 13:7 fulfilled in Matthew 26:31 and Mark 14:27

    Isaiah 53:12 fulfilled in Luke 22:37

Chapter 27

Psalm 35:19; 109:3; 119:161 fulfilled in John 15:25

Chapter 29

Zechariah 11:12–13 fulfilled in Matthew 27:9–10

Chapter 30

Psalm 22:18 fulfilled in Matthew 27:35, Mark 15:24, and John 19:24

Psalm 69:21 fulfilled in Matthew 27:34 and John 19:28

Psalm 34:20 fulfilled in John 19:36

Zechariah 12:10 fulfilled in John 19:37

Isaiah 53:12 fulfilled in Mark 15:28

Isaiah 53:4 fulfilled in Matthew 8:17

Psalm 22:8 fulfilled in Matthew 27:43

Psalm 22:1 fulfilled in Mark 15:34

APPENDIX V

Old Testament Prophecies
Fulfilled in the New Testament, by Gospel Book

Old Testament Reference	Fulfilled in Matthew
Isaiah 7:14	1:23
Micah 5:2	2:6
Hosea 11:1	2:15
Jeremiah 31:15	2:18
Spoken, not written	2:23
Isaiah 40:3; Malachi 3:1	3:3
Isaiah 9:1–2	4:14–16
Isaiah 53:4	8:17
Malachi 3:1	11:10
Isaiah 42:1–4	12:17–21
Isaiah 6:9–10; John 12:39–40; Acts 28:25	13:14–15
Psalm 78:2	13:35
Isaiah 29:13	15:8
Zechariah 9:9	21:5
Psalm 118:26	21:9
Isaiah 56:7; Jeremiah 7:11	21:13
Psalm 8:2	21:16
Psalm 118:22–23	21:42
Psalm 110:1	22:44
Zechariah 13:7	26:31
Zechariah 11:12–13	27:9–10
Psalm 69:21	27:34
Psalm 22:18	27:35
Psalm 22:8	27:43
Psalm 22:1	26:46

OLD TESTAMENT REFERENCE	FULFILLED IN MARK
Malachi 3:1	1:2
Isaiah 40:3	1:3
Isaiah 6:9–10	4:12
Isaiah 29:13	7:6
Psalm 118:26	11:9
Isaiah 56:7; Jeremiah 7:11	11:17
Psalm 118:22	12:10
Psalm 110:1	12:36
Zechariah 13:7	14:27
Psalm 22:18	15:24
Isaiah 53:12	15:28
Psalm 22:1	15:34
Psalm 69:21	15:36

OLD TESTAMENT REFERENCE	FULFILLED IN LUKE
Isaiah 40:3–5	3:4–6
Isaiah 61:1–2	4:18–19
Malachi 3:1, Compare Isaiah 40:3	7:27
Isaiah 6:9–10	8:10
Psalm 118:26	19:38
Isaiah 56:7; Jeremiah 7:11	19:46
Psalm 118:22–23	20:17
Psalm 110:1	20:42–43
Isaiah 53:12	22:37

Old Testament Reference	Fulfilled in John
Isaiah 40:3	1:23
Psalm 69:9	2:17
Isaiah 54:13; Jeremiah 31:34	6:45
Isaiah 11:1, 10; Jeremiah 23:5; Micah 5:1–2	7:42
Psalm 118:26	12:13
Zechariah 9:9	12:15
Isaiah 53:1	12:38
Isaiah 6:9–10	12:40
Psalm 41:9	13:18
Psalm 35:19; 109:3; 119:161	15:25
Psalm 22:18	19:24
Psalm 69:21	19:28
Exodus 12:46; Numbers 9:12; Psalm 34:20	19:36
Psalm 22:16; Zechariah 12:10	19:37
Psalm 16:10–11	20:9

ABOUT THE COMPILER OF
THIS CHRONOLOGY

In 1992 Nikola Dimitrov experienced a miraculous conversion, receiving Jesus as his Lord and Savior. Since 1995 he has been a full time minister of the Gospel, serving as pastor, Bible teacher, preacher, and Christian educator. He started his first church in 1994, which is still standing today, and in 1998 he began his traveling ministry. Nikola is currently pastoring several church groups in Bourgas, Bulgaria and is frequently sought out as a speaker around the country. He also serves as a Bible teacher at the Apostolic Kingdom Institute in Stara Zagora, Bulgaria.

As editor-in-chief of Vetil Media Ministry, Nikola has translated and published more than thirty books into Bulgarian, as well as writing some himself. He is passionate for a glorious Church, without spot, wrinkle or any such thing. Nikola's dynamic preaching pointedly encourages believers to be everything the Lord created them to be. He then encourages his congregations to take responsibility in word and deed toward that end.

As a translator, Nikola has also produced and distributed around the nation nearly 1,000 Bulgarian versions of audio and video teachings by famous foreign preachers and teachers.

As part of a charity in Bulgaria, along with other volunteers, Nikola takes care of needy people from the minorities, distributing clothes, food, medicine, and school materials to children.

Nikola is married to Helen, and they have two lovely young-adult daughters, Annie (which means *grace*) and Mikaela (which means *who is like God?*). Both are part of Nikola and Helen's ministry, serving in the area of music.

Life in Glory Apostolic Christian Center is the mother church where Nikola and family recharge spiritually and for whose vision they work tirelessly. It is a vibrant, multi-ethnic community of believers in the heart of Bulgaria: www.lifeinglory.org.

THE PUBLISHER'S WORD

That Word begotten of God before all worlds, and which was ever with the Father, is made man.

In the beginning was that Word, and that Word was with God, and that Word was God. This same was in the beginning with God. All things were made by it, and without it was made nothing that was made. In it was life, and that life was the light of men.... This was that true light, which lighteth every man that cometh into the world. He was in the world, and the world was made by him: and the world knew him not.... But as many as received him, to them he gave prerogative to be the sons of God, *even* to them that believe in his Name, which are born not of blood, nor of the will of the flesh, nor of the will of man, but of God. And that Word was made flesh, and dwelt among us, (and we saw the glory thereof, as the glory of the only begotten *Son* of the Father) full of grace and truth.... For the Law was given by Moses, but grace and truth came by Jesus Christ.[1]

Dear reader and embracer of the inerrant Holy Bible Scriptures: Why read this book? Because the Word of God is valuable beyond measure. The four Gospels depict the birth, life, teachings, miracles and works of Jesus Christ, as well as His death, burial, resurrection, forty days of revealing Himself in His glorified body to His disciples, and His ascension to heaven to sit at the right

---

1. The Holy Gospel of Jesus Christ, according to John, Prefix and 1:1–4, 9–10, 12–14, 17; from the 1599 Geneva Bible (Dallas, GA: Tolle Lege Press, 2006).

hand of Father God, where King Jesus presently rules and reigns from the heavenly Throne Room.

Jesus is worthy to be studied, praised and worshipped, and fully and completely loved (if we do He calls us His friends). He has overcome death, and has set the captives free. He co-created the heavens and the earth. Christians—those who obey Him faithfully and seek His forgiveness when we fail due to our sin-infected nature—are so utterly grateful that we cherish and embrace the precious history told in these Gospels.

Pastor and friend Nikola Dimitrov has been led of the Spirit to assemble this chronological version of *The Four in One Gospel of Jesus*, dedicating a full decade of scholarship and effort to this work. It is a reader-friendly His-Story (history) of the incarnation of Jesus in the order the events occurred, blending the four Biblical Gospel books that tell of the New Testament era, written by apostles Matthew, Mark, Luke, and John. It is unique in its rigorous harmonizing and combining of texts, without any omissions from the original King James.

This is a serious and thorough undertaking, the methodology of which is explained in Appendix II (General Explanations), where the author names nine resources he consulted in his research. In 1979, Thomas Nelson republished a popular 19th century edition of *Matthew Henry's Commentary on the Holy Bible*, which included additional commentary by others, including a tabular harmony of the Gospels. The author carefully compared *The Four in One Gospel of Jesus* to the Matthew Henry harmony and found it to be a 99% match to that esteemed resource. This affirms our confidence in the accuracy of this work, and is due to the thoroughness of Pastor Dimitrov's methods. The book is meticulously crafted, with detailed Scripture references that reveal the compiler's process of interweaving the texts, and make it easy to refer back to the original Scriptures. With the modernizing of pronouns, verb forms, and a small handful of other archaic words, the text becomes more readable and accessible for readers not familiar with Early Modern English, the language of the King James Version, be they non-Christians or new Christians. This makes this *Four in One Gospel* a unique contribution in the market of Biblical resources, and a great evangelistic tool for those young in their faith. The singular chronological narrative also helps the mature Christian make connections and glean new meaning from seeing the order in which events occurred.

According to Dr. D. James Kennedy and Dr. Jerry Newcombe, there are thirty-three miracles recorded in the four Gospels. Jesus lived about thirty-three years on earth (all the miracles were performed in a three-year period). According to Fred Melden: "He (the Miracle Man, Jesus) came to us by a miracle and left us by a miracle." Miracle comes from the word "mirari" meaning "to cause wonder." Of course Jesus' greatest miracle is the transformation He can bring to a human soul.[2]

Come, reader friend, and allow the Gospel of Jesus Christ, perfectly blended together into one chronological narrative of His time and purposed work here on earth, to work that transformation in you. Encounter The Miracle Man, the Lord of all of us who can help you find your way in the journey, so that you may experience the Triune God's everlasting love here and now on earth, as it is in heaven. Joy to the World, the Lord Is Come!

> And from Jesus Christ which is that faithful witness, *and* that first begotten of the dead, and that Prince of the Kings of the earth, unto him that loved us, and washed us from our sins in his blood, And made us Kings and Priests unto God even his Father, to him, *I say, be* glory, and dominion for evermore. Amen.... I am Alpha and Omega, the beginning and the ending, saith the Lord, Which is, and Which was, and Which is to come, *even* the Almighty.[3]

Here is the concluding statement by Matthew Henry concerning the book of Revelation (Revelation 22:21):

---

2. D. James Kennedy and Jerry Newcombe, *Strength for Today* (Albert Lea, MN: D. James Kennedy Ministries, 2016).

3. The Revelation of Saint John the Apostle 1:5–6, 8; from the 1599 Geneva Bible (Dallas, GA: Tolle Lege Press, 2006).

The apostolical benediction, which closes the whole: *The grace of our Lord Jesus Christ be with you all, Amen.* Here observe,

1. The Bible ends with a clear proof of the Godhead of Christ, since the Spirit of God teaches the apostle to bless his people in the name of Christ, and to beg from Christ a blessing for them, which is a proper act of adoration.

2. Nothing should be more desired by us than that the grace of Christ may be with us in this world, to prepare us for the glory of Christ in the other world. It is by his grace that we must be kept in a joyful expectation of his glory, fitted for it, and preserved to it; and his glorious appearance will be welcome and joyful to those that are partakers of his grace and favour here; and therefore to this most comprehensive prayer we should all add our hearty *Amen*, most earnestly thirsting after greater measures of the gracious influences of the blessed Jesus in our souls, and his gracious presence with us, till glory has perfected all his grace towards us, for he is a sun and a shield, *he gives grace and glory, and no good thing will he withhold from those that walk uprightly.*[4]

Indeed, the grace of our Lord Jesus Christ be with you all. Amen!

GERALD CHRISTIAN NORDSKOG
February 22, 2017
The Father of Our Country,
President George Washington's birthday

---

4. Matthew Henry, *Matthew Henry's Commentary on the Whole Bible: Complete and Unabridged in One Volume* (Peabody, MA: Hendrickson Publishers, Inc., 1991).